Reform and Reaction

REFORM and REACTION

THE ARC OF KANSAS POLITICS

Edited by

Michael A. Smith and H. Edward Flentje

University Press of Kansas

© 2024 by University Press of Kansas
All rights reserved

Published by the University Press of Kansas (Lawrence, Kansas 66045), which was organized by the Kansas Board of Regents and is operated and funded by Emporia State University, Fort Hays State University, Kansas State University, Pittsburg State University, the University of Kansas, and Wichita State University.

Library of Congress Cataloging-in-Publication Data

Names: Smith, Michael A., 1970– editor. | Flentje, H. Edward, editor.
Title: Reform and reaction : the arc of Kansas politics / edited by Michael A. Smith and H. Edward Flentje.
Description: Lawrence, Kansas : University Press of Kansas, 2024. | Includes bibliographical references.
Identifiers: LCCN 2023044340 (print) | LCCN 2023044341 (ebook)
ISBN 9780700636617 (cloth)
ISBN 9780700636624 (paperback)
ISBN 9780700636631 (ebook)
Subjects: LCSH: Governors—Kansas. | Kansas—Politics and government—1951–
| BISAC: POLITICAL SCIENCE / American Government / State | POLITICAL SCIENCE / Political Process / Political Parties
Classification: LCC JK6851 .R44 2024 (print) | LCC JK6851 (ebook) | DDC 320.9781—dc23/eng/20240214
LC record available at https://lccn.loc.gov/2023044340.
LC ebook record available at https://lccn.loc.gov/2023044341.

British Library Cataloguing-in-Publication Data is available.

To Dr. Burdett "Bird" Loomis,
our friend, colleague, and mentor,
who gave us six decades of scholarship about
Congress, Kansas, and how to live well.
We miss you, Bird.

Contents

Preface ix

Introduction 1
MICHAEL A. SMITH AND CHAPMAN RACKAWAY

1 The End of the Old Kansas and the Reapportionment Revolution 8
BURDETT LOOMIS

2 Institutional Reform and the Bennett Governorship 28
H. EDWARD FLENTJE

3 Political Competition and Policy Activism in the 1980s: Governors Carlin and Hayden 54
H. EDWARD FLENTJE

4 The Finney Transition and Political Undercurrents 74
H. EDWARD FLENTJE

5 Contentious Republicans: The Graves Years 92
MICHAEL A. SMITH

6 Democratic Rule in Red-State Kansas: The Sebelius-Parkinson Years 113
MICHAEL A. SMITH

7 Political Strategy Shifts Rightward: The Brownback Years 137
CHAPMAN RACKAWAY

8 Brownback's Red-State Governance 174
H. EDWARD FLENTJE

9 Kansas Voters Reverse Course: The 2016 and 2018 Elections 199
PATRICK R. MILLER

Conclusion: The Arc of Kansas Politics   234
H. EDWARD FLENTJE

About the Contributors   241

Index   243

Preface

The idea for this book originated with the formation in 2010 of Insight Kansas, a group of university academics who take turns writing weekly columns on Kansas state politics that are published in dozens of newspapers around the state. Based on their work, Professor Burdett "Bird" Loomis envisioned the group producing a completely new book on Kansas politics that chronicled the state's political landscape since 1960. He spearheaded the project: outlined the book's initial organization, recruited authors, solicited a publisher, and edited early chapter drafts. Over time, the book took shape as contributors opted in and fell out and coverage expanded. *Reform and Reaction: The Arc of Kansas Politics*, a title coined by Bird, is the product of this extended process.

When Loomis first proposed this book, the existing collection of works on modern-day Kansas politics was rather thin and had become dated. James W. Drury's *The Government of Kansas*, in its sixth edition, was published in 2001 and gave little attention to state politics. Two books were widely available, both of them authored or coauthored by contributors to the current volume. Coeditor and contributor H. Edward Flentje published *Kansas Politics and Government* with Joseph A. Aistrup in 2010, taking a wide-angle view of the Kansas political culture from the nineteenth century to the present era, but its coverage missed the intense political turmoil that began in 2010. Loomis's own book, *Time, Politics, and Policy* (1994), featured an in-depth analysis of how Kansas policymakers managed their time, with a focus on the Kansas legislature's 1989 session. One other book, *Low Taxes and Small Government*, coauthored by Michael Smith, took an early look at and singular focus on Sam Brownback's infamous tax experiment. None of these books delved into how the politics of Kansas and its impact on public policy had changed over the past half century.

Reform and Reaction focuses on the connection of politics and public policy in Kansas from the postwar period through the elections of 2018. Attention is given to actions of political leadership by governors and legislators, as well as through court rulings, in shifting and shaping public policy.

Kansas state government began the postwar years in the doldrums but was jolted into action. The story of reform and reaction begins with the notorious "triple play" of Kansas politics in the late 1950s and moves quickly into the 1960s and the revolution resulting from court-ordered reapportionment of the Kansas legislature in line with one person, one vote. Subsequent and dramatic alterations in the composition of the legislature then fostered a "progressive renaissance" in which the political institutions of state government—legislative, executive, and judicial—were fundamentally transformed. These reforms led to a period of activism in public policy concerning taxes, economic development, infrastructure, and school finance, among others, from the 1970s into the early 1990s. That activism was then contested by a Republican alliance favoring liberty on economic issues and order on social issues. The alliance gained power and reversed course with an aggressive agenda: elimination of the state income tax, abandonment of merit selection in judicial appointments, and the blocking of selected federal grants. After a brief experience with this reversal, Kansas voters again changed direction and elected mainstream lawmakers who sought to restore a middle ground on public policy. These sixty years of the push and pull of politics and their impact on public policy are well worth recounting.

Bird Loomis was unable to see this book through to completion, as he passed in 2021. Professors Michael Smith and H. Edward Flentje, two primary contributors, stepped in to bring the project to its conclusion. Bird's spirit and enthusiasm for this work have guided the contributors and editors throughout.

Bird Loomis completed his PhD in political science at the University of Wisconsin–Madison and was lured to the University of Kansas in 1979. Bird was a gifted scholar, mentor, teacher, community activist, and arts patron. He was the go-to source on Kansas politics for national and regional newspapers and was often interviewed on television and radio for his insights into national and state politics. His legacy includes an extensive list of books and articles. His book on interest-group politics coauthored with Allen Cigler and Anthony Nownes is still considered one of the standards in the field. In *Time, Politics, and Policies: A Legislative Year* (1994), Loomis used extensive interviews and participant observation to document the impact of the Kansas legislature's short, rushed sessions on the policymaking process. He also authored books about the US Senate. His work on members of Congress focused on their individual orientations and behaviors, whereas earlier scholars tended to emphasize institutions and structures. Long before today's political dysfunction, Loomis was warning about the declining civility in Congress and the drive toward partisan advantage instead of good policy.

Bird took on several administrative roles at the University of Kansas, including department chair. He spent a good deal of time at the state capitol in Topeka and in Washington, DC, where he directed a highly successful internship program. He was one of the first recipients of the Kemper Foundation Teaching Award in 1996 for his work in establishing that internship. Loomis was active in the Robert J. Dole Institute for Politics after befriending Senator Dole while doing research on Congress. He served as the institute's interim director from 1997 to 2001. The institute's rich collection and program of guest speakers, media events, and discussion sessions often featured Bird as a speaker or contributor.

Burdett Loomis loved life. He enjoyed his family and the arts as well as public service, teaching, and research. His memorial service centered around his love of art and politics and was held at the Spencer Museum of Art at the University of Kansas. It was attended by hundreds, including Kansas governor Laura Kelly and congresswoman Sharice Davids.

Bird is sorely missed by his colleagues, students, and everyone who knew and admired him for his work at the university and in the Lawrence community, in Kansas state government, and in our discipline. We can think of no more fitting way to continue Bird's legacy than the publication of this book. It has been a labor of love, in honor of a good friend and a political science giant. This one's for you, Bird.

Introduction

Michael A. Smith and Chapman Rackaway

Starting well before statehood, Kansas's history contributed a remarkable chapter to the American story. While still a territory, Kansas was the center of a national controversy, a fabled free state that served as a rallying cry for abolitionists and frontiersmen alike. Kansas was a war zone prior to the secession of the Confederate states in 1861. Over the five-year span from 1854 to 1859, "Bleeding Kansas" was a prelude to the Civil War. John Brown's radical view of abolition was driven by another strong Kansas trait: evangelical Christianity. Religious faith, an American hallmark, is shot through Kansas history from its territorial founding to the 1991 Summer of Mercy, which midwifed the modern evangelical Christian movement. The farmer-labor populist movement of the late 1800s and early 1900s also had strong ties to Kansas.

Kansas was a pivotal player in the westward expansion of the American republic. A key junction of the nation's first coast-to-coast railway system is located in Kansas, and the interstate highway system began in the Sunflower State. More recently, Kansas has been seen as a bellwether, particularly within conservative circles.

This book chronicles the transformation of Kansas politics from 1960 to 2018. We describe a pattern we refer to as the arc of Kansas politics. In chapter 1, Burdett Loomis argues that one driver of this transformation was the US Supreme Court's "one person, one vote" decisions of the 1960s. Compliance with these rulings forced the state to abandon its old model of assigning one state representative to each county, with only twenty seats remaining to distribute among the more populous counties. The boundaries of Kansas Senate districts had to be redrawn as well, although these changes happened later and were less extreme. Passed by Kansas House members who knew they were eliminating their own districts, this mid-decade redistricting dramatically shifted representation in Kansas from rural to urban and suburban, setting the stage for a new type of Kansas politics. The populist bent that accompanied this trend away from county-based representation in state legislatures had some of its roots in Kansas.

Change took new forms in the 1970s, as discussed by H. Edward Flentje in chapter 2. Robert F. Bennett was one of several Kansas officials from both parties who successfully replaced a nineteenth-century governing structure with a modern one starting in the late 1950s and continuing into the 1960s and 1970s. Triggered by the notorious 1956 "triple play" incident in which outgoing governor Fred Hall managed to get himself appointed to the state supreme court, Kansans had had enough. Not surprisingly, many of the first reforms concerned the courts, including the adoption of the Missouri Nonpartisan Court Plan, otherwise known as merit selection for many (but not all) Kansas judges. Later, following the recommendations of several nonpartisan committees and commissions, the legislature sent several state constitutional amendments to the voters, who approved them. The governor's term was lengthened, obsolete agencies were eliminated or consolidated, and an elected auditor was replaced by a nonpartisan Legislative Division of Post Audit, among other things.

Bennett transformed Kansas politics both as a legislator and as governor, but he served only one term as the latter. In chapter 3, Flentje documents the campaign that led to Bennett's defeat by Democrat John Carlin, who criticized his opponent for not doing enough about utility costs. Once in office, Carlin proved to be something of a reformer himself. Like the father-and-son team of George and Robert Docking, each of whom served as governor, Carlin was not necessarily more liberal than his Republican opponents and in fact may have been more conservative on a few issues.

In this era, Kansas officials of both parties tended to be nonideological moderates who focused on bread-and-butter issues like agriculture, roads, and utility costs. In particular, Kansas Democrats distanced themselves from the national party, resulting in a period of great electoral and legislative success. Kansas Democrats won enough seats in the legislature to wield substantial power, even winning the majority for a few terms, and they won the governorship as often as the Republicans did. Government reforms such as those championed by Bennett were broadly popular in both parties. In addition to his signature issue of utility costs, Governor Carlin prioritized economic growth.

Republican governor Mike Hayden continued this tradition of moderation. The folksy western Kansan got along well with most legislative leaders.

Hayden emphasized agriculture and infrastructure, including a new state water plan, roads, and prisons. Overall, his governorship was a continuation of the moderate, bipartisan tradition that characterized the era.

Kansas politics began a significant shift toward symbolism and culture war issues during the period chronicled by Flentje in chapter 4. The defeat of pro–abortion rights Republican Hayden by antiabortion Democrat Joan Finney shook the system. Finney did not like the policy-oriented politics practiced by her predecessors, nor was she very adept at it. Finney's relations with the legislature were poor, even with legislators of her own party. She preferred to go over the heads of politicians and speak directly to the people. Finney had previously served as state treasurer, and her campaign background showed in her style as governor. Long before moving to Cedar Crest (the governor's mansion), Finney was a regular presence at parades, bean feeds, and similar events throughout Kansas. Despite her troubles, a new base funding formula for schools was passed during her single term, resolving a lawsuit and ushering in a new era in school finance. Finney was not a strong leader in this process, however, as most of the work was done by the legislature. This period also featured the 1991 Summer of Mercy, which brought antiabortion protesters from across the nation to Wichita. The chapter concludes with the 1994 elections, which resulted in a national Republican wave that flipped two Kansas US House seats from Democratic to Republican with the victories of Todd Tiahrt and Sam Brownback.

In chapter 5, Michael A. Smith highlights an era in which the dual strains of Kansas politics—practical governance and culture war—vied for attention and votes. At one end of the continuum, Governor Bill Graves defeated Jim Slattery in a race in which they agreed on most issues. Graves then introduced modest tax cuts and another major infrastructure bill, while cautiously avoiding most culture war issues, including abortion rights. Graves subscribed to the old-school, bipartisan tradition of Kansas governors. To paraphrase Governor Robert Docking, these politicos believed that state government should be "austere, but adequate." This was a balancing act for Graves, particularly when he was being hammered from the right by culture warriors who wanted to talk about abortion, homeschooling, taxes, and guns. Voters appeared to ratify Graves's position with his landslide reelection in 1998. However, other races told a different story.

Culture war politics also achieved big victories in the 1990s. Sam Brownback beat both an establishment Republican and a well-connected Democrat to win a US Senate seat in 1996, one of Graves's biggest disappointments. To pull off the upset, Brownback organized evangelical churches and their allies, including homeschoolers and the Focus on the Family organization. Two years later, GOP chair David Miller shattered tradition when he resigned his post to run against a sitting governor from his own party in the primaries. Graves won handily, but change was afoot. In 2000, the Kansas Board of Education removed certain aspects of evolution from the recommended science curriculum, infuriating Graves. This decision flip-flopped for the next several years, depending on which side held a narrow majority on the board.

Smith continues this discussion in chapter 6, covering the Sebelius and Parkinson administrations. These two shifted the governor's office from Republican to Democratic but continued the austere but adequate tradition. Kathleen Sebelius stressed compliance with the state's base state aid per pupil (BSAPP) school funding formula, first approved during the Finney administration and the subject of numerous ongoing lawsuits. A former insurance commissioner, Sebelius also expanded health care coverage, working with moderate allies such as her successor as insurance commissioner, Republican Sandy Praeger. A moderate Republican–Democratic alliance had clearly emerged, leading one of this book's contributors to label Kansas a "three-party state." For the more conservative "polar alliance," critical issues included abortion rights and guns. On the latter, a bipartisan team overcame Sebelius's veto power to pass both concealed-carry permits for handguns and Kansans' right to own automatic weapons. Lieutenant Governor Mark Parkinson ascended to the governorship when Sebelius took the job of secretary of health and human services in the Obama administration. It was an eventful two years, as Parkinson was forced to cope with the economic crisis of 2008–2009 and the resulting loss of tax revenue. He also continued the work begun during Sebelius's governorship to rebuild after the catastrophic Greensburg tornado. His signature act was brokering a deal to allow a new coal-fired power plant in exchange for renewable energy credits.

In chapter 7, Chapman Rackaway documents how polar alliance Republicans secured control of the Kansas GOP through both public campaigning and less visible efforts. Behind the scenes, party operatives like Amanda Adkins rebuilt the Republican Party's capacity to raise money and recruit candidates. The disastrous leadership of Kris Kobach and Christian Morgan had left the party in disarray, with almost no money, no message, and multiple Federal Election Commission (FEC) fines. Kobach had focused on a "loyalty committee," essentially punishing moderates with a loss of power and ultimately pushing them to the margins or out of the party altogether. Meanwhile, polar alliance Republicans were winning at the polls. Attorney general Phill Kline's single term in office was characterized by a flurry of legal actions against Planned Parenthood in an attempt to restrict abortion. Kline also argued that Kansas laws allowed same-sex and opposite-sex relationships to be treated differently with regard to statutory rape charges, a decision reversed by the US Supreme Court. Of more long-term significance was the continued rise of US senator Sam Brownback, who built a solid base of support and won reelection twice.

In chapter 8, Flentje recaps the Brownback era in Kansas government. Winning the governorship easily in 2010, Brownback abruptly ended the austere but adequate tradition and replaced it with the policies of economist Arthur Laffer, whom he hired as a consultant. Decades earlier, Laffer had argued that tax cuts produced so much economic growth that they paid for themselves, and Brownback was hooked. A 2012 tax cut became his signature act. Brownback then announced his Glide Path to Zero—that is, zero state income taxes. Unfortunately, the increased state revenue did not materialize, and the state budget experienced annual crises during this period. An attempt to replace the BSAPP formula with block grants led to new lawsuits and lasted only about a year. Reserve funds of the Kansas Department of Transportation (known colloquially as the Bank of KDOT) were depleted to fill the budget hole created by the tax cuts. Social services were cut as well. No economic growth materialized during this time that could be attributed to the tax cuts, and Kansas's economic fate was similar to that of other states in the region.

In 2012, Brownback and his allies targeted moderate Republican state senators, including some in leadership positions. They managed to defeat several moderates in the primaries, cementing the conservative majority. In 2014, Brownback was reelected governor. Although his Democratic opponent, Paul Davis, was well funded, many considered his campaign too cautious and conventional. Money poured into the state on both sides, including many independent expenditures intended to influence the Pat Roberts–Greg Orman US Senate race. Despite his reelection, Brownback's popularity continued to erode, and during his second term, one survey ranked him as America's least popular governor.

There was bound to be backlash, and it came in 2016. In chapter 9, Patrick R. Miller documents the 2016 elections and their aftermath. Moderate Republicans, Democrats, and the affiliated groups that supported them all agreed on the themes of the election: pro–school funding, anti-Brownback. Brownback's allies were hammered in both the primaries and the general election. Moderates won six seats from conservatives in the state senate and eight in the house, and they also fought to win some of the seats open due to retirement. For their part, Democrats picked up twelve seats in the house and one in the senate.

The result was restoration of the moderate Republican–Democratic alliance, but only with regard to budget issues. In 2017, the coalition reversed the 2012 tax cuts, restored the BSAPP formula for schools, and put the school funding lawsuits on hold. However, the coalition included many rural Republicans who were more conservative on polar alliance issues such as abortion rights and guns. The new anti-Brownback coalition held together *only* on the issues that got them elected: taxes and schools. Brownback accepted a new job as US ambassador of religious freedom, and Lieutenant Governor Jeff Colyer ascended. Colyer had been a stalwart Brownback supporter, even putting his own money into the 2014 reelection campaign. However, Colyer's style as governor was lower key, and he did not fight the legislature on the tax cut reversal it had already passed over Brownback's veto.

In 2018, Colyer was defeated by the narrowest of margins in the GOP primary by secretary of state Kris Kobach, who had transformed that office into a clearinghouse for anti–illegal immigrant laws, including a controversial proof-of-citizenship law for voter registration that was overturned by the federal courts in 2018. Kobach preferred polar alliance politics, anti-immigration policies, and public stunts, such as riding in a parade in a vehicle featuring a fake machine gun. Kobach's strength was rallying the polar alliance base, but he was no organizer, as evidenced by his ruination of the Kansas GOP during his tenure as party chair. In a three-way race that featured the return of independent Greg Orman, Democratic state senator Laura Kelly pulled off a victory with a plurality, but not a majority, of the vote. Kelly's term would feature many high-profile clashes as the legislature once again turned increasingly conservative.

As this book goes to press, Kansas faces even more challenges. Rural districts became geographically larger in 2022 to make up for population losses. Meanwhile, Johnson County has grown so much that it and Wyandotte—the two core counties of the Kansas City area's Third District—can no longer be kept together in a single district. The paradoxical combination of anti-immigration politics and a growing reliance on immigrants will probably continue for some time. The big First District will likely remain deep-red Republican, but its expansion brings new sources of resistance, including university students; frustrated doctors, nurses, and teachers; and growing populations of people of color. The Third District's trend toward Democrats—Joe Biden won Johnson County by eight points in 2020, the first Democrat to win there since Woodrow Wilson—may be a long-term shift or a response to the Trump phenomenon. The defeat of a statewide referendum to restrict abortion rights in August 2022 suggests that culture war politics are here to stay, but support on those issues is shifting.

In rural Kansas, the state government has finally begun earnest efforts to save the High Plains Aquifer, but climate change complicates the project. Escalating tension with China under both the Trump and Biden administrations threatens one of agriculture's biggest export markets. Finally, there are few rural Democrats left to defend farm subsidies, so if the GOP's libertarian strain ever triumphs over old-school distributive politics, these programs may be cut or ended.

Climate change also brings challenges. Hotter temperatures and altered rainfall patterns will transform agriculture. For example, cotton is becoming an increasingly popular crop in western Kansas. The oil economy is highly volatile due to changes in the energy sector, although the demand for natural gas will probably continue for some time. Kansas has also been aggressive about harnessing wind power. A major outlet for corn—used as a base for ethanol biofuel—is likely to dry up if there is widespread replacement of internal combustion engines with electric vehicles. The upside is that it takes huge amounts of water to turn corn into ethanol, so curtailing this process would help relieve pressure on Kansas's water supply. These entangled and self-perpetuating problems constitute just a few of the issues that will define Kansas politics in the near future.

Austere but adequate may no longer be the state's dominant governing philosophy, but it remains a pretty accurate description of life in much of Kansas—for now, anyway.

CHAPTER ONE

The End of the Old Kansas and the Reapportionment Revolution

Burdett Loomis

On November 8, 1960, John F. Kennedy, age forty-three, was elected president of the United States, replacing Kansan Dwight D. Eisenhower, age seventy. This generational changing of the guard signaled the end of one era, grounded in two world wars and the Great Depression, and the beginning of a new one. The 1960s witnessed revolutionary changes in civil rights and health care, a new phase of US military interventionism, and, by the end of the decade, the landing of Americans on the moon.

National politics and policies certainly affected Kansas, but irrespective of these developments, the state was ripe for change. Kansas experienced a 14.3 percent population growth in the 1950s, reaching almost 2.2 million residents, and the baby boom produced a surge in school-age students. Even so, the state failed to keep up with national population increases, losing one congressional seat (from six to five) in the wake of the 1960 census. More generally, the state continued its inexorable decline in rural population, with just 40 percent of Kansas residents living in rural areas in 1960; this would drop to less than 25 percent in 2020.[1]

In 1960, public school enrollment stood at 460,000, up from 324,000 in 1950; this increase, typical for all states during the baby boom, placed great demands on Kansas public education, which was administered and funded almost completely at the local level. The sharp rise in public university enrollment would not come until the mid-1960s, but state policymakers knew that, with more K–12 students and more of them seeking higher education, this was inevitable.

In some ways, 1950s Kansas was prescient and pathbreaking. It provided the title case for *Brown v. Board of Education*, the Supreme Court's historic 1954 school integration decision. The Kansas Turnpike, an innovative superhighway (with speed limits of eighty miles per hour), was built remarkably quickly: it was legislated into existence in April 1953, and its entire 236 miles of road opened in October 1956. More generally, however, despite some residual populism, Kansas was scarcely in the forefront of policy changes among the states, and its structure of government owed more to its nineteenth-century origins than to any major twentieth-century modifications. This would all change in the late 1960s and throughout the 1970s, but Kansas in 1960 was only beginning to respond to the immense demands the next fifteen years would bring.

In 1960, Governor George Docking proposed a state budget of $325 million, with $85 million (including $31 million in federal pass-through funds) being spent on all levels of education. In short, the state spent relatively little money on all governmental functions and very little on education, especially given the growing demands fostered by increased enrollment.[2] It also continued to foster an archaic organizational system in which virtually every school represented its own little district, with a total of more than three thousand such units. This was local control and funding run amok. At the outset of his first two-year term as governor, John Anderson singled out public education for reform, and in 1964 he outlined a "school foundation" bill that would consolidate and better fund K–12 schools. He concluded: "If we are to improve the quality of education in our state . . . , it is imperative that we take the first step to eliminate the schools in our state that are so small that an adequate program cannot be offered in an economic manner."[3] The legislature's actions in the 1960s backed up Anderson's proposals, as state funding quickly rose and the number of school districts shrank from 2,416 in 1960–61 to 311 in 1970–71.[4] Remarkably, state spending on K–12 education rose from $29 million in 1960 to $357 million in 1975.

The legislative policy agenda between 1960 and 1975 often addressed traditional issues such as agriculture, but it was dominated by education and governmental reform and reorganization. Even though Governor Robert Docking was not a policy innovator, he understood the state's needs as its school population grew, its governing responsibilities increased, and its governmental structures proved inadequate to address their rapidly expanding responsibilities. In 1960–75, overall governmental spending rose sharply. Federal grants increased from $94 million in 1960 to more than $335 million in 1975, yet the state's own spending just kept pace with the federal share of state operating expenses and actually decreased slightly over these fifteen years, from 26.25 percent in 1960 to 25.92 percent in 1975.[5]

Higher education systematically expanded over the 1960s and 1970s, with the University of Kansas's student population rising by 73 percent from 1965 to 1977 as new buildings sprouted and more faculty members were hired. In 1964, Wichita State University officially became part of the state university system, thus giving the relatively small state of Kansas three research universities, three regional institutions (Emporia, Fort Hays, and Pittsburg), and nineteen community colleges. Kansas's expansive geography, and its attendant politics, probably contributed to producing this large number of institutions as much as any objective educational needs did. Even as legislators funded these universities, the schools generated political problems, most notably at the University of Kansas, where protests against racism and the Vietnam War became violent, capped by the burning of the student union in 1970.

For all the revamping of education policy and funding, the most profound governmental achievements in 1960–75 (and slightly beyond) were the broad and deep institutional changes passed by the legislature, ordered by the governor, and ratified by the voters through constitutional amendments. Kansas in 1960 had a minimal, ill-coordinated administrative state; an underpaid, amateur legislature; and governors who normally served for two two-year terms. In short, Kansas government looked far more like its nineteenth-century precursor than a modern administrative state. In just over fifteen years, this changed—and profoundly so—as governors, legislators, and citizens combined to yank the state into the late twentieth century. This meant wholesale revisions in the state constitution, along with legislative reforms and reorganization orders from the governor.

The most important constitutional amendments were proposed by the legislature and (largely) passed in 1972 and 1974 referenda. Although these changes came on Governor Robert Docking's watch, he was more an acquiescent presence than a driving force as legislative leaders pressed these issues. Many of the seventeen amendments simply cleaned up antiquated language or incorporated the reapportionment requirements that flowed from 1960s court cases (see later). But others were sweeping, such as the two 1972 amendments that restructured both the executive and judicial branches.[6] These amendments resulted in four-year terms for governor and lieutenant governor, who would run as a team; a cabinet-style executive branch under far stronger gubernatorial leadership; and a governor with substantial power to reorganize the executive branch, subject to legislative approval.

Governor Docking used his reorganizing authority to create a cabinet of new departments, each with a secretary who served at the pleasure of the chief executive. This replaced a decentralized series of boards that had been difficult to coordinate, especially as their responsibilities increased in the 1960s. Moreover, as the state budget grew, control over spending became more important. The cabinet system consolidated budgeting power within the executive, and the legislature reacted by establishing its own fiscal staff. In addition, it created the independent Legislative Division of Post Audit to audit state agency spending and perform specific studies at the request of the legislature.[7]

In addition, a 1972 constitutional amendment unified the judicial branch under the administrative leadership of the state supreme court's chief justice. Not to be outdone, the Kansas legislature, in the wake of its historic 1960s redistricting and reapportionment, modernized its own structure and process. It strengthened the capacity of the Legislative Research Department, added appropriations staff to match the governor's newly acquired power over budgeting, and created the Division of Legislative Post Audit to provide more oversight capabilities. Given its part-time status, the legislature enhanced its year-round continuity by refashioning the seven-member Legislative Coordinating Council and overhauling the interim committee system. Legislators' salaries rose to about $10,000 in total compensation (salary plus per diem) by 1977. This remained a modest sum, but considering the $5-a-day salary of 1960, it represented a sharp increase. Led by senators Bob Bennett (Overland Park) and Glee Smith (Pawnee County), house speaker Pete McGill, and house minority leader Pete Loux, the legislature responded effectively to the consolidation of power under the governor in the executive branch. In 1976, its efforts were rewarded as Legis-50, the Center for Legislative Improvement, honored the Kansas legislature as the most improved in the nation.[8] With only modest changes, the reforms of the 1970s have remained in place, although legislators' total compensation averaged $25,000 per year in 2021—failing to keep up with the pace of inflation over the past fifty years.

In 1960, John Kennedy was elected president of the United States, setting off fifteen years of immense policy change and political turmoil. Many of these new policies shaped the Kansas government, virtually demanding that the state greatly increase its administrative, legislative, and judicial capacities—changes that were long overdue. If reforms in Kansas were not quite so revolutionary and fraught over the next fifteen years, they were profound and long lasting. Kansas governance in 1975 was more like that of 2020 than 1960. In short, the architects of a refashioned Kansas policy process built a stable structure for the next half century of governance. But for all their success, the most profound alteration in Kansas politics and policymaking during the 1960–75 period came not by choice but by judicial fiat. In the wake of both national and state court cases, Kansas was forced to radically reapportion its state house and senate districts in the 1960s. Even though the state had become increasingly urban and suburban by the 1960s, the Kansas Constitution required the house to be grossly malapportioned in favor of rural areas. It would take six years, excruciating political pain, and consummate deal making, but historic adjustments were in place by 1968. Only then could the legislature modernize itself and join the other branches of government in setting a new course for Kansas.

The Shock of Reapportionment and Redistricting Hits Home, 1962–68

> I know there are a lot of representatives in this House who would have preferred never to take this step [of reapportionment]. Yet they bled and died and voted for this bill when the chips were down because we had no other alternative. They deserve a lot of credit.
> *Kansas House Speaker Clyde Hill, February 25, 1966*

In 1960, Kansas politics and many of its policies reflected decisions made in the late 1800s rather than conditions in the mid-twentieth century. Of particular importance were the overlapping splits between rural and urban factions and east-west factions in the state legislature. The state senate, though scarcely a perfect exemplar of "one person, one vote" districting, was roughly apportioned on a population basis. Indeed, after some redistricting in the mid-1960s, one study found that the Kansas Senate's district boundaries were the second most equitable in the nation.[9]

Conversely, the 125-seat Kansas House was grossly malapportioned due to a constitutional requirement that each of the state's 105 counties have one representative; this left the growing urban and suburban counties seriously underrepresented.[10] Only after the US Supreme Court's landmark reapportionment decisions in the 1960s did Kansas legislators seriously address the issue of redistricting, and even then, their overall approach in 1962–66 resembled a caricature of Elisabeth Kubler-Ross's five stages of grief (denial, anger, bargaining, depression, and acceptance). Remarkably, the rural-dominated legislature eventually accepted its fate, led by one of its most powerful members: Representative Jess Taylor, from the least populated county in the state, located on the Colorado border.

The Kansas legislature implemented redistricting in 1962–68, with particular emphasis on the all-important house redistricting decision of 1966, when the century-old rural-urban divide morphed into partisan divisions that reflected various bases of power. Rural Republicans, who had dominated the legislature (and Kansas politics in general), were forced to build new coalitions and address issues they could previously afford to ignore. In many ways, the Kansas Republican Party, despite its numerical advantage among the electorate and usually in the legislature, has never regained its solid, rural-based footing of pre-reapportionment days. In 1974, first-term senator Bob Dole veered right in the wake of the *Roe v. Wade* decision and narrowly won reelection, while state senator Robert Bennett won the governorship by moving to the left against conservative Democrat Vern Miller. These divergent tendencies have remained part of the Kansas Republican Party for more than thirty years and have helped Democrats win both elections and policy victories disproportionate to their numbers in the electorate. Still, contemporary divisions in Kansas politics have their roots in the reapportionment decisions of the 1960s.

Setting the Reapportionment Stage: Kansas's Nineteenth-Century Legacy

The Kansas Constitution established a 40-person senate and a 125-member house and guaranteed each county one representative in the lower chamber, as long as at least 250 voters had cast ballots in the previous election. The number of counties stabilized at 105 in the late nineteenth century, and the

Kansas House was locked into a representational scheme that ensured rural dominance, even as urban areas steadily grew in absolute numbers and as a proportion of the state's population over the next sixty-plus years. Although legislators would occasionally reallocate the twenty "floating" house members, the requirement that each county have at least one representative remained a bedrock element of Kansas politics since statehood (1861). Indeed, when the initial judicial challenge to Kansas apportionment arose in 1962, it focused on population equality for districts in the state senate, which had no constitutionally mandated geographic basis for representation.[11] In short order, however, a more sweeping and substantive suit was filed by a Hutchinson, Kansas, group that included the publisher of the local newspaper (a traditional power base for many Kansas politicos). That case, known as *Harris v. Shanahan*, argued for the complete reapportionment of both house and senate seats, thus anticipating the Supreme Court's 1962 *Baker v. Carr* ruling. Indeed, the Kansas petitioners sought to influence *Baker* by submitting an amicus brief in support of the Tennessee plaintiffs in that case.[12] The interplay between state judicial rulings and federal decisions would continue through the 1960s, as the US Supreme Court clarified its one person, one vote rulings and the Kansas Supreme Court applied them with increasing specificity to the state legislature.

Building on a series of articles for which the *Hutchinson News* would win a Pulitzer Prize, the plaintiffs laid out their case. The facts pointed to the overwhelming malapportionment of the Kansas legislature, especially the house. For example:

- Thirty-nine percent of the Kansas populace controlled the Kansas Senate; the twenty-seven smallest senate districts—a two-thirds majority—had a total of 845,000 residents (based on the 1960 census).
- Thirty-four percent of the people controlled two-thirds of the Kansas House, with 63 of the 125 seats representing a total population of 403,000, or 18 percent of the state's 2.2 million residents. In other words, just over a third of the population controlled a two-thirds majority of the house.
- The state's four largest counties contained more than 800,000 residents, but their 37 percent of the population elected only fifteen representatives (less than the population that elected more than two-thirds of that chamber).[13]

Moreover, the senate districts—allegedly drawn to reflect population—had not been meaningfully reapportioned since 1886, and twenty-seven of the forty districts had exactly the same boundaries in 1961 as in 1886.[14]

The numbers reported by the *Hutchinson News* and the *Harris* plaintiffs were never seriously questioned; rather, rural legislators and their allies argued that the Kansas Constitution had purposely designed the house of representatives to reflect geographic divisions and not population. The apportionment inequities in the legislature exemplified the overall influence of nineteenth-century structures and decisions on state politics and policymaking in 1960. The state budget stood at $366 million in 1960. There was no state retirement system, and as noted earlier, legislators received a salary of $5 a day, with an additional $7 for expenses. In 1963, there was one female legislator out of 165, and 53 of 125 house members listed their occupation as farmer. There were more than three thousand separate school districts in the state, the vast majority of them existing in hundreds of small towns.

In many ways, Kansas resembled other midwestern and southern states, where rural forces dominated the political process throughout the twentieth century, often relying on grossly unrepresentative legislatures whose status was reinforced by constitution and custom. In Kansas, divisions in the legislature reflected this powerful underlying rural bias; even as statewide elections began to favor some Democrats and urban legislators became more vocal about malapportionment, rural legislators and their constituents continued to view their dominance of Kansas politics as their birthright.

The Stages of Reapportionment: Denial and Anger in the Early 1960s

Although both a Republican and a Democratic plan for reapportioning the Kansas House surfaced in the legislature's short 1962 "budget session," it took *Baker v. Carr* for reapportionment to gain the full attention of Kansas lawmakers. The US Supreme Court not only ruled that apportionment was a justiciable issue; both legal observers and politicians believed that the court was also inclined to support a definition of fair representation that emphasized equality rather than some more flexible interpretation (e.g., geographic units, particular communities of interest).[15] *Baker v. Carr* had an immediate impact on Kansas, in that the district court ruling in *Harris v. Shanahan* explicitly cited *Baker*; by July 1962, the district court had declared invalid the "legal basis of *both* the House and Senate apportionments."[16]

Although both chambers fell under the court order, legislators initially focused on the senate, where the state constitution did not impede redistricting to achieve relative population equality among districts. Before the end of 1962, the Kansas Legislative Council's Federal, State, and Local Committee issued a report calling for senate districts to be reapportioned based on population during the 1963 legislative cycle.[17] As one media report stated in November 1962, reapportionment in the 1963 session seemed inevitable, and the only question was how it would be accomplished.[18] The question of when might have been relevant as well, given that the legislature proved to be in no hurry to redistrict both chambers. In fact, the legislature joined a national movement to overturn *Baker v. Carr* and its implications for equal representation by population. In early 1963, Senate Concurrent Resolution 4 passed handily in both chambers, as Kansas and fifteen other states called for a constitutional convention to prohibit federal courts from regulating the reapportionment of state legislatures.[19] By 1963, apportionment had also become a partisan issue, with all minority Democrats in the senate and twenty-eight of thirty-three in the house voting against this resolution.

Still, the senate engaged in good-faith efforts to redistrict. In 1962, populations in senatorial districts ranged from 16,280 to 323,574, and one major proposal stipulated that district populations would range from 48,232 to 60,602, not varying by more than 12 percent from the median.[20] In the senate, bargaining began almost immediately, but in the house, there was only denial and anger.

Over the course of the mid-1960s, many house members with rural constituencies reluctantly confronted the court mandates, both state and national, to redistrict. In early 1963, rural GOP representative Ross Doyen proposed a districting plan that would reduce the house to 105 seats, one for each county (with populations ranging from 2,500 to well over 300,000).[21] This plan would resurface periodically (such as in 1966). There was little chance that it would be adopted, but its presence suggests that the denial and anger stages of "grief" over reapportionment continued into the 1960s, even as bargaining on new alignments were well under way.

The Kansas Supreme Court's decision would not come until January 21,

1963, eighteen days into the legislative session. In essence, the court deferred to the legislature, assuming that it could successfully reapportion both chambers before the 1964 elections.[22] Although the senate did manage to redistrict itself along roughly equal population lines in 1963, the court declared its map invalid for various technical reasons. It then suggested that the governor call a special session for both the senate and the house, the latter having blatantly disobeyed the court's order to redistrict.[23]

In 1964, the house made a pass at redistricting but did not attack the core issue of malapportionment—the requirement that each county have its own representative. The house rearranged the deck chairs for the twenty remaining seats, dividing them up among the largest five counties instead of the largest thirteen. Despite this step, the five most populous counties remained badly underrepresented, containing 41 percent of the population but accounting for only 20 percent of house members. Rural Republicans in the house remained in denial, even as both the Kansas and the US courts moved toward a one person, one vote interpretation of the state and federal constitutions.

Meanwhile, the senate went about the business of fixing the clerical errors of its 1963 remapping plan in Senate Bill 2 (the only legislation entertained by the upper chamber during the 1964 special session). The house approved the bill, and Governor John Anderson signed both measures (house and senate) into law on February 24, 1964. On March 30, the Kansas Supreme Court ruled both plans legal and ceased judicial action in *Harris v. Shanahan*.

The success was short-lived, however. On June 15, 1964, the US Supreme Court ruled in *Reynolds v. Sims* that *both* state legislative chambers must base their apportionment solely on population. In short order, *Long v. Avery* was filed in federal district court, identifying both Kansas chambers as malapportioned. A three-judge federal panel convened on June 26, but it abstained from hearing this challenge until the Kansas Supreme Court decided another case. *Harris v. Anderson* was also filed on June 26, with the goal of forcing state legislators' hand by seeking a judgment on the Kansas House's compliance with the Fourteenth Amendment's equal protection clause. The case began in mid-December 1964, and given the *Reynolds v. Sims* ruling, the outcome was not in doubt. Still, state legislators would mount one last effort at obstruction during the 1965 session.

Introduced on January 14, Senate Concurring Resolution 1 called on Congress to either propose a constitutional amendment allowing states to apportion one legislative chamber in any manner they chose or call a constitutional convention. The resolution passed both chambers, but to no avail. On March 1, the Kansas Supreme Court decided *Harris v. Anderson* in favor of the plaintiff, thus ruling that the house reapportionment approved just a year earlier was invalid.

On April 2, the three-judge federal panel resumed its activity. By December 28, *Long v. Avery* was decided, first concurring with the decision in *Harris v. Anderson* and calling for redistricting of the Kansas House by the end of the 1966 special session. Next, the panel declared that the senate reapportionment plan was not up to the one person, one vote standard; however, given the four-year senate election schedule, it imposed a deadline of April 1968. As suddenly as the victories of 1964 had been won, they were now overturned. The Kansas legislature simply had to face the music. By late 1965, anger and denial had largely given way to depression and acceptance. Nevertheless, legislators engaged in vigorous give-and-take bargaining once they accepted the necessity of reapportionment. Not surprisingly, given the composition of the house, rural representatives found a way to salvage bits of their previous power.

Designing Their Demise: Kansas Representatives Comply with One Person, One Vote

By 1966, time had run out for the grossly malapportioned Kansas House of Representatives. Well before Republican governor William Avery set February 15 as the official start of the special legislative session on reapportionment, most lawmakers recognized that they had to redistrict; if they did not, the courts would be forced to act in their stead. Quoting a legislator from Washington State, which had previously undergone reapportionment, Representative Lawrence Slocombe quipped, "It's like getting up on the operating table and taking out your own appendix without an anesthetic."[24] There would indeed be pain, assuaged only by considerable amounts of liquid self-medication during the two-week session.

Representative Jess Taylor, chairman of the Legislative Apportionment Committee and perhaps the most powerful foe of redistricting, had finally accepted the inevitability of change. In a late 1965 letter to fellow legislators, Taylor not only called for cooperation to achieve redistricting but also came

Jess Taylor
The 1960 *Kansas Legislative Directory* featured the following biography: "Jess Taylor, Tribune, was born in Iowa on Feb. 1, 1897; spent 20 years in Texas and Oklahoma, and has lived in Greeley Co., since 1930. A farmer and stockman. Member Masonic and Odd Fellows lodges, American Legion and Baptist church. Past president County Farm Bureau and Tribune Rotary club. President Wheatland Electric Co-op, and Master Farmer. Is married and has three children. Enjoys all sports. Serving his sixth term; was House Speaker 1957–58." (Source: Kansas Legislative Administrative Services)

close to prophesying the precise conditions the courts initially found acceptable.[25] Despite his fierce ideological and constituency-based opposition to reapportionment, Taylor's letter highlighted the reluctant pragmatism that would characterize much of the redistricting process. He would prove to be an ideal candidate to lead the house's self-surgery, in that he was a highly respected legislator from the most rural district in the state; he had previously served as speaker, winning the high regard of virtually all legislators. As chair of a key committee, Taylor combined formal authority with informal respect as he proceeded to end rural dominance in the legislature.

With almost a year to react after the Kansas Supreme Court's *Harris v. Anderson* decision, house members had plenty of time to agree informally on certain ground rules for redistricting. These included commitments to keep the 125 house districts within senatorial district boundaries, observe county lines whenever possible, and maintain district population variations within 10 percent of the median figure of 17,583.[26] Kansas attorney general Robert Londerholm advised the legislature to err on the side of equality, not political expediency, noting, "Our best chance for successful legal defense before the courts would come from a reapportionment plan drawn in the spirit of 'how close to equal can it be made' rather than 'how far from equal can it safely stray.'"[27] Given that the ultimate meaning of one person, one vote remained uncertain, legislators had to guess at what would be acceptable, and they tended to stretch the boundaries of equal representation, even when complying with the court order.

As the special session began, legislators knew that their actions would profoundly alter the composition of the house, but the immediate question was how to go about producing the requisite set of large-scale changes. In the past, legislative redistricting had been largely at the margins, as the twenty "floating" seats (beyond the 105 guaranteed to each county) were shifted among the most populous counties, most recently in 1960. By early 1966, the actual work of drawing up proposals fell mainly to separate groups of legislators from particular geographic areas. Taylor did not believe statewide maps would be appropriate early in the game; instead, he encouraged affected legislators to work together (under the guidance of committee members) to remap the four most populous counties, including the relevant cities, on their own. In fact, Taylor decided that the four most populous urban districts would receive forty-seven seats, more than doubling their number of representatives. Only after legislators from these population centers had completed their task would the rural legislators begin the unenviable job of deciding who among them would lose seats. To that end, Taylor created several bipartisan, regional task forces to draw the lines within their respective areas. The self-surgery metaphor remained appropriate, in that representatives would be responsible for drawing their own region's district lines; only after all the groups had done this would a full map be considered.

Despite Taylor's leadership, a general spirit of cooperation, and near-universal agreement that the house had to redistrict, the onerous job of reapportionment generated real tensions between urban and rural forces, as well as between the political parties.[28] Indeed, during the first meeting of the Apportionment Committee, Representative Kenith Howard argued that his all-Republican Johnson County (suburban Kansas City) delegation deserved eleven house members instead of the ten it had been offered. Taylor responded, "I wouldn't do that at this stage in the game.... You boys should be satisfied with ten members—you are getting double representation."[29] Taylor was making the rules, and he was doing so in a way that benefited, if just slightly, his fellow rural legislators.

Howard's argument rested on the fact that, mathematically, Johnson County was entitled to 10.6 representatives. Taylor pointed out that, under this logic, another large Kansas county (Sedgwick) would have to receive 19 representatives, as it was mathematically entitled to 18.6. "That would mean that somebody else would have to give up seats," said Taylor.[30] That "somebody" was the group of rural representatives, whose ranks were already being decimated.

After this meeting, Taylor held a press conference at which he unveiled a map consisting of 125 districts, all of them equal within 1 percent of population. However prescient (if unintentionally so) this might have been, his purpose was scarcely pure, in that the map contained many districts described as resembling "birds' heads and dogs' hind legs." "You've got a double barreled monster by the tail here," said Taylor. "You can get pretty close to equality but when you do you have something that looks like this."[31] Journalists described reaction to the so-called computer map as a "Boo!" effect.[32] Ironically, such maps would become common over the next forty years, as population equality became the defining feature of legislative districts. In 1966, however, Taylor made his point, and legislators sought mutual accommodation rather than absolute equality.[33]

During the 1966 budget session, the Legislative Apportionment Committee unsurprisingly ratified Taylor's allocation of seats to urban areas by a vote of fourteen to one. Thus, Kansas's four largest counties stood to receive 47 of the 125 house seats. The committee sided with Taylor, recommending that Johnson County receive ten representatives (up from five), Sedgwick County (Wichita) eighteen seats (up from nine), Wyandotte County (Kansas City) eleven seats (up from five), and Shawnee County (Topeka) eight seats (up from three). The other 101 counties would split the seventy-eight remaining seats.[34]

Attendance at these preliminary meetings was described, in yet another medical metaphor, as "tooth pulling without Novocain [for rural members]."[35] Still, there was resistance. Various lawmakers sought to finesse the court's clear meaning by offering plans to elect the entire chamber at large, while perhaps requiring nominations on a county-by-county basis. Such a tactic was both a political and a constitutional nonstarter, and it fell to Taylor to address it. Much as he had presented the stalking horse "computer map" a month earlier, on the special session's opening day, Taylor introduced a plan for statewide at-large elections for the house. Although this proposal was labeled "a mockery of the legislative process," Taylor shepherded the bill to committee approval by a vote of thirteen to three.[36] Like the computer map, Taylor's arguably facetious plan had tactical and cautionary elements drawn from contemporary American state politics: in 1964, Illinois had elected its entire 177-member assembly on an at-large basis—an action subject to extreme criticism from most quarters. Taylor was standing, symbolically at least, with his rural counterparts. "I have men who look at the [computer] map and say they would rather run at large than accept what is suggested," he said.[37] Upon its introduction on the house floor, the bill was immediately assigned to committee and left for dead.[38] More purposeful work ensued.

By the session's third day, Wyandotte and Sedgwick, two of the four most populous counties, had submitted agreed-upon proposals for redistricting. Once again, Johnson County was running into difficulties.[39] This time, its all-Republican delegation could not choose between two competing maps. To make matters more complicated, and despite Taylor's allotment of ten seats, the five Johnson County legislators continued to push for eleven. Nevertheless, the committee was determined to move ahead. Within a week, it had approved a plan that set the districts for the four most populous urban-suburban counties, more than doubling their representation. Taylor maintained a little extra clout for rural Kansans by denying these rapidly growing counties two additional representatives, which they arguably deserved from a statistical perspective. Still, this was a minor victory, and the difficult task of agreeing to eviscerate the state's rural representation remained.

With the urban counties' districts tentatively drawn, the road was clear to consider the only serious statewide proposal. On February 23, 1966, the regional remapping plans, drawn up by subgroups of affected legislators, were compiled, and House Bill 504 was officially introduced.[40] As the Kansas House prepared to redistrict itself, the capital community held its collective breath. Although the outcome was uncertain, house members would determine their own fate, as state senators (who did not have to worry about redistricting in 1966) would bow to the wishes of their legislative counterparts. Less than a week before the special session began, on February 11, a three-judge federal panel declared that the reapportionment order for the Kansas Senate would be stayed until after the senators' four-year terms were up in 1968.[41] Deferring to the house, the senate would play only a passive, technical role in the 1966 redistricting process.[42]

Absent potential senate meddling or complicated interchamber negotiations, house members went about their legislative work with dispatch. Their reconstructive surgery would not take long, and remarkably, there would be little conflict over the final product. By now, in Kubler-Ross's terms, the affected legislators had passed through depression to a kind of fatalistic acceptance of both their individual fates and the overall decline in rural influence. Lawmakers raised just two challenges. The first came with an amendment that proposed the single at-large remedy, which died before being offered.[43] The second challenge was a last-gasp motion to strike the bill from the legislative calendar, which failed (by a vote of 29–75).[44] House Bill 504 passed by a margin of 88–36.

The reapportionment finale was described as a "masterpiece of understatement," due to both the sense of inevitability and the legislative skills of Taylor, house speaker Clyde Hill, and other key lawmakers.[45] With both practicality and irony, Taylor voted *against* the bill he had done so much to facilitate. "If the folks in my district learned I had voted for this," he said, "they would hang a sign around my neck which read 'Dead Duck.'"[46] Feet propped up on his desk, his head "wreathed in pipe smoke," Jess Taylor could take satisfaction in his accomplishment, guiding a complex bill through a reluctant chamber to produce a broadly consensual outcome. To the best of his ability, he had protected rural interests, within the overall mandate of equal representation. Moreover, he had created his own western Kansas district that would allow him to win reelection until his retirement in 1972.

Nevertheless, the bill would turn a minimum of thirty-eight members out of office. Although most of the opposition came from rural legislators, three disgruntled Johnson County representatives also voted no.[47] A few groups of house members, including the Johnson County diehards, attempted to convince the senate to add substantive amendments, but it quickly and overwhelmingly approved the house plan, with just a handful of minor and procedural changes.[48] Any possibility of senate tampering was eliminated both by its expectation of reciprocity in its own redistricting in 1968 and by the circulation of a measure by the house majority floor leader that outlined potential plans to remap the senate during the current special session.[49]

On March 2, 1966, the house passed the senate's version by a margin of 79–40, and Governor Avery signed it five days later. As the new maps became law on March 8, Attorney General Londerholm submitted a motion for the Kansas Supreme Court to rule on the bill's constitutionality. Two weeks later, the court stated that the new apportionment was constitutional; on March 25, judicial involvement in house redistricting officially ceased, at least for the time being.[50]

Under this remapping plan, populations in 123 of the 125 districts varied by less than 9 percent from the average. With populations of 15,680 to 19,521, the new districts came close enough to the perfect 17,583 to satisfy the one person, one vote standard. And despite Governor Avery's prediction that this remapping would not cause "drastic changes in state government," he had just signed into law Kansas's most sweeping reapportionment bill since 1873.[51]

At the margins, however, the Taylor-inspired redistricting did relatively well for rural legislators, at least within the constitutional constraints. This was especially true for house districts in western Kansas; in the final remap, of the twenty-two house districts in the western half of the state, only one had a population that exceeded the average (17,583).[52] At the same time, Sedgwick (Wichita) and Johnson (suburban Kansas City) Counties received slightly less than their fair share of representatives.

Still, the new law had a deep and immediately recognizable impact on the urban-rural power struggle. Kansas's four most populous counties now had forty-seven representatives, sixteen short of the sixty-three votes needed for a simple majority.[53] In one historic two-week session, an anachronistic legislature had managed to usher in the era of equal representation. Jess Taylor (an anachronism in his own right), who represented far more cows than people, witnessed the end of an era, if not the end of his own political career. Fittingly, the house adjourned with a tribute of sorts to the man who represented the Kansas county with the smallest population (less than 2,500). Presenting Taylor with a decorated cow's skull, his fellow legislators sang:

> Yes we drew the lines with courage
> And we drew the lines with care.
> till we had a jigsaw puzzle . . .
> Foul or Fair.
> So we serenade our leader
> whose courage never failed.
> And vote to be forgotten
> with the rest.
> We're poor little cows who have lost our vote.
> Moo! Moo! Moo![54]

Beyond 1966

The extended, if ultimately anticlimactic, struggle over reapportionment and redistricting in Kansas set the stage for substantial changes over the next few years. Although redistricting politics would continue into the early 1970s, as one person, one vote rules were more clearly articulated by the courts, in 1966 the Kansas House seriously addressed the major inequities, and the Kansas Senate followed suit in 1968. The 1966 election produced a fiscally conservative Democratic governor, Robert Docking, who would serve for eight years and oversee, in conjunction with some farsighted and politically skilled legislative leaders (mostly Republicans), the thorough overhaul of Kansas government, from the legislature to the executive and the judiciary.

Although the state continued to be dominated by Republican officeholders, the new state legislative boundaries increased Democratic numbers in both chambers and led to substantial Democratic influence. Most notably, between 1966 and 1986, Democrats controlled the governor's office for sixteen years; thus, having even substantial minorities in either chamber meant that the vetoes of Democratic chief executives could be sustained.

Perhaps most importantly from a partisan perspective, the breakdown in rural Republican control of the legislature meant that the GOP's ideological factions grew stronger as social conservatives came to dominate the party, albeit incrementally, from 1974 to 1994 (and beyond). In the end, the demise of rural Republican control over the Kansas legislature allowed the essential modernization of state government in the post–Great Society era. The end of rural GOP dominance also led, if indirectly and at a distance, to the emergence of the three-party state—moderate Republicans, socially conservative Republicans, and Democrats—which has redefined Kansas politics since the early 1990s.[55]

Notes

1. University of Kansas Center for Regional Studies, "Kansas Statistical Abstract," 1965.

2. Governor's Budget Report, 1960.

3. "Proposal No. 20—School Foundation Program," June 5, 1964, Spencer Research Library, University of Kansas.

4. Institute for Social and Environmental Issues, University of Kansas, "Kansas Statistical Abstract," 1971.

5. Marvin A. Harder and Raymond G. Davis, *The Legislature as an Organization* (Lawrence: Regents Press of Kansas, 1979), 143.

6. H. Edward Flentje and Joseph A. Aistrup, *Kansas Politics and Government: The Clash of Political Cultures* (Lincoln: University of Nebraska Press, 2010), 38.

7. Flentje and Aistrup, 84.

8. John Carlin, "Message to the Legislature," January 23, 1979, https://kslib.info/DocumentCenter/View/1126/John-William-Carlin-Governors-Message-1979.

9. Stephen M. Smith, "Legislative Reapportionment in Kansas in the 1960s: A Case Study" (PhD thesis, University of Kansas, 1968). This work, along with that of former representative William K. Hall, "The Reapportionment of the Kansas House of Representatives, 1966" (MA thesis, University of Kansas, 1966), proved invaluable in providing insights and background material for this chapter.

10. Smith, "Legislative Reapportionment."

11. Smith, 12.

12. Walter Sandelius, "The Reapportionment Problem in the State Legislatures: A Solution in the Courts?" *Your Government* 17 (December 4, 1961).

13. John Marshall, "1966 Last Emergency Session," *Chanute Tribune*, July 25, 1987.

14. Marshall.

15. Royce Hanson, *The Political Thicket, Reapportionment, and Constitutional Democracy* (Englewood Cliffs, NJ: Prentice-Hall, 1966), 56.

16. Smith, "Legislative Reapportionment," 123; emphasis added.

17. Smith, 25.

18. Smith, 28–29.

19. Smith, 37–38.

20. Smith, 42, 48.

21. Ray Morgan, "Rural Kansas Legislators Take Aim at Cities," *Kansas City Star*, January 11, 1963.

22. Smith, "Legislative Reapportionment," 33–34.

23. Smith, 62–110.

24. Jack Coffman, "'Surgical' Chore Begins," *Topeka State Journal*, February 15, 1966.

25. Smith, "Legislative Reapportionment," 125, 127.

26. Hall, "Reapportionment of the Kansas House," 58.

27. Hall, 59.

28. "Interview with Former Rep. Robert Harder, January 21, 1966," *Topeka Capital*, March 13, 2008.

29. *Topeka State Journal*, January 18, 1966.

30. *Kansas City Star*, January 28, 1966.

31. *Topeka Capital*, January 23, 1966.
32. Smith, "Legislative Reapportionment," 137.
33. *Topeka Capital*, January 23, 1966.
34. Hall, "Reapportionment of the Kansas House," 63.
35. *Topeka State Journal*, January 18, 1966.
36. *Kansas City Times*, February 16, 1966.
37. Smith, "Legislative Reapportionment," 144.
38. Smith, 145.
39. Smith, 147.
40. Smith, 153–154.
41. *Kansas City Star*, February 11, 1966.
42. Smith, "Legislative Reapportionment," 167.
43. Smith, 75.
44. Smith, 76.
45. *Topeka Daily Capital*, February 26, 1966.
46. *Topeka Daily Capital*, February 26, 1966.
47. Smith, "Legislative Reapportionment," 163.
48. *Topeka Daily Journal*, March 1, 1966.
49. Hall, "Reapportionment of the Kansas House," 77.
50. Smith, "Legislative Reapportionment," 174–177. Additional court cases would bring Kansas districting in line with the Supreme Court's criteria for equal representation.
51. *Topeka Daily Journal*, March 8, 1966.
52. *Topeka Daily Journal*, March 3, 1966.
53. *Topeka Daily Journal*, March 3, 1966.
54. *Topeka Daily Journal*, March 1, 1966.
55. See, most prominently, Thomas Frank, *What's the Matter with Kansas* (New York: Henry Holt, 2004). See also Allan J. Cigler and Burdett A. Loomis, "After the Flood: The Kansas Christian Right in Retreat," in *Prayers in the Precincts*, ed. Mark Rozell and Clyde Wilcox (Washington, DC: Georgetown University Press, 2000).

CHAPTER TWO

Institutional Reform and the Bennett Governorship

H. Edward Flentje

"When anything is going to happen in this country, it happens first in Kansas." So asserted the state's renowned journalist William Allen White, who in 1922 saw Kansas as a national laboratory for political change. He was referring to crusading abolitionists prior to the Civil War, constitutional prohibitionists in 1880, insurgent populists in the 1890s, and Bull Moose progressives in the early 1900s. White chuckled as he said, "These things come popping out of Kansas like bats out of hell. Sooner or later other states take up these things."[1]

Twenty years later, White's exuberance for Kansas at the forefront of political reform had cooled. He wrote in his 1946 autobiography that the progressive instincts of his Republican Party had become "chastened, weary, and disillusioned." Further, "greedy, egoistic forces in that party . . . controlled its organization . . . and kept right on running the farm."[2] A more pointed critique came in 1983 from journalists Neal Pierce and Jerry Hagstrom, who concluded that Kansas was "scarcely the place where thing happen 'first.' Indeed, nowhere on the American continent can the eclipse of a region or a state as a vital force—a focal point of creative change or exemplar of national life—be felt so strongly and poignantly as in Kansas."[3]

In truth, a progressive resurgence took shape in the postwar years that would transform the executive, legislative, and judicial institutions of Kansas.

A Progressive Resurgence

As Kansans celebrated the centennial of territorial settlement in 1954 and statehood in 1961, many forces came together to prod the state forward on institutional reform. The Commission on Intergovernmental Relations—created in 1953 by Congress at the urging of Kansas-grown President Eisenhower—called for states to update their constitutions to address the requirements of an ever-changing modern society.[4] In 1964, the US Supreme Court ruled in *Reynolds v. Sims* that state legislative representation must be apportioned based on "one-man, one-vote," undoing a century of malapportionment in Kansas. Also in 1964, with assistance from the Ford Foundation, the Citizens Conference on State Legislatures was launched to promote the improvement of state legislatures throughout the country. The Citizens Conference undertook a fifty-state study to assess and rank each legislature based on whether it was functional, accountable, informed, independent, and representative.[5] The study ranked Kansas twenty-third on these criteria and made twenty-six specific recommendations—constitutional, statutory, and procedural changes—for the improvement of its legislature.

At the same time, a transformation of state governorships was under way across the country. Larry Sabato tracked these changes from 1950 through 1975 and found "a modern avalanche of reform." Various steps were being taken "to increase accountability and efficiency of government by giving the state governor the authority to match his responsibility in the executive branch."[6] Many states were lifting constitutional restraints and strengthening the chain of command and the governor's appointing authority, realigning the office of lieutenant governor, and reducing the number of elective state executives, among other alterations.

Homegrown political shenanigans, however, triggered immediate attention to institutional change. The infamous "triple play" of 1956–57 occurred when Kansas's incumbent Republican governor Fred Hall sought reelection but was defeated in a divisive primary. Democrat George Docking won the race for governor in the general election. Days before Hall was set to step down as governor, William Smith, a friendly Republican justice, resigned from the Kansas Supreme Court, allowing the outgoing governor to appoint his replacement. Hall then resigned as governor, elevating Republican lieutenant governor John McCuish to the governor's chair. The new interim governor promptly appointed Hall to the court.

Kansans were outraged at these political antics, and in response, Kansas lawmakers moved to insulate the Kansas Supreme Court from partisan politics with a constitutional amendment patterned after the Missouri Plan for the nonpartisan appointment of judges. Voters overwhelmingly ratified that proposition in 1958. The amendment, now part of the judicial article of the Kansas Constitution, provided for the screening of supreme court nominees through a "nonpartisan nominating commission." Once appointed to the court, a justice was required to stand periodically for retention on the court but was prohibited from having a "party designation" next to his or her name on the retention ballot. In addition, sitting justices were required to avoid political activity. The amendment stated: "No justice of the supreme court... shall directly or indirectly make any contribution to or hold any office in a political party or organization or take part in any political campaign."

Broad-ranging constitutional self-assessment followed and marked the beginning of a "progressive resurgence" in institutional change.[7] In 1957, Governor George Docking created a Commission on Constitutional Revision. In 1961, newly elected Republican governor John Anderson continued the trend with a reconstituted second commission. In 1964, the Kansas Bar Association initiated a comprehensive review of Kansas courts in association with the Citizens' Conference on Modernization of Kansas Courts. In 1968, state lawmakers blocked Democratic governor Robert Docking's call for a constitutional convention and created their own Citizens' Committee on Constitutional Revision. Subsequently, lawmakers cooperated with Docking to establish the Kansas Commission on Executive Reorganization in 1970. These bodies studied and laid the groundwork for changes that would transform the state's executive, legislative, and judicial institutions throughout the 1970s and beyond.

From 1970 through 1974, the Kansas legislature deliberated over possible constitutional changes, refined the language of these proposals, and placed twenty constitutional amendments on the ballot. All were approved by the voters.[8] Francis Heller described these changes in the state's founding document as "wholesale revision by the incremental method."[9]

Executive Reform

These changes dramatically strengthened the governor's formal authority over the executive branch of state government and included the following:[10]

- The governor's term of office was extended from two years to four years, with a limit of two successive terms.
- The governor and lieutenant governor would now be nominated and

elected jointly, and the office of lieutenant governor as an independently elected state executive was eliminated.
- The governor was authorized to submit executive reorganization orders to the legislature for the purpose of transferring, abolishing, consolidating, or coordinating any state agency, in whole or in part, as the governor determined to be necessary for efficient administration. Such executive reorganization orders would take effect unless vetoed by either chamber of the legislature within sixty days of submittal by the governor.
- The offices of state auditor, state printer, and state treasurer were removed from the constitution and made subject to statutory change.

These changes followed from the findings of the Kansas Commission on Executive Reorganization, which concluded: "The executive branch of state government is an organizational jungle. . . . Kansas has nearly 200 agencies, boards, and commissions, committees, councils, and other groups for whose actions the governor is at least theoretically responsible. It is obviously impossible for anyone to govern this state as long as this inadequately structured organization exists. The governor should be the chief executive . . . [and so] give him the powers commensurate with his responsibilities."[11] In addition, the commission recommended the establishment of a cabinet structure for the executive branch and the consolidation of executive agencies into fewer departments, each headed by an official selected by and responsible to the governor.

Governor Robert Docking moved promptly in 1972 to implement the commission's organizational plan. On his recommendation, state lawmakers restructured by statute the Departments of Administration and Revenue; in line with the cabinet model, each was headed by a secretary appointed by the governor with the consent of the senate and serving at the pleasure of the governor. Then, in 1973, Docking exercised the governor's newly acquired constitutional power of executive reorganization and issued Executive Reorganization Order No. 1, which abolished the existing Board of Social Welfare and placed its functions in a newly established Department of Social and Rehabilitation Services, headed by a secretary. The governor similarly created the Department of Health and Environment by executive reorganization order in 1974. Not to be outdone, the legislature established a Division of State Planning and Research headed by a director serving at the pleasure of the governor.

Executive reorganization along cabinet lines substantially expanded gubernatorial authority to appoint and remove executive officials. These augmented powers allowed governors to direct the discretionary actions of subordinate officials informally through verbal instructions and more formally through executive orders, proclamations, memoranda, and various other policy directives.

Constitutional amendments reshaping the executive branch also enhanced gubernatorial powers by narrowing the number of executives running for statewide office from seven to four. The lieutenant governor would be chosen by and run on the ticket with the governor. The elected offices of auditor and printer were abolished, and the office of state treasurer was removed from constitutional status and made subject to change by statute or executive reorganization order. Only the attorney general and secretary of state remained as independently elected constitutional executives who could lay claim to a political base separate from that of the governor.

Constitutional change also enhanced the potential tenure of the governor. Extending the term of office to four years removed the constraints of a two-year term and gave the governor more time to master the duties of office and exercise leadership.

Judicial Reform

Judicial reform through court unification was initiated by statute and substantially clarified through revision of the judicial article of the state constitution in 1972. The movement toward court unification was actively promoted by the Kansas Bar Association and its sponsorship of the Citizens' Conference on Modernization of Kansas Courts.[12] In 1965, the Kansas legislature passed the Judicial Department Reform Act, which gave supreme court justices supervisory responsibility over district courts and created the position of judicial administrator, who was appointed and supervised by the chief justice to assist in the operation and administration of the courts.

Additional reforms followed. According to Kansas Supreme Court Chief Justice Harold Fatzer, a consensus developed by the Citizens' Conference on Modernization of Kansas Courts advocated court unification fortified through constitutional amendment.[13] Its work was folded into the broader Citizens' Committee on Constitutional Revision for submission to the governor and the legislature for final refinement. Fatzer explained that except for the provisions related to nonpartisan selection, the constitution's existing article on the judiciary was designed for litigation that prevailed a hundred years ago: "We now find that the present system cannot adequately handle the caseload. . . . In order to assure prompt, fair, and efficient justice, this state must have constitutional judicial reform."[14]

The constitutional changes of 1972 completely rewrote the judicial article. The 1958 provisions for the nonpartisan selection of Kansas Supreme Court justices were retained intact, but the structure of the state judiciary was consolidated as follows:

- Judicial power was unified into one court of justice composed of one supreme court, district courts, and other courts as provided by law.
- The supreme court was granted general administrative authority over all state courts.
- The supreme court was granted authority to temporarily assign district court judges to other districts or to serve temporarily on the supreme court.
- The supreme court was authorized to discipline, suspend, or remove other state court judges for cause after an appropriate hearing.
- The voters of each judicial district were authorized to adopt a method of nonpartisan selection of district court judges.

Court unification led to the eventual elimination of numerous courts of limited jurisdiction that had been created by lawmakers over time. This, in turn, resulted in more balanced workloads among judges. The amendment retained the district courts, with judges elected by voters to four-year terms, but it directed the legislature to allow the voters of each judicial district to opt for a nonpartisan method of selection. The legislature enacted implementing legislation for this provision in 1974. Then, in 1975, lawmakers created the Kansas Court of Appeals as an intermediate court to hear appeals from district courts and even out the appellate workload of the Kansas Supreme Court.

The constitutional amendment allowed "the discipline, suspension, removal, or retirement of judges for cause by means other than the cumbersome remedy of impeachment," according to Fatzer.[15] Also, all justices and judges were prohibited from practicing law during their terms of office.

Legislative Reform

The US Supreme Court decisions in *Baker v. Carr* (1962) and *Reynolds v. Sims* (1964) forced fundamental legislative reform by requiring the legislature to be apportioned in accordance with the one person, one vote principle. Provisions requiring each of the state's 105 counties to have at least one seat in the Kansas House were struck from the constitution. Further, Article 10 was revised to adopt periodic reapportionment of the legislature in ten-year cycles, based on US census data.[16] Compliance with these US Supreme Court rulings began in advance of constitutional changes and dramatically shifted legislative representation in Kansas from smaller rural jurisdictions to larger urban and suburban parts of the state (see chapter 1).[17]

The changing complexion of representation in the legislature driven by reapportionment fomented change, and a push forward came from within. An informal, ad hoc alliance of bipartisan legislators took shape in the early 1970s. The energy of newly arriving backbenchers was channeled through emerging legislative leaders: Democrat Pete Loux of Wichita (house minority leader, 1969–75) and Republicans Duane "Pete" McGill of Winfield (house speaker, 1973–76) and Wendell Lady of Overland Park (house minority leader, 1977–78; house speaker, 1979–82). Republican representative Clyde Hill of Yates Center, the elder statesman of the alliance, lent the younger activists the credibility of his experience: he had been elected to the Kansas House in 1954, served as speaker for two sessions (1966 and 1967), and then continued in other leadership roles through his ninth term in the house (1973–74).[18]

Most of the reformers had attended meetings of the national Citizens Conference on State Legislatures and had carefully studied the conference's 1971 report, *The Sometime Governments*, which provided a template for change. Former Republican representative Jim Maag recalled: "We didn't want our legislature to be ranked last in the nation."[19]

Importantly, in 1971, the legislature created by statute the Legislative Coordinating Council to govern legislative operations. The seven-member council consisted of the legislative leadership—the speaker, speaker pro tem, and majority and minority leaders of the Kansas House and the president and majority and minority leaders of the Kansas Senate. It replaced the long-standing Legislative Council, which had comprised twenty-six legislators, mostly senior members, plus the lieutenant governor as chair. The former council had been in place since the 1930s and served as the primary mechanism for interim studies of legislative and policy issues, but it had lost credibility with rank-and-file legislators over time. The outgoing council acknowledged its shortcomings, reporting that, "in the period following reapportionment of the legislature, many new, younger members wanted to be more involved in the total legislative process and they challenged old institutions which they felt were obstacles to such involvement."[20]

According to Richard Ryan, former director of the Kansas Legislative Research Department, the move to replace the old Legislative Council resulted in part from growing confusion and duplication related to interim studies. Increasingly, in the late 1960s and early 1970s, certain standing committees operated in conflict with the traditional role of the Legislative Council.[21] Participation in interim study committees was expanded significantly under the Legislative Coordinating Council.

The newly established Legislative Coordinating Council was charged with governing legislative activities, as follows: (1) oversee and establish rules for legislative committees, except for those committees conducting specific statutory assignments; (2) create and appoint legislative study committees and determine topics for study; (3) select, remove, and supervise the heads of the Legislative Research Department, the revisor of statutes, and the Division of Legislative Administrative Services; and (4) oversee legislative expenditures and prepare a budget for the legislature.

Once the Legislative Coordinating Council was launched, its members pushed forward a reform agenda. In 1972, 1973, and 1974, the council appointed a Legislative Budget Committee composed entirely of top leadership. Though intended as an interim committee for budget oversight, the committee became the vehicle for considering additional steps for institutional change.[22] Over three years, the Legislative Budget Committee made proposals for updating and cleaning up the legislative article of the constitution, clarifying legislative rules and procedures, refining and strengthening the powers of the Legislative Coordinating Council, and implementing changes in the legislative article ratified in November 1974.

A whirlwind of activity took shape in the 1973 and 1974 legislative sessions under the leadership of senate president Robert Bennett and house speaker Pete McGill. They presented joint messages at the beginning of both sessions as guides for legislative action. The Democratic minority leaders—Pete Loux of the house and Jack Steineger of the senate—cooperated in making institutional reform a bipartisan endeavor. Beyond its regular legislative work, the Kansas legislature compiled a substantial record on institutional improvement in 1973 and 1974:

- It submitted constitutional amendments to voters for ratification, including:
  — procedures for apportioning legislative representation every ten years, based on US census data;
  — elimination of the constitutional office of state printer; and
  — revision and updating of the legislative article.
- It enacted legislation on campaign finance reform, requiring disclosure and regulating campaign contributions and expenditures for all state elective offices.
- It enacted legislation establishing guidelines for ethical conduct by state officers and employees and regulating such conduct.
- It created the Commission on Governmental Ethics to administer campaign finance reforms and compile guidelines for the conduct of state officers and employees.
- It created the Division of State Planning and Research, headed by a director appointed by the governor.
- It enacted legislation giving voters the option of nonpartisan selection of district court judges.
- It enacted legislation establishing the president of the senate, not the lieutenant governor, as that chamber's presiding officer.
- It supported the following action on executive reorganization:
  — cleared the implementation of Executive Reorganization Order Nos. 1 and 3, creating the Department of Social and Rehabilitation Services and the Department of Health and Environment, respectively, each headed by a secretary serving at the pleasure of the governor; and
  — abolished the office of state auditor and transferred its duties.

Bipartisan reforms of the state legislature, which began in the mid-1960s and continued through 1974, would earn Kansas national recognition in 1976 as the "most improved" state legislature in the nation.[23]

Historically bare-bones legislative staffing and support grew substantially in the early 1970s. Research assistance was extended to interim committees, and secretarial assistance for individual legislators was expanded during legislative sessions. Office space was steadily made more available in the capitol building for legislators, and space for legislative committee meetings was increased. Elementary technology, such as telephones and microphones, became more widely available.

With the elimination of the elected state auditor, the legislature created the Legislative Post Audit Committee and the Legislative Division of Post Audit headed by the legislative post auditor. The ten-member Post Audit Committee provided for the representation of majority and minority parties and was charged with selecting, removing, and directing the legislative post auditor and determining matters to be audited. Audit reports would advise the committee, the governor, and the legislature as a whole whether state agencies were following the law, achieving intended results, and operating efficiently.

In 1974, the Legislative Coordinating Council also established a fiscal analysis staff within the Legislative Research Department. Historically, the legislature had relied on the budget office, which assisted the governor in preparing the executive budget, to respond to legislative inquiries on budgetary issues. Legislative dependence on a budget staff serving two masters—the governor and the legislature—became increasingly unworkable.[24] A separate fiscal analysis staff gave legislative committees charged with reviewing the governor's budget an independent capacity to analyze executive agency budget requests and recommend the appropriation of state funds.

Also in 1974, the legislature authorized the Legislative Coordinating Council to appoint a legislative counsel to represent the legislature in any matter and render advisory opinions on issues submitted by legislators or legislative committees.[25] Additional legislative action authorized the revisor of statutes to develop in phases a comprehensive legislative information system to assist in searching statutes and other documents and preparing bills and resolutions.

Beginning in the late 1960s and continuing through the mid-1970s, the legislature also formalized procedures regulating legislative operations. For example, it passed laws on:

- Pre-session organizational meetings for the selection of legislative leaders

- Pre-filing of bills
- Compulsory process for investigating committees
- Provision for open meetings and notice of meetings
- Prohibition on taking binding action through secret ballot
- Provision for compensation and expenses of legislators and legislative officers
- Provision for calling a special session of the legislature
- Pre-session orientation meetings for members-elect
- Convening of the legislature

These reforms brought clarity and consistency to legislative operations and decision making and were in line with recommendations by the Citizens Conference on State Legislatures and suggestions by individual legislators.[26]

In 1974, Kansas lawmakers enacted landmark legislation on campaign finance and governmental ethics. The Citizens Conference on State Legislatures had directed attention to the states in general and Kansas in particular on conflicts of interest and the regulation of lobbyists, and it called for every legislature to have "carefully drawn ethical guidelines."[27] However, legislative action on such matters had stalled in Kansas. Consideration of this issue came to a head in the wake of the Watergate scandal and the resignation of Vice President Spiro Agnew at the national level. Kansas legislators' attention became more focused in January 1974 when a Shawnee County grand jury brought bribery charges against five firms and nineteen individuals, including Governor Docking's brother plus the governor's former assistant, in connection with the awarding of a $54 million state construction contract.[28]

Senate president Bennett and house speaker McGill announced their intention to make action on campaign finance a priority in the 1974 legislative session. A proposal drafted by an interim committee on elections provided a starting point for deliberations.[29] Bennett, the prime mover for the legislation, pushed for early action by the senate and later led negotiations in conference committee discussions; house minority leader Loux, who had kept the issue alive over earlier interims, gave the measure strong bipartisan support.[30] The enacted legislation required full disclosure of all campaign contributions and expenditures in elections for state office by all candidates, political parties, and political committees.[31] These requirements included:

- Prohibition on receiving campaign contributions or making campaign expenditures without first appointing a campaign treasurer
- Provisions for filing reports on campaign contributions and expenditures by all candidates for state office, political parties, and political committees at specified intervals
- Limitations on campaign contributions by individuals, organizations, or committees
- Limitations on campaign expenditures by candidates for state office and congressional offices

A bipartisan Commission on Governmental Ethics was established to enforce these requirements and to rule on violations of the law.

Companion legislation on the ethical conduct of state officers and employees also moved forward from the senate. The enacted legislation charged the Commission on Governmental Ethics to administer the guidelines on ethics, which included the following:[32]

- Prohibition on the solicitation and acceptance of gifts
- Disclosure of substantial financial interests by all elected officials and candidates, individuals subject to confirmation by the senate, and employees
- Prohibition on state officers, employees, or their business associates making representations before a state agency without first filing a disclosure statement
- Registration of lobbyists

Bennett and McGill also closed down hospitality rooms sponsored by lobbyists near the statehouse. Harold Stones, a lobbyist for the Kansas Bankers Association at that time, remembered being asked to meet with the two legislative leaders. He recalled Bennett saying: "We need you to shut down your hospitality room. It looks bad. The people think it's bad. Our members are traipsing back and forth at all hours. We need the bankers to take the lead."[33] The bankers association complied, and other lobbyists followed suit. The closures generated headlines and allowed Bennett and McGill to distance the legislature from the unfolding Watergate saga as well as the taint of scandal embroiling Governor Docking at the time. Overall, the new laws governing campaign finance and ethical conduct led to decades in which the political institutions of the Kansas government were free of serious scandal.

In sum, the state government was undergoing an institutional transformation. Most nineteenth-century shackles on the state's executive, judicial, and legislative functions had been cut loose. Against this backdrop of fundamental change, how would Kansas voters assess these reforms? How would they respond to a leader of reform? These questions would be addressed in part in the 1974 campaign for governor.

The 1974 Race for Governor

The 1974 gubernatorial contest would not begin to take shape before the incumbent four-term governor, Robert Docking, announced his political plans. Governor Docking, a conservative Democrat, remained popular, and pundits speculated that he might challenge Republican Bob Dole for a US Senate seat rather than run for reelection as governor. Meanwhile, Democrats considering a run for either office were left waiting in the wings.

Docking delivered his decision to a statewide gathering of Democrats in early March: "I will not seek reelection as governor. I will not seek election as U.S. senator. I will return to private life. My decision is firm."[34] Within the month, attorney general Vern Miller, a top vote-getter for Democrats, declared that he would enter the race for governor, and that announcement cleared an uncontested path for Miller to win the Democratic nomination.

On the Republican side, Kansas Senate president Robert Bennett had emerged from the 1974 legislative session in a strong position to make a run for governor. He had led bipartisan lawmakers through a progressive resurgence—two productive legislative sessions that transformed the executive, judicial, and legislative institutions of Kansas. But his quest for the governorship would not be a cakewalk. Legislative leadership had not proved to be a stepping-stone to the governor's office. Indeed, not one of the thirty-three Kansas governors elected from 1861 through 1972 had risen to the position of chief executive while serving as a legislative leader.[35]

Bennett had first been elected to the Kansas Senate in 1964, when institutional reform was in a formative stage. He was reelected in 1968 and 1972 and rose steadily as a force in the senate, serving as chair of the Committee on Commercial and Financial Institutions and vice chair of the Assessment and Taxation Committee. He was actively engaged in tax policy as well as revision of school finance legislation in 1970–71 and a complete rewrite of the School District Equalization Act of 1973.[36] In 1973, Bennett's colleagues elected him president of the senate.

Leroy Towns, a statehouse reporter at the time, remembered Bennett as being thoughtful, even scholarly, in legislative deliberations and described him as exceptionally skilled in interpersonal relations.[37] He was capable of working congenially across political factions and had a reputation for reading the minutiae in every bill under consideration, being well prepared and forceful in floor debate, and outworking the opposition. Rarely did a colleague look forward to facing off against Bennett in a legislative contest.

Bennett initially declined to run for governor. Before the opening of the 1974 legislative session, he firmly announced: "I am not now, nor do I have any present or prospective intentions of becoming a candidate for the Republican nomination for governor of Kansas in 1974." He explained that he wanted to continue his contributions to "future modifications and improvements which should move the legislative branch to the position of equality [with the executive branch] which the constitution mandates." After the legislature adjourned slightly more than three months later, Bennett declared a change of heart: "I will be a candidate for the Republican nomination for Governor of Kansas." His earlier announcement, he rationalized, had allowed the legislative session to proceed without devolving into "partisan shambles," making it "one of the most productive sessions in recent state history." Further, he sensed "an intensified concern among many Kansans about the future of executive leadership of this state, [and] the ability of that leadership to work with a revitalized legislature."[38]

In his campaigns for state office, Bennett would seldom escape opposition in the primaries.[39] In 1964, his first race for the state senate, he faced a two-term house incumbent and won by just 54 votes out of 8,300 cast, the margin confirmed by a recount. His campaign for governor drew three primary opponents, including two with strong regional draws: Don Concannon of western Kansas and Forrest Robinson of Wichita. Bennett eked out a narrow victory with 32.4 percent of the vote, defeating Concannon by only 530 votes out of 208,000 cast; Robinson came in a strong third with 56,000 votes. Bennett prevailed by building up vote margins in his eastern Kansas City base.

The Republicans' competitive primary campaign had unfolded without creating any damaging divisions. Clyde Reed of the *Parsons Sun* observed: "The GOP emerged from a four-way contest for the governorship without scars. The race was clean all the way and there will be no feuds to carry into the general election."[40] Bennett's campaign organization promptly built bridges with his primary opponents. Robinson was named field director to work on the general election, and Concannon was recruited to join the campaign in an advisory capacity.

With the party nominations for governor settled, Bennett faced an uphill battle. A couple weeks after Bennett's primary victory, an independent media survey showed Miller leading statewide among potential voters, 56 to 32 percent.[41] Miller was ahead in every congressional district, including Bennett's own Kansas City area district, and among every category of voter—urban and rural, men and women, and all age groups. Bennett was undeterred, declaring, "We're closing the gap."

Miller's law-and-order persona represented a stark contrast to Bennett's legislative service. Miller had made a name for himself as sheriff of Sedgwick County with an aggressive, highly personal brand of law enforcement that only escalated when he became attorney general. His legendary exploits included jumping out of the trunk of police cars at drug raids in university towns and seeking to enforce state liquor laws on interstate trains and planes that crossed Kansas territory or airspace. In the waning days of the gubernatorial campaign, Miller donned a disguise to bust up a drug-buying operation.

Bennett responded by focusing on personal competence, modernization of state government, and the need for a governor with broad expertise in public policy. His message on the campaign trail reiterated these themes: "Government is a complex business with a $1.3 billion budget. . . . You need some experience, some knowledge of state government to run a business like that."[42] He called for increased spending on education at all levels and vowed to remove state highway decisions from the "politics of road building."

Bennett repeatedly challenged Miller to debate during the campaign, but the Democrat resisted. Bennett taunted: "His lack of familiarity with state issues will undoubtedly show up. . . . If necessary, we will debate empty chairs."[43] When Miller advanced a proposal for a state spending lid, Bennett blasted back: "The spending lid could easily be used to avoid the responsibility the governor has to veto irresponsible legislation. . . . Any governor who shirks the responsibility to veto a bad bill shouldn't be seeking the office."[44] Miller eventually consented to one debate near the end of the campaign.

Bennett could not ignore the public attention and media focus on his stylish Vandyke beard and the debate over whether he should shave it off. "We do on occasion get several questions about it," he conceded to a civic club audience. He quipped that someone had suggested T-shirts featuring his bearded visage and the caption: "Not just another pretty face."[45]

Bennett's productive legislative experience earned him favorable treatment from statehouse reporters and garnered a clear majority of newspaper endorsements across the state. They essentially echoed Bennett's campaign themes and the striking contrast between Miller's image and Bennett's substance. Typical on the editorial pages were the words of Henry Jameson of the *Abilene Reflector-Chronicle*: "The biggest thing that Vern Miller . . . has going for him is his name and public image of a truck-jumping, club raiding and publicity wise attorney general. On the other hand the Republican candidate, Senator Bob Bennett, is a genuinely capable man with years of experience in government and the administrative process. . . . Boiling it all down to the qualifications of the two candidates . . . there is in our opinion no comparison."[46]

By Election Day, Bennett had closed the gap. He squeaked by, beating Miller by a slender margin of 3,677 votes out of 784,000 cast and falling just short of 50 percent of the vote, as a third-party candidate picked up 12,000 votes. Bennett carried his home county of Johnson by 25,000 votes, compared to Miller's 17,000 in Sedgwick County. Bennett also built a 14,000-vote advantage in three state university communities in Douglas, Riley, and Lyon Counties.

Governor Robert F. Bennett

In January 1975, Bennett stepped into a governor's office that he had helped transform over the prior ten years. He became the first Kansas governor to serve a four-year term with a lieutenant governor of his own choosing. He would be held publicly accountable for the newly organized cabinet departments headed by secretaries serving at his pleasure. He would have at his disposal broad constitutional powers of executive reorganization and would face a revitalized legislative institution. As governor, Bennett would continue taking steps toward reform of the executive branch and leave his distinct imprint on the expanded duties of the state's chief executive.

Bennett moved promptly on reorganizing the executive branch.[47] In his first legislative message, delivered ten days after assuming office, he announced his support for abolishing the politically tainted state Highway Commission and replacing it with a broader Department of Transportation. Former governor Docking had been reluctant to take on the Highway Commission, but Bennett's support of the reorganized department quieted opposition from entrenched highway interests and secured a smooth path to enactment by the legislature. Also in 1975, the governor sought to eliminate the elective offices of state treasurer and insurance commissioner, but his executive orders were rebuffed by members of his own party.

In 1976, Bennett issued executive reorganization orders to establish the Departments of Economic Development and Human Resources, and both cleared without legislative opposition. Over his four-year term he would issue eleven executive reorganization orders, and all but three moved forward without legislative objection. In 1977, the legislature established the Department on Aging as a cabinet agency and made the secretary of the Department of Corrections subject to selection and removal by the governor. By the end of his term, Bennett would have nine cabinet department heads—representing roughly half the state budget—serving at his pleasure.

In addition to moving forward on executive reorganization, Bennett put executive reform into practice. For example, in advance of creating the Department of Transportation and within days of assuming office, Governor Bennett articulated his philosophy for managing the new department to the leading special-interest group on road construction, the Kansas Contractors Association:

> During my administration, I will not tolerate the utilization of the department for political patronage—for political purposes—nor will I allow the people of this state to become the victims of "special deals"—"controlled bidding"—or any other chicanery—whether it be for partisan or personal gain. I assure you that should any employee of the department violate this precept, he will be discharged forthwith. Likewise, should any contractor or supplier encourage the violation of this precept, he will be dealt with in a summary fashion. . . . As

a Kansan—a lawyer—a former legislator—and now as your governor—I have many friends and supporters but—when they deal with state government—in the offering of either material or service—they will deal as strangers.[48]

In the wake of prior scandals, he chose words that would leave little doubt about his desire to reshape the administration of state government.

Once lawmakers created the new Department of Transportation, Bennett recruited and appointed a professional department head, explaining:

> I campaigned on the reorganization of our Highway Commission into a Department of Transportation [because] I felt highway funds should be allocated on the basis of need as determined by travel and condition of the roads rather than upon the basis of political clout and patronage. . . . In keeping with this commitment . . . I recruited, not a politician, but an experienced engineer and planner to be the Secretary of this new department. For the first time in my memory the governmental head of the department supervising the maintenance and construction of the highways was not the political pal or ally of the governor, appointed to carry out his bidding, but rather an experienced professional dedicated to improving the transportation system of this state within the funds available.[49]

Highway boosters, most often local newspaper editors, would dispute Bennett's highway policy and administration throughout his term.[50] They would rally area residents to claim that their roads were worse and their share of highway funds less than in other parts of the state. The governor, however, stood fast in defending his transportation secretary and his policies on the allocation of highway funds, even though he would suffer political consequences.

Bennett wanted to insulate his administration from politics and explicitly expressed his intentions to his personal staff. As governor-elect, he instructed staff members that their services and courtesies should "be available to all Kansans, regardless of political affiliation," and that no action of his office should "be dependent upon past contributions or future offers of contributions, either to my campaign or to the Republican Party." Any staff member violating this policy, he directed, "shall be subject to immediate dismissal" and possibly prosecution for violation of the law. Similarly, any staff member found to "threaten political reprisal" would be subject to prompt removal.[51]

Bennett also acted to ensure strict enforcement of the law on conflicts of interest, which he had championed as senate leader. In June 1975, he issued an executive order directing all executive branch officials and employees to comply with prohibitions on the acceptance of gifts or entertainment, as outlined in the law. He warned that any failure to comply could result in "termination or other disciplinary action." Any questions about the propriety of conduct or specific application of the law, he advised, should be referred to the Governmental Ethics Commission.[52]

As his campaign for reelection was under way in 1978, Bennett directed executive officials and employees to avoid political impropriety in carrying out their official duties. He cited statutory prohibitions on political activity but also issued specific guidelines directing that supervisors should not solicit political contributions from their employees and that no political activity should be undertaken in the workplace. Campaign paraphernalia, he warned, should not be displayed, worn, or distributed at an employee's place of employment.[53]

Governor Bennett believed passionately that effective and efficient administration could best be achieved by insulating that administration from undue political influence and that he could draw a bright red line between politics and government. Former statehouse reporter Leroy Towns served as Bennett's press secretary and described the governor as follows: "Bennett was a genuine, good government guy. He revered government and had a disdain for politics. He felt prior governors had allowed state government to become tainted with politics and wanted to change that. As senate president, he had become bothered about the politics influencing the awarding of state contracts, particularly those involving state highways. He was adamant about stopping that."[54]

Bennett was also committed to making merit-based appointments. As he acted on these precepts, he experienced pushback from legislators and local party officials, among others. As a result, he spent extensive time explaining and defending his philosophy as chief executive.[55] In one instance, a close political ally demanded that Bennett fire the secretary of a major cabinet department who was a holdover from the prior governor's administration. Bennett responded with a lengthy defense of the secretary:

> I don't think he is perfect, he has made errors, and we certainly have had our disagreements but when I review the vast number of programs, most with federal restrictions, which he is expected to run, the number of institutions which

he is expected to supervise, and the number of local providers and clients that he is expected to serve, I marvel at his ability to keep his sanity let alone his balance. When I get upset with a dispute that he hasn't been able to resolve, which doesn't occur that often, I start to think how I would like to spend a day, a week, or a month trying to administer that department.... I quickly come to the conclusion that a solution to the dispute is essential but that it lies more in my personal involvement to improve communication and engender compromise as distinguished from replacing one of the combatants.[56]

The governor firmly believed that persuasion and logic could carry the day with those who questioned his administration.

While tending to executive reorganization and exercising his expanded appointment authority, Bennett acted aggressively on a parallel course to shape a gubernatorial agenda on public policy. Without a clear electoral mandate, he deployed the resources available to leave his stamp on state policy and the state budget. The executive's budget staff was immediately available to him as governor-elect and assisted him in recommending his first budget. Still, based on his legislative experience, the governor was aware of the historic domination of state government by the budget staff, and he established a counterbalancing policy analysis staff within the newly created Division of State Planning and Research.[57]

Bennett brought his legislative experience and lawyerly style into deliberations on both policy and the budget. He wanted all the facts on each case brought to bear, and he welcomed diverse perspectives and multiple voices. He sought a complete understanding of issues and consumed extensive background research on topics large and small. His legislative experience led to his mastery of subjects such as school finance and taxation, which he could dispose of with dispatch. But half the state budget and many other problems that landed on the governor's desk were beyond his direct experience, and for those he depended on his policy and budget staff for assistance.

The governor adopted a problem-solving mode on matters outside his expertise. As a legislative leader, he had valued and promoted the extensive use of interim committees to study and address issues. As governor, his alternative to such committees was the gubernatorial task force, which he deployed to deal with a range of topics, from broad issues such as water resources to narrower concerns involving interagency coordination. He used task forces to bring diverse voices into the discussion, identify and define issues more clearly, further public understanding, and explore alternative approaches to resolution. Task forces also served as screening mechanisms for development of the governor's annual legislative message and budget.

During his term as governor, Bennett used task forces to tackle a wide range of issues.[58] For example, a task force consisting of top business executives surveyed management issues in the administration of state government and identified areas of potential cost savings. A task force on problems confronting youth assembled public and private stakeholders and recommended investments in prevention and family preservation. Another one on water resources, chaired by the lieutenant governor, engaged state executives, legislators, and interested parties to lay the groundwork for the establishment of a state water office and the development of a state water plan.[59]

Governor Bennett left a distinct mark on the Kansas governorship as an activist chief executive, chief policymaker, and chief manager of state government. He believed passionately in the cause of good government and in his ability to persuade Kansans to adopt a broad vision of "One Kansas!!" that could prevail over competing interests and divisions across the state, regardless of the issue.[60] He drew on his command of language and his skills in extemporaneous speech to communicate and explain the complexities of government and outline the wise course forward—in his view.

Kansans appeared to be persuaded, and Bennett campaigned for reelection in 1978 with confidence. He cited his accomplishments and advocated fiscal accountability.[61] He ran a positive campaign and avoided personal attacks on his opponents. Voting-age Kansans surveyed in August 1978 gave the governor a 60 percent approval rating. A similar number approved of "the way things are going in state government."[62] On the Sunday before Election Day, the *Topeka Capital-Journal* headlined: "Bennett Leads Carlin by 13 Points."

But the tide was turning, and it shifted sharply in the waning days of the campaign. Dairy farmer and speaker of the Kansas House John Carlin attacked Bennett with campaign ads depicting the governor as part of "a cadre of overweight, sweaty, cigar-smoking men muscling money out of the taxpayer."[63] Bennett ignored the attacks, and Carlin achieved a slim but clear victory, winning by a margin just short of 16,000 votes out of 736,000 cast. Bennett had lost ground, compared with his 1974 tallies, in rural counties, in counties with concentrations of state employees, and in counties experiencing local turmoil over highway funding.[64]

Robert Bennett would depart after one term as governor, but his imprint on the governorship would live on. He was the first Kansas governor elected from a position of legislative leadership, and he would be succeeded by two governors—John Carlin (1979–87) and Mike Hayden (1987–91)—similarly elected while serving as leaders in the legislature. Both of them would follow Bennett's example as an activist chief executive. Both would establish their respective legacies in public policy—Carlin on economic development, and Hayden on infrastructure.

Bennett firmly established the cabinet model of gubernatorial administration. His commitment to merit-based appointments and governmental ethics set high standards for those who followed. Hayden served in the Kansas legislature during Bennett's term and observed:

> Bob Bennett should be remembered for cleaning up the political mess surrounding the old state Highway Commission. That commission had a long history of filling jobs through political patronage, turning a blind eye toward bid rigging, and having politics decide who got roads and who didn't. Bennett supported abolishing the old commission and creating the Department of Transportation. And his administration of the new department established a standard of public service that lives on to the present time.[65]

Hayden believed that his own initiation of a comprehensive highway program in 1987 succeeded in part due to the support of a credible and professionally managed Department of Transportation.

As governor, Carlin experienced Bennett's change in gubernatorial administration from a different perspective, as many local partisans expected him to restore patronage jobs and to do so quickly. But as he tried to explain: "The rules changed and the governor could no longer dictate who got those highway jobs in counties across the state. . . . I always believed that you do things right, this is the way you operate: we're going to put good people in, but it was hell."[66] Carlin recalled that Docking Democrats across the state were very upset, and his lieutenant governor abandoned the post over the controversy.

Robert F. Bennett contributed extraordinary leadership during the progressive resurgence in Kansas from the mid-1960s through the late 1970s. As a legislative leader and as governor, he applied his exceptional skills to the work that transformed the legislative, executive, and judicial institutions of the state.

Notes

1. Quoted in Kenneth S. Davis, *Kansas* (New York: W. W. Norton, 1976), 170–171.
2. Davis, 176; William Allen White, *The Autobiography of William Allen White* (New York: Macmillan, 1946), 546.
3. Neal R. Pierce and Jerry Hagstrom, *The Book of America* (New York: W. W. Norton, 1983), 585.
4. US Commission on Intergovernmental Relations, *A Report to the President for Transmittal to the Congress* (Washington, DC: US Government Printing Office, 1955).
5. Citizens Conference on State Legislatures, *The Sometime Governments: A Critical Study of the 50 American Legislatures* (New York: Bantam Books, 1971), 217–220.
6. Larry Sabato, *Goodbye to Good-Time Charlie: The American Governor Transformed, 1950–1975* (Lexington, MA: Lexington Books, 1978), 66–67; see also 63–96.
7. H. Edward Flentje and Joseph A. Aistrup, *Kansas Politics and Government: The Clash of Political Cultures* (Lincoln: University of Nebraska Press, 2010), 35–40.
8. One of the amendments ratified in 1970 attempted to revise two articles with one amendment and was struck down by the Kansas Supreme Court for this reason.
9. The discussion of constitutional changes is drawn in part from the excellent review by Francis H. Heller, *The Kansas Constitution: A Reference Guide* (Westport, CT: Greenwood Press, 1992), 25–34.
10. This section draws heavily from chapter 5 of Flentje and Aistrup, *Kansas Politics and Government*.
11. Kansas Commission on Executive Reorganization, *Reorganizing Kansas State Government for Maximum Effectiveness, Efficiency and Economy* (Topeka, January 1971), v, 6–7, 9.
12. Wesley E. Brown, "Some Views Concerning the Modernization of Kansas Courts," *Judicial Council Bulletin*, October 1964, 4–6.
13. Harold R. Fatzer, "The Proposed Judicial Article," *Judicial Council Bulletin*, October 1972, 3–5.
14. Fatzer, 3.
15. Fatzer, 4.
16. Final agreement on the use of census data would not be resolved until 1988. See Heller, *Kansas Constitution*, 112–115, for an initial review of litigation over whether university students and military personnel should be counted at their physical location or their place of legal residence. A number of other changes were made in the legislative article of the early 1970s to bring the constitution in line with court action, shift minor provisions between sections, make procedural adjustments, and remove obsolete provisions (see Heller, 70–82). See also Kansas Legislative Coordinating Council, *Report on Kansas Interim Studies to the 1973 Kansas Legislature, Part I, Special Committees*, December 1972, 268–274.

17. Marvin Harder and Carolyn Rampey, *The Kansas Legislature: Procedures, Personalities, and Problems* (Lawrence: University Press of Kansas, 1972), 18–25.

18. David Heinemann, who served in the Kansas House at the time, confirmed that Loux was "a silent mover behind the scenes." David Heinemann interview, April 2, 2021. Richard Ryan, former director of the Legislative Research Department, noted McGill's early push for reform. Richard Ryan interview, June 7, 2021. Hill served as vice chair of the 1972 Legislative Budget Committee, was a member of the 1973 Legislative Budget Committee, chaired the 1973 Special Committee on Ways and Means, and was chair of the House Ways and Means Committee in 1973 and 1974. Hill was also active in court consolidation as former chair of the House Judiciary Committee.

19. James S. Maag interview, March 26, 2021. Maag served in the Kansas House from 1969 through 1976; he was assistant majority leader in 1973–74 and speaker pro tem in 1975–76.

20. Kansas Legislative Council, *Report and Recommendations Submitted to the 1971 Legislature, Part I*, December 10, 1970, 220.

21. Ryan interview, June 7, 2021. Ryan served on the staff of the Kansas Legislative Research Department during the period under study and as director of the department from 1978 through 1996.

22. See Kansas Legislative Coordinating Council, *Report on Kansas Interim Studies to the 1973 Kansas Legislature, Part I, Special Committees*, December 1972; *Report on Kansas Interim Studies to the 1974 Kansas Legislature, Parts I and II, Special Committees*, November 1973; and *Report on Kansas Interim Studies to the 1974 Kansas Legislature, Parts I and II, Special Committees*, December 1974. Richard Ryan points out that the Legislative Budget Committee initiated the revenue-estimating committee, composed of legislative and executive staff plus consulting economists from state universities, that still produces revenue estimates today. The committee process has avoided conflicting revenue estimates between the legislative and executive branches in Kansas for nearly fifty years. Ryan interview, June 7, 2021.

23. H. Edward Flentje, ed., *Selected Papers of Governor Robert F. Bennett: A Study in Good Government and "Civics Book" Politics* (Wichita: Center for Urban Studies, Wichita State University, 1979), 1.

24. For a short history of this development, see Marlin Rein and Sherry Brown, *The Appropriating Process in Kansas* (a publication of the Kansas legislature), November 1982, 3–12.

25. This bill was passed by overriding Governor Docking's veto. See Kansas Legislative Research Department, *Highlights of the 1974 Legislature*, March 23, 1974, 3.

26. See Kansas Legislative Coordinating Council, *Report on Kansas Interim Studies to the 1973 Kansas Legislature, Part I, Special Committees*, December 1972, 289–291.

27. See Citizens Conference on State Legislatures, *Sometime Governments*, 130–133, 166–167, 219.

28. *Salina Journal*, January 23, 1974, 1–2.

29. Kansas Legislative Coordinating Council, *Report on Kansas Interim Studies to the 1974 Kansas Legislature, Part II, Special Committees*, November 1973, 60-1–60-26.

30. Lynn Hellebust interview, April 16, 2021. Hellebust was on the staff of the Kansas Legislative Research Department and served as principal staff member for the elections committees during their deliberations on this legislation. Later in 1974, he became the first director of the Commission on Governmental Ethics.

31. Kansas Legislative Research Department, *Highlights of the 1974 Legislature*, 2.

32. Kansas Legislative Research Department, *Highlights of the 1974 Legislature*, 2–3.

33. Harold Stones interview, April 6, 2021.

34. *Wichita Eagle*, March 3, 1974, 1.

35. Walter Stubbs might be considered the one exception. He was elected governor in 1908 and reelected in 1910 after serving in the legislature from 1903 to 1908. He was elected speaker of the Kansas House for the 1905 session but did not hold a top leadership position in 1907 or 1908. Another possible exception is Frank Hagaman, who was never elected governor but was elected lieutenant governor in 1948. He served as governor for forty-one days when Governor Frank Carlson vacated the office after being elected to the US Senate in 1950. As lieutenant governor, Hagaman would have presided over the Kansas Senate, as prescribed in the state constitution at the time.

36. Harder and Rampey, *Kansas Legislature*, 86–98.

37. Leroy Towns interview, April 1, 2021.

38. Flentje, *Selected Papers of Bennett*, 8–9, 9–10.

39. Bennett's only primary without opposition was his first race for reelection to the state senate in 1968.

40. Quoted in Charles Pearson, "The State's Political Scene," *Wichita Eagle*, September 1, 1974, 21.

41. *Wichita Eagle*, August 30, 1974, 15.

42. *Wichita Eagle*, July 4, 1974, 14.

43. *Wichita Eagle*, September 13, 1974, 39.

44. *Wichita Eagle*, October 12, 1974, 54.

45. *Wichita Eagle*, July 4, 1974, 14.

46. Quoted in Charles Pearson, "Another Go at the Candidates," *Wichita Eagle*, October 20, 1974, 39.

47. See Flentje and Aistrup, *Kansas Politics and Government*, 106–120, for a review of executive reorganization.

48. "Speech to Kansas Contractors Association," Kansas City, MO, January 16, 1975, in Flentje, *Selected Papers of Bennett*, 217.

49. Letter to Donald M. Skoglund, *Arkansas City Daily Traveler*, August 4, 1976, in Flentje, *Selected Papers of Bennett*, 219.

50. See Flentje, *Selected Papers of Bennett*, 215–229.

51. "Memorandum to Staff of the Governor Elect," n.d., in Flentje, *Selected Papers of Bennett*, 236.

52. "Executive Order No. 75-8 Establishing Standards of Conduct for State Officials and Employees Concerning Conflicts of Interest," June 26, 1975, in Flentje, *Selected Papers of Bennett*, 238–240.

53. "Memorandum to All Agencies under the Supervision of the Governor Concerning Political Activity," July 7, 1978, in Flentje, *Selected Papers of Bennett*, 255–256.

54. Towns interview, April 1, 2021.

55. See Flentje, *Selected Papers of Bennett*, 223–257.

56. Flentje, *Selected Papers of Bennett*, 254.

57. This domination is reflected in a quotation in Harder and Rampey, *Kansas Legislature*, 62: "The governor is governor, but Mr. Bibb is king." Longtime budget director Jim Bibb dominated much of state government under prior administrations and supported the legislature's move to establish its own fiscal analysis staff in the early 1970s. Governor Bennett recruited the author of this chapter to become director of the Division of State Planning and Research and establish a staff capacity for policy analysis in support of the governor.

58. See Flentje, *Selected Papers of Bennett*, for task forces on energy emergency management (155–156), the future of the Kansas transportation system (224–225), effective management (270), water resources (279–280), state development (285–286), management policy (286–287), library resources (287), problems of youth (291), state data processing and review (296–297), and aging (297).

59. See the reports of the Governor's Task Force on Effective Management, August 1977; Governor's Task Force on the Problems of Youth, 1978; and Governor's Task Force on Water Resources, December 1977 and 1978.

60. See Flentje, *Selected Papers of Bennett*, 30, for the governor's extemporaneous remarks on "One Kansas!!" at a Kansas Day banquet, January 27, 1978.

61. "Statement on Taxation and Spending [to the Republican Platform Committee]," August 22, 1978, in Flentje, *Selected Papers of Bennett*, 32–36.

62. Flentje, *Selected Papers of Bennett*, 324.

63. "Be Willing to Take Some Risks to Make Things Happen: A Conversation with Former Governor John W. Carlin," *Kansas History: A Journal of the Central Plains* 31 (Summer 2008): 124.

64. Flentje, *Selected Papers of Bennett*, 325–326.

65. Mike Hayden interview, April 6, 2021.

66. "Be Willing to Take Some Risks," 131–136.

CHAPTER THREE

Political Competition and Policy Activism in the 1980s
Governors Carlin and Hayden

H. Edward Flentje

Legislative reapportionment, combined with constitutional reform of the state's political institutions in the 1960s and 1970s, ignited a period of political competition and policy activism that would continue into the early 1990s. Experienced legislative leaders—Robert Bennett, John Carlin, and Mike Hayden—advanced to the governorship, but neither Bennett nor Hayden won a second term. Legislative seats were tightly contested as well. Republicans controlled the state senate by narrow majorities but would lose their majority in the house twice during this period. Even with this intense partisan competition, highly productive policy initiatives in economic development, tax reform, and public infrastructure emerged.

Political Competition

Party registration in Kansas stabilized during the 1980s after the turmoil of the 1970s. The Republican Party remained dominant, as its share of registered voters edged upward slightly from 40 percent in 1980 to near 45 percent in 1990 and the percentage of unaffiliated voters declined. Democrats maintained their numbers, claiming slightly less than 30 percent of registered voters during this period.[1]

Surveys conducted in the 1980s showed that party alignments in Kansas reflected national demographic patterns. Republicans were predominantly Caucasian and Protestant, had higher levels of education and income than Democrats, and identified as conservative rather than liberal. A plurality of Kansans considered themselves politically moderate, and those identifying as conservative or liberal did not view themselves as extreme.[2]

In the early 1990s, political scientists Allan Cigler and Burdett Loomis described party politics in Kansas as "two-party competition in a one-party state." They characterized Kansas voters as "committed Republicans in national politics [who] frequently behave like unaligned voters in state elections."[3] In the three presidential elections of the 1980s, Kansas voters gave Ronald Reagan a 27-point margin over Jimmy Carter in 1980 and a 34-point margin for reelection over Walter Mondale in 1984. George H. W. Bush secured a tighter but respectable 15-point margin over Michael Dukakis in 1988. In 1992, however, Bush's margin over Bill Clinton narrowed to five points (39–34), as Ross Perot garnered 27 percent of the total vote.

Kansas's two US senators, Bob Dole and Nancy Kassebaum, coasted to election by wide margins in this period, the closest race being Kassebaum's initial election in 1978, in which she prevailed in a nine-way primary and then defeated former congressman Bill Roy in the general election with a comfortable 56 percent–44 percent margin. Nevertheless, moderate Democrats held two of five congressional seats for most of the period.[4] Democrat Dan Glickman defeated incumbent Garner Shriver in 1976 and then won reelection eight times in 1978 through 1992, representing the south-central Kansas district around Wichita. Jim Slattery won an open seat in 1982 in the northeastern corner of the state that included Topeka and was reelected five times before vacating the seat to run for governor in 1994.

Republican domination in national elections stood in stark contrast to highly competitive races for state office. Party control of the governor's office shifted three times in the four gubernatorial elections held in 1978 through 1990, with vote margins averaging one-half of 1 percent of the total votes cast. Republicans Robert Bennett and Mike Hayden won open contests for the governorship in 1974 and 1986, respectively, but lost to John Carlin and Joan Finney when they sought reelection, due in part to Republican factionalism. In their reelection bids, both Republican governors survived multiple primary challengers, who garnered 31 percent of the primary vote against Bennett in 1978 and a remarkable 54 percent against Hayden in 1990.

Interparty contests for state legislative seats were highly competitive as well. Republicans controlled the Kansas Senate throughout the period, but only by small margins. After losing six seats in 1976 in the aftermath of Watergate, Republicans began the 1979 legislative session with a bare 21–19 majority in the state senate. They regained two seats in 1980 and another in 1984 before losing two in 1988 and ending the period with a 22–18 edge at the start of the 1991 legislative session.

Party competition for the Kansas House was more volatile. Democrats gained control of the house in 1976 for only the second time in Kansas history, the first time being in 1912. They immediately lost control in 1978 and entered the 1979 legislative session on the short end of a 69–56 Republican majority. Republicans increased their majority through the next three elections, attaining a high of 76–49 for the 1985 legislative session, during the last half of Governor Carlin's second term. Then they lost ground in the next three elections, eventually surrendering control in 1990, for the third time in state history, by a slim 62–63 margin.

Gubernatorial Contests: Carlin and Hayden

Few observers would have predicted either Carlin's election to the governorship in 1978 or Hayden's in 1986. Both had risen in state politics and served as speaker of the Kansas House, just as Bennett had served as president of the Kansas Senate. Both came from farming backgrounds and rural upbringings. But similarities in their elevation to the governor's office end there.

Carlin's rise in state politics was dramatic: first elected to the Kansas House in 1970 at age thirty-two, he was selected as minority leader in 1975, advanced to speaker in 1977, and was elected governor in 1978. Two huge breaks boosted Carlin's political career. First, after serving as assistant minority leader beginning in 1973, Carlin stepped up as minority leader two years later when Pete Loux accepted a full-time executive appointment from Governor Bennett. Carlin's second break came when Democrats captured control of the Kansas House in the 1976 elections and Carlin became speaker. Ironically, within a little more than a year, he was challenging the incumbent governor who had cleared the way for Carlin's elevation to statewide visibility.

Carlin's rise illustrates how an agile, energetic centrist Democrat could succeed in the competitive arena of Kansas politics in the 1970s and 1980s. He gave up the speakership to jump into the governor's race in the face of formidable odds, first taking on two well-known primary opponents and then challenging an incumbent governor with high approval ratings. Carlin prevailed handily in the primary, garnering 55 percent of the vote in a three-person race, later asserting: "I outworked and out-organized my opponents. I was organized in every single county."[5]

The general election was another story. Bennett was widely viewed as an intelligent and competent governor, but he came across as aloof and much too urbane for rural Kansans. According to the governor's own polls, he had a 60 percent approval rating in August 1978, but Carlin attacked by making utility rates a campaign issue. He blamed the governor for rising utility rates and inattention to the impact of the state's first nuclear power plant on ratepayers. He promised to cut utility rates by removing the state sales tax on utility bills and, in line with Democratic governors George and Robert Docking before him, vowed to rein in state spending. Bennett ignored his challenger, and on the Sunday before the election, the *Topeka Capital-Journal* reassured the incumbent governor with the headline "Bennett Leads Carlin by 13 Points." But on Election Day, Carlin eked out a narrow victory, 49.4 percent versus Bennett's 47.3 percent, a margin just short of 16,000 votes. Aggregate vote totals showed that Bennett had lost ground in the state's rural counties compared with 1974—a shift of nearly 20,000 votes toward Carlin, the dairy farmer from Smolin.

Carlin showed similar savvy during his reelection campaign in 1982. Once again, he made the election about an issue—this time, a state severance tax on oil and gas. He had advocated enactment of a severance tax in the 1981 and 1982 legislative sessions to reduce the reliance on property taxes to fund schools, but Republican legislative majorities blocked his tax plan and helped set up the governor's reelection campaign. Carlin's Republican opponent, first-time candidate Wichita businessman Sam Hardage, played into the governor's hand by proposing higher gas taxes. Carlin easily framed a populist message for voters: he chose to tax a few rich oil companies rather than impose a tax burden on every Kansas family. The governor coasted to reelection, winning 53 percent of the vote—a margin of 66,000 votes.

Given the constitutional limit of two consecutive terms, the 1986 race for governor was wide open, and the Republican primary became a hotly contested seven-way race. Speaker of the Kansas House Mike Hayden did not appear to be a likely prospect. First elected a state representative in 1972 at age twenty-eight, he had emerged as a capable and respected legislative leader during his seven terms in the house—advancing past senior colleagues to chair the powerful Ways and Means Committee in 1979 and winning election as speaker without opposition in 1983 and 1985. However, Hayden's northwestern Kansas district was an unlikely base for a gubernatorial candidate. Moreover, he had a fourteen-year legislative record to defend. Most recently, during the 1986 legislative session, he had supported Carlin's one-cent sales tax increase to break a deadlock and had voted against popular proposals on liquor-by-the-drink and pari-mutuel wagering.

Hayden began to seriously consider the governorship in 1985 and believed his rural background might be an asset in a race expected to attract multiple candidates. He raised enough money to conduct a benchmark poll in October and used the results to develop a strategy. In contrast to Carlin's issue-oriented campaign, Hayden focused on candidate image. Since he was largely unknown to voters statewide, his campaign would highlight the personal characteristics likely to be most attractive to voters: Hayden came from a farm family, had been raised in a small town in western Kansas, was a Vietnam veteran, and had served fourteen years in the Kansas legislature, including four years as speaker of the Kansas House. This strategy would carry particular weight in the primary election, which focused on personalities and qualifications rather than issues.[6]

Hayden announced his intention to run for governor in the first week of January 1986, but by the June filing deadline, three other formidable candidates had entered the primary race: Wichita business executive Larry Jones, Pizza Hut millionaire Gene Bicknell, and incumbent Kansas secretary of state Jack Brier. Jones and Bicknell would each spend nearly $1.5 million on their campaigns, more than five times the amount spent by the Hayden campaign. A February poll by the *Topeka Capital-Journal* demonstrated the challenge facing Hayden. Only 8 percent of those surveyed could identify him as an active candidate for governor. Further, a head-to-head matchup against his eventual Democratic opponent Tom Docking showed Hayden trailing by a staggering 55 percent–27 percent margin.

Hayden hit the campaign trail at the close of the legislative session in May and rarely stopped before the August primary. A network of friendly Republican legislators allowed him to reach audiences in every corner of the state. He buffered issues through his mastery of state policy and reinforced his positive image through stump speeches and campaign commercials. His work paid off when he garnered 36 percent of the primary vote and won a plurality of votes in 92 of 105 counties, including Shawnee and Douglas, two of the state's five large urban counties. His closest competitor, Jones, obtained 31 percent of the votes, trailing Hayden by 14,000 votes. Polling immediately after the primary showed that his strategy had worked: 69 percent of those surveyed could now identify Hayden, and 81 percent had a favorable impression of him.[7]

Hayden immediately worked to consolidate support among his primary opponents, and his primary victory gave him a surprising postelection bump in the polls, pushing him ahead of Docking. However, the race tightened as Election Day got closer. Docking was campaigning as lieutenant governor, having joined Carlin's winning ticket in 1982 at age twenty-eight. The Docking name was golden in Kansas politics, as Docking's father and grandfather had won six two-year terms as governor—grandfather George, 1957–61, and father Bob, 1967–75. No single issue dominated the campaign, although Hayden championed highway improvement and enactment of a death penalty. The latter issue arose from Carlin's repeated vetoes of death penalty bills and Docking's opposition to the death penalty.

Hayden narrowly prevailed on Election Day, 51.9 to 48.1 percent, with a margin of 32,000 votes. He built a lead of nearly 58,000 votes in the one hundred smaller, mostly rural counties, which offset his 26,000-vote deficit in the five largest counties. Rural voters in the heavily Republican Big First District in western Kansas gave him a 25 percent margin, approaching a total of 50,000 votes.

Policy Activism

Constitutional amendments adopted in the early 1970s modernized the Kansas governorship and created greater potential for executive initiative at the state level. President Reagan's tax cuts in the early 1980s at the national level initiated a retrenchment and resulted in a vacuum for broadening the scope of state responsibility. Former governor Bennett (1975–79) had left his imprint on a revitalized governorship, and from 1979 through 1990, Carlin and Hayden would act aggressively as they utilized their gubernatorial powers and reshaped public policy in fundamental ways. Both governors believed government could serve the common good and drew on their experience as legislative leaders to advance progressive agendas. Both were policy activists in a tradition traceable to Kansas governors serving in the early decades of the twentieth century.

Professor Burdett Loomis describes these political actors as "policy entrepreneurs" who work in the overlapping realms of politics and policymaking. They address public demands, set policy agendas, and develop policy alternatives, and in doing so, they shape public policy. Policy entrepreneurs seek "windows of opportunity" within "the context of long-term trends, various cycles, and impending deadlines."[8]

Governor John Carlin

Governor Carlin believed that "good government is good politics," according to Professor Joe Pisciotte. In other words, if a governor "thinks in the best interests of the state," he or she "will be on solid ground politically."[9] Carlin showed special skills in managing the interplay of politics and public policy and channeling public demands into policy initiatives. These skills were required as Carlin faced solid and growing Republican majorities in both houses of the Kansas legislature.

Carlin later reflected on the success of bipartisanship during his governorship: "Republican legislators in those days wanted to do what was best for the state. And so consequently we got a lot done." After his reelection in 1982, the governor announced that he would not challenge Kansas's senior US senator, Bob Dole, in 1986. He believes that strategic decision cleared the way for him to work with Republican lawmakers on issues confronting the state. According to Carlin, "At least 80 percent of what I did successfully was done in the second term by partnering with Republicans."[10]

In the huge array of state actions taken during Carlin's eight years as governor, his imprint on state policy stands out in three areas: initiatives arising from his issue-oriented campaigns in 1978 and 1982, actions taken to reform inequities in property taxes, and a dramatic expansion in the scope of state authority for economic development.

As noted, Carlin single-mindedly campaigned on utility rates in 1978 and the severance tax in 1982. In both cases, he identified and elevated issues for broad public discussion, crafted a populist message of fighting for the public interest against special interests, and swung public understanding and opinion his way through his campaigns. In 1978, his target was rising utility rates, along with the powerful electric utilities that seemed immune to public scrutiny. Dramatic cost overruns in construction of the state's first nuclear power plant, rate hearings across the state, and the likelihood of dramatic increases in the cost of electricity provided the backdrop for Carlin to bring the utility issue to public attention. Candidate Carlin latched on to the idea of cutting utility rates by exempting them from the state sales tax, and once he was elected, state lawmakers complied with the voters' verdict. According to Carlin, this act, coupled with adjustments made by the state's regulatory body, meant that ratepayers "would pay 15 percent less for their electricity."[11]

As governor, Carlin first presented his proposal for a severance tax in 1981 as a way to fund schools and highway improvements, but lawmakers balked. His target this time was the state's well-heeled oil and gas producers, a "booming" industry with "soaring profits" that was "jeopardizing the education of our children," according to the governor.[12] After lawmakers defeated his severance tax proposal again in 1982, Carlin took his case to the voters in his reelection bid, and they sided with the governor. Carlin secured a severance tax in the next legislative session, though at a substantially lower level than he originally sought.

The taxation of property, according to the Kansas Constitution, was to be "uniform and equal," but like most states, Kansas had fallen short of this standard for most of its history. Indeed, as the mid-1980s approached, Wichita State University professor Glenn Fisher concluded that in Kansas, the assessment of property for tax purposes "was incredibly bad."[13] Legislative measures to address this issue over the past thirty years had stalled, and various taxpayer groups threatened court action to rectify the situation.

In his 1980 message to the legislature, Carlin warned that court-ordered reappraisal would dramatically shift the tax burden, and he urged legislative action to protect homeowners and farmers. The governor's insistence forced the consideration of a constitutional amendment for property "classification" that would, in combination with reappraisal, roughly maintain the existing tax burden among major classes of property. The Carlin administration's active engagement with legislative leaders eventually produced a classification amendment coupled with mandatory statewide reappraisal based on more modern and centralized appraisal technology. Like many controversial policies, the reappraisal and classification bill passed only in the waning days of the 1985 legislative session, as pressures increased under the capitol dome. Voters adopted the amendment by a two-to-one margin in November 1986 and "set in motion the most comprehensive attempt to reform property tax administration in Kansas history," according to Fisher.[14] Carlin could claim victory and pass along to his successor the political backlash associated with implementing the reform.

Kansas approached the mid-1980s with an economy in the doldrums. Growth in the three pillars of the state's economy—aviation, oil and gas, and agriculture—had stalled. In a report commissioned by the Kansas legislature and leading business groups, University of Kansas professors Tony Redwood and Charles Krider concluded that "the state economy fell further, started to recover later, and has grown more slowly than the national economy, in relation to the most recent 1980–82 recession." Their report called on government "to take bold, new actions to encourage economic development."[15]

During his last two years as governor, Carlin forcefully championed a debate on the state's role in stimulating the economy. In his 1985 message to the legislature, he asserted that "the status quo is no longer acceptable," and he called on lawmakers to "return to our roots and be progressive once again." Being competitive, according to the governor, "translates into promoting economic development in the broadest sense of the term."[16] His economic agenda initially tackled archaic liquor and banking laws, then expanded dramatically in 1986 to include constitutional amendments authorizing a state-owned lottery, pari-mutuel wagering, and local property tax exemptions for economic development, plus a loosening of constitutional restrictions on "internal improvements" (an archaic term meaning state investments designed to stimulate the economy). The governor also proposed a one-cent sales tax increase "to fund the future" and help pay for both state obligations and new economic initiatives.[17]

Carlin assembled a coalition of business leaders primarily from the state's normally contentious metropolitan centers—Kansas City and Wichita—to promote his jam-packed economic agenda. Once these two urban hubs were politically aligned, legislation and constitutional amendments moved smoothly and with bipartisan support through the legislative process. In 1986, voters approved the liquor, lottery, pari-mutuel, and internal improvements amendments by wide margins and narrowly approved the amendment for property tax exemptions. Tax and budget measures expanding the scope of state authority for economic development were enacted by lawmakers in 1986. With the adoption of this broad array of initiatives, Carlin dramatically affirmed that government could and should act to stimulate the state's economy.

Governor Mike Hayden

As a policy activist, house speaker Mike Hayden had started thinking about the next phase of public policy well ahead of his announcement that he would run for governor in 1986. In the waning days of a productive legislative session in 1985, he crafted a joint resolution authorizing the creation of a Special Commission on a Public Agenda for Kansas that would "identify public issues critical to the future of Kansas" and "identify policy choices available to Kansas in responding to these issues."[18] He quietly spearheaded adoption of the resolution, as well as funding and staffing for the commission, which he would then chair through its reporting date of July 1, 1986. The commission's work helped Hayden formulate a policy focus should he be elected governor.[19]

Within a month after Hayden took office, there was little doubt what his priority as governor would be. He named a secretary for transportation on inauguration day and shortly thereafter directed the secretary to work with a gubernatorial task force in "charting the course for a comprehensive Kansas highway program. . . . Development of a new highway program may be the most important step Kansas can take for long-term economic growth."[20] Hayden instructed the task force to report no later than August 1, and he stated his intention to call a special session of the legislature to expedite action on his recommendations.

In focusing on highway investment, Hayden was following through on major findings of the special commission he had chaired in 1985 and 1986 and a central theme of his gubernatorial campaign. In its study of capital finance and public infrastructure, the commission reported: "State expenditures on capital improvements have declined consistently and dramatically relative to construction costs, overall state expenditures, and personal income over the past twenty to twenty-five years . . . [and] falls substantially below various national projections of infrastructure needs." The commission noted that investment in state highways, water projects, and prisons, among other capital requirements, had stalled. More aggressive debt financing was identified as a solution "to rectify financing inequities . . . and allow the state to move ahead with backlogged projects and avoid the increased cost of construction due to project deferral."[21]

Along with putting highways on the state's agenda, Hayden's first legislative session as governor was heavily occupied with overseeing implementation of the constitutional amendments on taxation, gambling, and liquor adopted by voters in 1986.[22] Each amendment required specific enabling legislation, budgeting, and staffing to carry out the state's new obligations. Competent implementation of property classification and reappraisal ushered in historic advancements in the administration of property taxes. Gambling amendments required the organizing and staffing of agencies from scratch to oversee state-owned and -operated lottery and pari-mutuel wagering and ensure scandal-free administration of those functions. Initiating liquor-by-the-drink required mechanisms for licensing and oversight that would close a hundred-year-old chapter in Kansas's struggle to regulate intoxicating liquors.

Also, as a first step in addressing deficiencies in capital investment, the Hayden administration secured the creation of the Kansas Development Finance Authority in 1987. This entity, designed to manage professional and competitive debt financing of state investment, "moved Kansas into the twentieth century" in the field of capital finance.[23]

Hayden's drive for quick action on highways, however, immediately encountered roadblocks. At the close of the 1987 legislative session, he crisscrossed the state to champion a major highway initiative. Once his task force submitted its report in late July, he called a special session of the legislature for late August and presented lawmakers with the largest public works program in Kansas history. The governor's comprehensive highway plan included substantial new construction, accelerated maintenance, and expanded aid for local roads, all supported through sizable increases in highway user fees. Lawmakers balked at the magnitude of Hayden's initiative and the tax boost it required, leaving the governor empty-handed on highways in 1987.

Hayden's aggressive action on highways reflected his view of the Kansas governorship as a position with great potential for leadership. As he later noted, his "no nonsense, straightforward" style had worked well for him as a legislative leader, committee chair, and speaker. He listened carefully but, when necessary, could also act with authority, describing his approach as: "Here's what we got to do, let's get the job done."[24] His assertive style could push politics aside if doing so would help accomplish a policy objective; it could also require two steps forward and one step back.

Hayden and legislative leaders would step back in 1988 (an election year), only to regroup with allies to push for a comprehensive highway program in the 1989 legislative session. The governor, in concert with an interim committee of the legislature and grassroots lobbying, would reframe the highway issue and generate favorable publicity and support from local stakeholders after the 1988 legislative session ended. By December, the committee had placed a major highway initiative on the table. Hayden called for legislative action, but he allowed legislative advocates allied with lobbyists to move the highway package forward in 1989. After a chaotic struggle in the legislature over the size of the package as well as its financing, legislative leaders squeezed out the necessary votes to produce a comprehensive highway program that served all parts of the state.[25] This breakthrough on highways allowed the governor and lawmakers to turn their attention, in the final days of the 1989 legislative session, to two other unresolved issues on Hayden's agenda: financing for a new state prison and the state water plan.

Hayden's special commission had drawn attention to stalled plans for new correctional facilities in 1986. Governor Bennett had failed to secure legislative approval for a new correctional facility during his term, and Governor Carlin had shelved the issue during his eight years in office. Hayden recruited a secretary for the Department of Corrections with experience in new prison construction, and the governor addressed the issue of prison overcrowding immediately upon taking office in 1987 and again in 1988, approving facility upgrades and expanded capacity at existing facilities. Early in 1988, plans for a new state prison were given a major boost when federal judge Richard Rogers, formerly president of the Kansas Senate, ordered the release of prisoners from overcrowded state facilities and threatened additional releases. Hayden cited the judge's order when he pointed out the need for additional prison capacity to reluctant lawmakers and then recommended "the construction of a new, multi-security facility" at a cost of $55 million.[26] Judge Rogers kept the pressure on lawmakers by ordering additional prisoner releases. On the last day of the 1989 legislative session, immediately after enactment of the landmark highway plan, legislators agreed to construct a new prison with a capacity of 640 beds, the first maximum-security prison built since the first decade of Kansas statehood.

Environmental issues had motivated Mike Hayden's first run for the Kansas legislature in 1972, and his imprint on environmental policy during his fourteen years in the legislature had earned him recognition as a leader on issues related to natural resources. On becoming governor, he named a special assistant on environment and natural resources to advocate for his environmental priorities. For Hayden, no environmental issue had higher priority than establishing permanent financing for a broad range of water-related projects affecting agriculture, wildlife, recreation, health, and other environmental matters.[27]

Governor Carlin had developed and secured the adoption of a comprehensive state water plan, but without any method of financing it. Hayden focused public attention on environmental issues, secured appropriations to start implementing parts of the water plan in 1987 and 1988, and led a discussion of the benefits of having stable, long-term funding of the water plan. In 1989, he proposed to the legislature a dedicated water plan fund financed through diverse sources, including user fees and general revenue. After back-and-forth haggling over the magnitude of agricultural fees, Hayden, in alliance with former governor Carlin, helped round up the necessary votes. In the last hour of the wrap-up session, legislators agreed to $16 million a year dedicated to implementation of the state water plan.[28]

At the end of the 1989 legislative session, Hayden could point with pride to historic achievements: an eight-year, $1.8 billion comprehensive highway package; a new $55 million high-security prison; and a dedicated state water plan fund of $16 million annually. These initiatives addressed issues he had been mulling over for years, well before his election as governor. The *Wichita Eagle* editorialized, "Perhaps at no time in state history was more done to ensure a better future for Kansas than during the seven-day wrap-up session."[29] Loomis concludes, Hayden acted as "both strategic politician and persistent policy entrepreneur who sought to take advantage of specific, long-awaited windows of opportunity."[30]

On the sidelines, a few detractors had questioned Hayden's leadership and tried to diminish his contributions to the final outcome, but the governor understood the give-and-take of the process better than his critics, and he had key lieutenants intimately engaged to help push his agenda forward. As senate majority leader Bud Burke noted, "Every time there was a kink in the hose, he was there to work it out." House majority leader Robert H. Miller added, "When we get up and read the newspapers, the sausage will look pretty good."[31]

Mike Hayden was fond of saying, "You play the hand that is dealt you," and he was dealt a wicked hand on property taxes. In November 1989, property owners across the state began receiving their tax bills based on the reappraisal initiated by the legislature in 1985 and the property classification amendment adopted by voters in 1986. Hayden had supported these measures as a legislative leader, and as governor, he had overseen the three-year reappraisal of all Kansas properties and the modernization of the appraisal process. The results ignited a firestorm of protests. As Hayden bluntly summarized: "Reappraisal is a politician's nightmare. If your taxes go up, you're mad. If they don't, you deserve it."[32]

The governor's political dilemma related to property taxes was complicated by tax reform at the national level, instituted by President Reagan just days before Hayden's election in 1986. National reforms lowered tax rates for all taxpayers at the expense of those benefiting from real estate tax preferences, such as real estate developers and "passive investors." At the same time, reappraisal at the state level hit owners of underappraised commercial properties, and classification shifted property taxes onto commercial and industrial properties. In sum, a confluence of state and national tax reforms hammered many real estate investors with sizable hikes in both local property taxes and national income taxes.[33]

Hayden foresaw the looming property tax issue in 1988 and called on lawmakers to enact a "shock absorber" fund to soften the impact of unexpected tax shifts on property owners. However, lawmakers hesitated to act without knowing exactly what tax shifts would occur. Once reality hit in late 1989, Hayden maneuvered to control the political damage, including calling a special legislative session on property taxes, but little could be done. As Hayden later reflected: "We did the right thing from a policy standpoint," but "I also knew politically it was probably the kiss of death."[34] Property taxes became the dominant issue in the 1990 elections.

One other thorny issue complicated Hayden's reelection bid in 1990. His campaign had sidestepped the issue of abortion in 1986 by maintaining that it was a federal matter. In the summer of 1989, however, the US Supreme Court forced the governor's hand by ruling in *Webster v. Reproductive Health Services* that states had latitude in regulating abortion. True to his style, Hayden addressed the issue forthrightly and sought a middle ground, proposing modest regulatory measures while affirming women's constitutional right to terminate a pregnancy.[35] Abortion opponents were not satisfied and would eventually support the governor's opponents in both the primary and general elections. The ultimate irony for Hayden came in the 1990 general election, when he ran as a "pro-choice" Republican against a woman who was a "pro-life" Democrat.[36]

The 1990 Elections

In 1990, both former governor Carlin and incumbent governor Hayden would be candidates for governor, but not against each other, as it turned out. On the Democratic side, congressmen Dan Glickman and Jim Slattery were both rumored to be testing the waters for a gubernatorial bid, but after the blockbuster legislative session of 1989 boosted Hayden's standing, they bowed out. Carlin then stepped into the void, along with state treasurer Joan Finney.

Finney had a grandmotherly demeanor and seemed an unlikely winner against Carlin. She had switched from Republican to Democrat in 1974, was elected state treasurer that year, and had been reelected to that office three times since then. In the heavy policy activity of the 1970s and 1980s, however, she stayed on the sidelines and rarely engaged. She was decidedly outmatched by the former governor's experience and mastery of public policy and ran a shoestring campaign. But, as he later reflected, Carlin underestimated Finney. She excelled at retail politics, having "gone to every damn bean feed, for sixteen or twenty years, that the Democratic Party had ever held."[37] In addition to her grassroots appeal, Finney was aided by gadfly Fred Phelps, a third candidate in the race who repeatedly badgered Carlin in public forums, claiming that he caused highway deaths through his support of liquor-by-the-drink. In the end, Finney unexpectedly edged out an overconfident Carlin, 47 to 46 percent—a margin of less than 2,000 votes, or roughly 1 percent of the total number cast. Phelps garnered 7 percent of the vote, or nearly 12,000 votes.

Hayden faced primary challenges too, as well as a Republican electorate deeply divided on property taxes and abortion. Wichita real estate executive Nestor Weigand fueled anti-tax sentiment and hammered the governor on property taxes with a million-dollar media-driven campaign. Ironically, Weigand had been active in both state and national realtors' associations that had failed to prevent the double whammy on the real estate industry by the state and national tax reforms of 1985 and 1986. Four other candidates jumped into the race, the most significant being Wichita-area attorney Richard Peckham, who campaigned against Hayden on the abortion issue. The governor fought off his challengers and nosed out Weigand in a narrow victory, 44 to 42 percent, or a margin of 8,000 votes; Peckham drew 29,000 votes, just short of 10 percent of the total cast.

Hayden's primary battle weakened him going into the general election; by contrast, Finney's primary victory over a successful two-term governor of her own party gave her a huge boost. The governor had expected to be running against Carlin, a race in which the property tax and abortion issues would have been largely neutralized. Hayden struggled to challenge Finney, whose textbook answer to most complex issues was to "return government to the people" through initiative and referendum. Weigand did little to help Hayden unify Republican voters, and a third-party candidate, Christine Campbell-Kline, entered the race under the Independent Party label. The National Organization of Women endorsed Hayden, unhelpfully highlighting the abortion issue.[38] The property tax issue, compounded by Finney's appeal among antiabortion voters, doomed the governor's reelection. Finney prevailed over Hayden 49 to 43 percent, with a margin of 47,000 votes; Campbell-Kline siphoned off 69,000 votes, or 9 percent of the total.

A Maturing Bipartisan Consensus

Kansas politics in the 1980s exhibited a progressive resurgence traceable to the earliest days of the twentieth century. Legislative reapportionment in the 1960s and constitutional reforms in the 1970s spurred this renaissance in Kansas government and policy. Underpinning this activism in public policy was the broadly shared belief that government could play an affirmative role in serving the common good and addressing public problems. State government could and should play an active part in ensuring that Kansans had high-quality schools and excellent state universities, good roads, and aid for vulnerable citizens. Kansans at that time expected no less.

Republicans and Democrats competed fiercely for state office in this period, but once the victors took office, they came together to find policy solutions. The governorship shifted between the parties in every election but one from 1978 to 1994. Republicans narrowly held majorities in the state senate but lost control of the state house twice, in 1976 and 1990. Within this context, both Carlin and Hayden drew on gubernatorial powers modernized in the 1970s and set aggressive agendas for state action. Even so, every significant policy initiative of the 1980s required bipartisan support. Carlin's economic proposals could not have been enacted without Republican votes, and Hayden's infrastructure plans required Democratic support. Tax increases during this period—the severance tax, sales taxes, and highway taxes—were all adopted through bipartisan coalitions.

Although competition between Kansas Republicans and Democrats characterized state elections from the 1950s through the 1980s, critical elements of state policy seemed immune to these interparty disputes. Key decisions made in different time frames throughout the twentieth century were reinforced and gained broad legitimacy, largely insulated from the rough-and-tumble of partisan campaigns. This bipartisan consensus was largely unwritten and generally unspoken, but when legislative votes were needed, coalitions regularly formed across party lines. Candidates for office conducted competitive campaigns on numerous issues, but they rarely threatened existing agreements on achieving a balanced tax policy, accepting federal assistance when available, or making appointments to office based on merit. Retracing this maturing bipartisan consensus helps explain the political turmoil that would come with the election of Sam Brownback as governor in 2010.

Tax Policy

State lawmakers in the 1980s continued to move the financing of state and local obligations away from a reliance on property taxes. State sales tax increases were enacted in 1986 and 1989 not only to finance state initiatives in economic development and highway improvements but also to expand state aid to public schools, which relied heavily on property taxes. City and county governments also adopted local sales taxes to relieve pressure on property owners. The state income tax was simplified and made more equitable. With a prod from state courts, administration of the property tax was transformed, and perceived inequities among classes of property were rectified. Slowly but steadily, the state moved toward a more balanced tax structure that would become known as the "three-legged stool" of state and local finance. This bipartisan tax policy sought balance and diversity in the three primary revenue sources—property, income, and sales taxes—to achieve lower tax rates overall, reduce competition with other states, and promote tax fairness.

Federal Assistance

The Great Depression combined with the leadership of Governor Alf Landon (1933–37) helped Kansans shed their cultural reluctance to accept federal assistance and the requirements associated with such assistance.[39] Landon moved swiftly to procure all federal funds available for emergency relief in the 1930s and campaigned for constitutional amendments in 1936 that allowed Kansas to participate in the social welfare and unemployment provisions of the Social Security Act of 1935. The state's commitment to equalizing health care would be profoundly deepened by its participation in Medicaid, established through amendments to the Social Security Act in 1965. State officials followed Landon's lead to take full advantage of Medicaid and the many federal grants-in-aid enacted during LBJ's Great Society of the 1960s. Kansas governors and legislators would wrangle with federal officials from time to time over the strings attached to federal dollars, but in the end, they would act to maximize federal funds flowing into the state. This pattern of acceptance of federal dollars would continue unabated on a bipartisan basis throughout the 1970s and 1980s.

Merit-Based Appointments

Governor Robert Bennett critically broadened state government's commitment to merit-based appointments during the progressive resurgence.[40] Through executive reorganization and the recruitment of professional executive leadership, he abruptly ended the vestiges of political patronage in the Highway Department. He also ordered that all executive appointments be made on a nonpartisan, merit basis, with due consideration given to achieving balance in factors such as race, sex, and geography. As an attorney, he was often personally acquainted with nominees for judicial appointments and conscientiously sought to make those appointments based on qualifications and not partisan considerations.

Governors Carlin and Hayden shared Bennett's desire to eliminate partisanship and followed his lead on merit-based judicial appointments. As a Democrat, Carlin resisted partisan pressure to restore patronage in both executive and judicial appointments and "took a lot of heat" for that decision.[41] Hayden required background checks on all judicial nominees and defended his appointments based on qualifications. His modest suggestion to the

Supreme Court Nominating Commission that geographic balance be considered in nominations to the state's highest courts drew a strong retort from the commission's chair, and the matter was dropped.

The bipartisan consensus on balanced tax policy, acceptance of federal funds, and merit-based appointments would continue through the 1990s and the first decade of the twenty-first century until being challenged by Sam Brownback after his election as governor in 2010.

Notes

1. Allan Cigler and Burdett Loomis, "Kansas: Two-Party Competition in a One-Party State," in *Party Realignment and State Politics*, ed. Maureen Moakley (Columbus: Ohio State University Press, 1992), 169–171.

2. Cigler and Loomis, 171.

3. Cigler and Loomis, 178.

4. Kansas lost one congressional seat due to reapportionment after the 1990 census. As a result, it has had four seats from the 1992 elections to the present.

5. "Be Willing to Take Some Risks to Make Things Happen: A Conversation with Former Governor John W. Carlin," *Kansas History* 31 (Summer 2008): 123.

6. H. Edward Flentje, ed., *Selected Papers of Governor Mike Hayden: Advancing a Progressive Agenda* (Wichita: Hugo Wall School of Urban and Public Affairs, Wichita State University, 2002), 3–5. See also "Being Close to the People: A Conversation with Former Governor Mike Hayden," *Kansas History* 32 (Spring 2009): 56–62.

7. Flentje, *Selected Papers of Hayden*, 5.

8. Burdett A. Loomis, *Time, Politics, and Policies: A Legislative Year* (Lawrence: University Press of Kansas, 1994), 8, 16.

9. Joe P. Pisciotte, ed., *Selected Papers of Governor John Carlin, 1979–1987: An Index of Social and Political Change* (Wichita: Hugo Wall School of Urban and Public Affairs, Wichita State University, 1993), 12.

10. "Be Willing to Take Some Risks," 131.

11. Pisciotte, *Selected Papers of Carlin*, 636.

12. Pisciotte, 755–761, 772–773.

13. Glenn W. Fisher, *The Worst Tax? A History of the Property Tax in America* (Lawrence: University Press of Kansas, 1996), 169.

14. Fisher, 175–179.

15. Anthony Redwood and Charles Krider, "Kansas Economic Development Study: Interim Report and Recommendations" (Report No. 103, Institute for Public Policy and Business Research, University of Kansas, January 1986), 8, 12.

16. Pisciotte, *Selected Papers of Carlin*, 107, 106.

17. Pisciotte, 113–121.

18. H. Edward Flentje, ed., *Kansas Policy Choices: Report of a Special Commission on a Public Agenda for Kansas* (Lawrence: University Press of Kansas, 1986), vii.

19. The author of this chapter served as coordinator of the special commission.

20. Flentje, *Selected Papers of Hayden*, 57.

21. Flentje, *Kansas Policy Choices*, 138–139.

22. Flentje, *Selected Papers of Hayden*, 262–263.

23. Flentje, 264.

24. "Being Close to the People," 62–63.

25. Loomis, *Time, Politics, and Policies*, 107–129.

26. Flentje, *Selected Papers of Hayden*, 152.

27. Flentje, 85–86.

28. Loomis, *Time, Politics, and Policies*, 142–148.

29. Cited in Loomis, 149.

30. Loomis, 160.

31. Loomis, 151, 150.

32. Loomis, 151.

33. Flentje, *Selected Papers of Hayden*, 159–160.

34. "Being Close to the People," 70.

35. Flentje, *Selected Papers of Hayden*, 250–252, 257–258.

36. In 2019, the Kansas Supreme Court ruled in *Hodes & Nauser v. Schmidt* that the Bill of Rights of the Kansas Constitution "affords protection of the right of personal autonomy, which includes the ability to control one's own body, to assert bodily integrity, and to exercise self-determination. This right allows a woman to make her own decisions regarding her body, health, family formation, and family life—decisions that can include whether to continue a pregnancy." Republican lawmakers proposed a constitutional amendment to nullify the court's ruling, but Kansas voters overwhelmingly rejected that amendment in August 2022.

37. "Be Willing to Take Some Risks," 137.

38. Maralee Schwartz, "Being a Woman Is No Guarantee," *Washington Post*, November 3, 1990.

39. H. Edward Flentje and Joseph A. Aistrup, *Kansas Politics and Government: The Clash of Political Cultures* (Lincoln: University of Nebraska Press, 2010), 154–160.

40. H. Edward Flentje, ed., *Selected Papers of Governor Robert F. Bennett: A Study in Good Government and "Civics Book" Politics* (Wichita: Center for Urban Studies, Wichita State University, 1979), 233–257.

41. "Be Willing to Take Some Risks," 131–132.

CHAPTER FOUR

The Finney Transition and Political Undercurrents

H. Edward Flentje

In 1990, Kansas voters turned their backs on the policy activism of the prior twenty years and elected state treasurer Joan Finney as governor. Both former governor John Carlin and incumbent governor Mike Hayden sought the governorship that year, only to be rejected by the voters. As governors and former legislative leaders, Carlin and Hayden had been instrumental in making remarkable changes in tax policy, infrastructure improvement, and economic development and in revising archaic liquor and gaming laws, among other issues. The two governors had drawn on the powers of a legislature and a governorship modernized in the 1970s in part by former governor Robert Bennett, also a former legislative leader. But in 1990, voters signaled a desire for a slowdown in the activism of those prior years, and Kansas politics entered a transitional period with Finney as governor.

The dramatic reforms in Kansas's political institutions and in state policy were largely immune to political undercurrents in both the state and the nation. These political forces and their underlying ideologies were scarcely hidden from view, nor were they completely new to the politics of the state. From their earliest days, Kansans not only supported use of the government to ensure social order but also restrained government to enhance economic liberty. In the early 1990s, a new, opportunistic alliance of these opposing cultural impulses would transform state politics. These emergent social and economic dogmas would challenge the pragmatic and progressive ideals that had dominated Kansas politics for a good part of the twentieth century. Retracing these undercurrents sheds light on the transitional nature of the Finney governorship and the political shifts that lay ahead.

Governor Joan Finney

Three governors with deep experience as state legislative leaders—Bennett, Carlin, and Hayden—were followed by Joan Finney, who presented Kansans with a dramatic contrast not only in political and governmental experience but also in gubernatorial style. She became the first woman and the first Catholic to win the Kansas governorship; she was the oldest, too, assuming office just short of her sixty-sixth birthday. She would also be the first Kansas governor not to seek reelection after an initial term.

Finney entered the governorship with a significant background in government but without policymaking experience. Her public service began in 1953 as a member of Republican US senator Frank Carlson's staff; she served in that capacity, first in Washington, DC, and later in Kansas, until the senator retired in 1969. After a stint in local government, she ran unsuccessfully in the 1972 Republican primary for a congressional seat that included Shawnee County and the northeastern corner of Kansas. Feeling that Republicans had discouraged her political aspirations, Finney was open to the entreaties of Democrats and switched parties in 1974. As a Democrat, she ran successfully for state treasurer and easily won reelection three times.[1]

"Joan Finney was the people's governor," the *Topeka Capital-Journal* editorialized at the time of her passing in 2001.[2] Warren Armstrong and Dee Harris, who compiled and edited selected papers from the Finney governorship, observed that she took office in "an era of disrespect for, distrust of, and skepticism about government" and was determined "to arrest that disturbing trend." Finney viewed her primary role as the people's representative and never became "the prototypical politician that the average citizen loves to distrust." With her "outgoing personality and unconventional style," she gained "special affinity with the people of Kansas that served her well throughout her four years in office."[3] One colleague recalled her political style: "She knew the grass roots better than just about anybody . . . and she honored the grass roots with trip after trip after trip across the state." Another remembered: "She'd walk in the parades, speak at chili suppers, campaign in bowling alleys and grocery stores, just picking up bits and pieces from the people."[4]

Finney brought to the office of governor sincere compassion for those she saw as wronged or disenfranchised. She and her two sisters had grown up during the Great Depression in a household headed by their mother after their father abandoned them. She had worked on tribal affairs as a US Senate staffer and showed an exceptional affinity for Native Americans, who participated in her inaugural ceremony. Finney granted Kansas tribes official recognition shortly thereafter.[5] Governor Finney had a long memory when she felt she had been disrespected or others had been slighted, according to Michael Johnston, who served as head of the Transportation Department during her administration.[6] For example, her animosity toward Republicans increased in 1975, a few weeks after she became state treasurer, when Governor Bennett tried but failed to abolish the position as an elective office through an executive reorganization order. Conversely, her long memory extended favorably to those who had spoken out in her defense or recognized her through even modest gestures.

The Governor as Policymaker

According to Armstrong and Harris, "Finney chose not to be heavily involved in the area of policy development, focusing instead on her role as representative of the people."[7] Thus, Johnston reported that he had little direct contact with the governor on policy issues. In contrast to the policy activism of her immediate predecessors, Finney was frequently dismissed by contemporaries as a "meeter and greeter" who rarely addressed substantive legislative issues. For example, when responding to an inquiry about Finney's position on a year-end budget issue, Democratic representative George Teagarden, chair of the House Appropriations Committee, reportedly replied in frustration, "I have never been in her office in two years."[8]

An important issue for Finney was authorizing voters to petition for and enact legislation directly through initiative and referendum. She had advocated for direct citizen action on legislative issues during her 1990 campaign and repeatedly called on lawmakers to place this constitutional change on the ballot. She appeared personally before the relevant legislative committees and party caucuses to appeal for action. She threatened to veto spending bills in 1991 if the legislature failed to act.[9] In 1993, following her impassioned plea before the house Democratic caucus, a constitutional amendment for initiative and referendum passed the lower chamber but died in the senate.[10] In a surprising move before leaving office, Finney financed and appeared in radio and television ads weeks before the 1994 election, asking voters to support candidates who favored initiative and referendum.[11]

On other issues, Finney was generally reactive rather than proactive. She positioned herself as a fiscal conservative and frequently spoke out against overspending and rising property taxes. During her first legislative session as governor, when her party enjoyed a one-seat majority (63–62) in the house and strong, veto-proof minority status (18–22) in the senate, she issued twenty-two vetoes, rejecting even some bills advanced by members of her own party; this triggered an immediate fracture with Democrats. Her message to the legislature was brash: "It is time for the Legislature to go home . . . 'Get the heck out of Dodge.' . . . If the Senate wishes to exercise their constitutional prerogative, and in fact override my vetoes, that is fine with me. That is part of the legislative process."[12]

Democrat Marvin Barkis, who served as speaker of the house in the 1991 and 1992 legislative sessions, found Finney nearly impossible to work with, noting, "She vetoed bills that Democratic legislators had worked hard to pass and did so without consultation, without reasons." Barkis believed Finney's defiance resulted from her inexperience and lack of a legislative agenda of her own: "She simply wanted to demonstrate her independence and power."[13] A perceptive insider described the governor this way: "She appeared to play her cards close to her chest, keep her options open as long as she could, avoid making any commitments and surprising as many as she could to keep opponents off guard."[14] Democrat Donna Whiteman, who served as house majority leader in the 1991 legislative session, said that Finney's inexperience, combined with house Democrats' status as a majority party for the first time in a dozen years, made for a tumultuous legislative session.[15]

Finney's breach with her party never healed, as a "chasm between her and Democrats in both houses of the legislature" widened. Veto overrides, which required a two-thirds majority in both houses, occurred regularly, even though the Democrats enjoyed sizable veto-proof numbers in both legislative chambers throughout her four years as governor. Democrats joined Republicans in overriding four of the governor's twenty-two vetoes in 1991 and thirteen of her thirty-nine vetoes in 1992. Finney issued 148 vetoes during her term—seventy on whole bills and seventy-eight on line items in appropriations bills—and thirty-two were overridden. This was far more overrides than any other governor in a similar time frame. In contrast, Democratic governor Carlin vetoed 103 bills and twenty-four line items over eight years, with no overrides.[16]

Given Finney's contentious relationship with the legislature and her reluctance to offer policy leadership, house speaker Barkis and senate majority leader Fred Kerr moved into the political vacuum and set the agenda for the 1992 legislative session, including groundbreaking legislation on school finance. Legislative action on this issue was spurred by a case before district court judge Terry Bullock, who ordered strict equality in education for students and total state control of school finance. In response to the judge's order, Finney created a task force that conducted preliminary work in advance of the legislative session, but serious work began at the initiative of house Democrats, led by Barkis and his tax and education committee chairs, once the session began. The court's action precipitated extended give-and-take between representatives of urban and rural constituencies throughout the 1992 legislative session. In the senate, Kerr persevered through the rejection of five conference reports and eventually patched together a bipartisan coalition that broke the deadlock on the sixth vote. Legislators consulted with the governor throughout the process, but she rarely engaged in the substantive details.[17]

In the absence of gubernatorial leadership, the legislature fundamentally rewrote the approach to school finance in Kansas by acknowledging that funding the public schools was a state obligation, shifting the financing of schools from property taxes to state sales and income taxes, assuring more equity among school districts with disparate wealth, and allocating state aid for school construction projects. Finney signed the School District Finance and Quality Performance Act in May 1992, and Judge Bullock applauded the legislature's work. The governor would subsequently highlight the fact that property taxes were cut in 291 of the state's 304 school districts by roughly $260 million statewide, due to a uniform and mandatory statewide levy for school finance. In contrast, she rarely mentioned that sales and income taxes rose by nearly $350 million or that school budgets jumped by nearly 10 percent in the first year after the law's passage.[18] The governor successfully pushed for the repeal of a few sales tax exemptions that composed a small part of the increased funding.

After the 1991 legislative session, speaker Barkis, in concert with house minority leader Robert Miller, organized the Special Committee on Children's Initiatives, with Barkis as chair and Miller as vice chair. Committee members included legislative and private-sector representatives who worked in collaboration with the governor's staff and officials in the Department of Social and Rehabilitation Services.[19] In December 1991, the committee produced "A

Blueprint for Investing in the Future of Kansas Children and Families," which led to the introduction of seventeen bills and resolutions in the 1992 legislative session. The legislature adopted most of the committee's recommendations, including mandatory school breakfasts and health assessments, the creation of a "children's budget," and a joint legislative committee on children and families, among other initiatives to coordinate schools, social services, and courts with respect to children. State lawmakers also created the Corporation for Change to conduct strategic planning related to investments in children and families.[20]

Barkis and Kerr left their mark on public policy but ended their legislative careers with the 1992 legislative session. Kerr announced that he would not seek reelection, and Barkis lost his seat in a bid for reelection. Republicans gained four seats in the house to retake majority control of that chamber. Republicans also added four seats in the senate, strengthening their majority, 26–14.

In 1994, Finney allowed a death penalty bill to become law without her signature, which ended, at least temporarily, twenty-two years of heated debate on the issue. The US Supreme Court had prompted that debate in 1972 by nullifying all state laws concerning capital punishment. Republican governors Bennett and Hayden had called for reinstatement of the death penalty during their terms, without success, even with Republican majorities in the legislature. Democratic governor Carlin had promised he would not stand in the way of reinstatement of the death penalty during his 1978 campaign, but when presented with a bill in 1979, he vetoed it, saying his personal beliefs prevented him from signing it. Republican legislatures presented Carlin with three additional death penalty bills, which he promptly rejected. Finney opposed capital punishment, but by allowing the death penalty bill to become law, she stated: "I am keeping the promise I made to the people of Kansas when they elected me."[21] The governor's inclination to represent the popular will overcame her personal objections.

The Governor as Manager

Finney thrived in person-to-person politics but not in administering the state government. Throughout her governorship, she entrusted day-to-day operations to a trio of women—Susan Seltsam, Gloria Timmer, and Finney's daughter Mary Holiday—who served variously as secretary of administration, budget director, and chief of staff. On most issues, this triumvirate functioned as intermediaries between the governor and her department heads. A cabinet member who dared to bypass these women and go directly to the governor risked their wrath. This tight internal funnel, combined with Finney's personal style, often proved frustrating to gubernatorial staff and agency heads.[22]

Finney valued loyalty, but her unique style did not contribute to a smooth administration, as her revolving-door appointments demonstrated. A statehouse reporter observed that the governor had promised "to be different," but "in her 18 months in office, Mrs. Finney's 10 cabinet posts have been held by 21 people."[23] Appointees who crossed her quickly lost their jobs. One cabinet officer was fired over questionable computer purchases, another over unauthorized travel, and another over the illegal granting of hunting permits. Others resigned when their moral indiscretions came to light. At one point, during a single week, three different individuals served as secretary of administration, a key cabinet position.

Finney sent a message to her appointees by personal example. She could become "impatient, even incensed with state employees who treated members of the public with rudeness or disrespect" and did not hesitate to intervene.[24] Even before assuming office, for example, she visited the women's prison in Topeka and had serious questions about the quality of treatment there. She handed the outgoing department head a long list of complaints she wanted addressed. Later, she ordered corrections officials at the Hutchinson facility to provide fans to inmates suffering through the summer heat. In another case, she appointed herself to the state Pension Board, ordered an immediate audit, and directed the recovery of questionable investments by the agency. At one point, she questioned a cabinet official over the purchase of a high-priced chair. In another instance, she instructed highway patrol officers to lighten up in ticketing overweight trucks carrying grain during harvest season.[25]

Finney decided not to run for reelection in the middle of her third year in office, according to her daughter and chief of staff Mary Holiday. She announced her decision in September 1993, well in advance of the 1994 elections. She was proud of her administration's accomplishments, but she had grown tired and was not looking forward to a difficult, uphill campaign. The legislative process often left her frustrated, and the political climate was changing, as demonstrated by deep divisions in the Republican Party.[26]

Political Undercurrents

While state government was undergoing a transition during the Finney governorship, political undercurrents were gaining steam. These forces were not new, nor were they unique to Kansas. However, the centrist tendencies of Kansas politics had pushed these opposing cultural impulses underground for much of the prior half century. In that period, both Republicans and Democrats, governors and legislative leaders, had operated largely from the political mainstream and just slightly to the right of center in shaping public policy. The activist governors of the 1970s and 1980s—Bennett, Carlin, and Hayden—were largely oblivious to the turmoil bubbling below the surface.

Kansans have long felt the urge not only to use the powers of government to ensure social order but also to restrain governmental powers to enhance economic liberty. In the early 1990s, these opposing cultural impulses allied in ways that would change the politics of both the state and the nation. In Kansas, reemergent social and economic dogmas would fragment Republicans, challenge those with centrist political leanings, and transform state politics. Examining these undercurrents sheds light on the political battles that lay ahead.

Social Order

A preference for social order has shaped Kansas politics throughout the state's history. New England Puritans came to the Kansas Territory in the mid-1850s to ensure that Kansas entered the union as a free state. Their moral fervor focused first on precluding slavery, but their vision of a good community was more extensive. The state's century-long struggle to control the evils of liquor, for example, left an indelible mark on the state's body politic.

Early Kansans banned intoxicating liquors in their city charters both before and after statehood. In 1880, voters enacted a constitutional prohibition on the manufacture and sale of intoxicating liquors, and elected officials spent the next hundred years trying to enforce that ban, with limited success. The desire for social order had its heyday early in the twentieth century when state lawmakers utilized governmental authority to curb a variety of perceived evils, such as drinking, smoking, gambling, and disreputable behavior in theaters and dance halls. Lawmakers even authorized the sterilization of certain individuals, in the belief that it would help control criminal behavior and mental deviance. This intense push for social order quietly subsided as the century progressed.[27]

The abortion controversy reignited certain cultural inclinations. In 1973, the US Supreme Court's decision in *Roe v. Wade* negated state laws restricting abortion, which existed in most states, including Kansas. The issue resurfaced in Kansas politics shortly thereafter. In 1974, first-term US senator Bob Dole, in a tight race for reelection against obstetrician Dr. Bill Roy, brought the issue to the fore. Dole called for a human life amendment to overturn the court's decision and demanded that Roy reveal how many abortions he had performed.[28] These tactics enlivened abortion opponents, and late in the campaign they blanketed cars in church parking lots with leaflets labeling Roy an "abortionist." Dole achieved a narrow victory, which Roy's supporters attributed to the abortion issue.

Surprisingly, abortion would not resurface in statewide campaigns for another fifteen years, but the issue was alive in other arenas. In 1976, Ronald Reagan endorsed a constitutional amendment to ban abortion when he challenged President Gerald Ford for the Republican Party's presidential nomination. But Kansas Republicans joined Governor Bennett in backing Ford over Reagan in what became a close fight for the nomination. Four years later, Reagan would prevail, and the national party platform embraced a constitutional ban on abortion and a right-to-life litmus test for judicial appointments. Reagan crafted an appealing message that blended faith and protection of the unborn child with his opposition to big government.[29]

Quietly and systematically, abortion opponents were organizing at the grassroots level. In 1981, Right to Life of Kansas formed in Topeka, and in 1984, Kansans for Life organized in Wichita. Church groups established pregnancy counseling centers in a dozen Kansas communities during this time.[30] In 1988, the Reverend Pat Robertson lured evangelical Protestants and Catholics into Republican politics by challenging Dole's presidential bid in party caucuses across Kansas.

Another US Supreme Court decision, *Webster v. Reproductive Health Services* (1991), gave states broader leeway in regulating abortion and forced the issue onto the Kansas agenda. Churches and community groups, both pro and con, reengaged. Antiabortion protesters were arrested in Wichita after blocking an abortion clinic. Pro-choice Republican governor Hayden was compelled to weigh in on the issue in the 1990 legislative session and sought a middle ground, but his actions divided Republicans.[31] As he sought reelection, Hayden drew challengers supported by the state's growing antiabortion constituency in both the primary and general elections. His opponent in November, Democrat Joan Finney, distanced herself from Hayden by promising to sign any legislation restricting abortion, saying simply, "I am a Catholic [and] sick of abortions."[32] The issue helped sink Hayden's reelection prospects that fall.

The political energy incited by the abortion issue reached a peak in the 1991 Summer of Mercy, as abortion opponents who gathered in Wichita gained the national spotlight. More than twenty-five hundred protesters were arrested for blocking clinics. Finney, Wichita mayor Bob Knight, and US district court judge Patrick Kelly clashed in a chaotic political confrontation that galvanized protesters.[33]

Momentum then shifted antiabortion forces toward legislative action. In 1992, the Kansas legislature adopted restrictions on abortion, but these failed to satisfy abortion opponents, who fielded Republican candidates for state and local offices that year, without dramatic success.[34] However, abortion opponents often filled vacant precinct committee posts and quietly took over much of the Republican Party organization in suburban Johnson County, urban Sedgwick County, and other parts of the state.

The antiabortion movement also broadened its agenda for social order in line with diverse national initiatives associated with the Religious Right. Activists promoted prayer in public schools, vouchers for private schools, and homeschooling; they opposed sex education and gay rights, among other issues. Lecturing at Kansas State University in 1993, Pat Robertson attacked feminism as "a socialist, anti-family political movement that encourages women to leave their husbands, kill their children, practice witchcraft, and destroy capitalism."[35] In the 1994 elections, these advocates of employing governmental authority on behalf of social order would find political allies among those who preferred economic liberty.

Economic Liberty

A deep-seated preference for individual liberty and limited government unleashed an unprecedented boom during Kansas's first thirty years of statehood.

By 1890, "1.4 million immigrants had flooded into Kansas; most of the state's fifty-two million acres had moved from the public domain into private hands; two hundred thousand farms were opened; nine thousand miles of railroad track had been constructed; and 106 counties, 1,509 townships, 329 cities, and 9,284 school districts had been organized across the state."[36]

That boom would turn to bust by the late 1880s, sparking a populist revolt led by insurgent farmers. These populists called attention to the inequities imposed on them by creditors and railroad interests, and after the turn of the century, progressive Republicans would introduce a regulatory regime that tempered the state's embrace of laissez-faire economics. Kansans then steered a more centrist course, but their belief in economic liberty, free markets, and limited government continued to underpin the politics of the state.[37]

As Governors Bennett, Carlin, and Hayden led Kansas lawmakers through a period of governmental reform and policy activism in the 1970s and 1980s, an ideological challenge was emerging across the nation. While hostility to an affirmative government had various champions and surfaced in numerous ways, its devotees believed in free markets, economic liberty, and limited government. Their ideological framework called for stimulating economic growth through tax cuts, less regulation, and reductions in the scope of government. Beginning in the early 1970s and continuing well into the twenty-first century, Charles and David Koch of Koch Industries in Wichita and economist Arthur Laffer would be instrumental in reviving a belief in economic liberty and small government in Kansas.

At a young age, the Koch brothers immersed themselves in various sources of libertarian thinking. Their father, Fred Koch, had helped found the John Birch Society, a Far Right, anti-communist organization that fiercely advocated limited government and opposed the redistribution of wealth by government. The brothers developed several vehicles to advance their libertarian leanings. In 1974, Charles formed the Charles Koch Foundation, reframed two years later as the CATO Institute, a think tank for the advocacy of individual liberty, limited government, and free markets. CATO became the "organizing hub" for a nationwide libertarian movement. Charles also purchased the *Libertarian Review* as an outlet for the movement, and both brothers became involved in the Libertarian Party.[38]

Charles Koch boldly asserted his ardent libertarian thinking, writing in 1978, "Large numbers of businessmen . . . want nothing more from government than to be left alone. . . . [O]ur goal is to *roll back* government. We should consistently work to reduce *all* taxes, our own and those of others. . . . Do not cooperate voluntarily; instead, resist wherever you can. . . . And do so in the name of *justice*."[39] He advocated the recruitment of libertarian talent, specifically scholars who were "willing to dedicate their lives to the cause of individual liberty." He called for a libertarian movement that would deter governmental intervention, including at the state and local levels, and spark tax revolts, such as Proposition 13 in California. In 1980, Charles persuaded his brother David to seek the vice-presidential nomination of the Libertarian Party, whose platform included the elimination of income taxes.

Charles and David Koch began to provide seed money for libertarian endeavors. They sponsored free-market professorships, conferences, and lectures at universities across the country. Most prominent was the establishment of the Mercatus Center at George Mason University in 1980, self-described as "the world's premier university source for market-oriented ideas." In the 1980s, the brothers turned their attention more directly to grassroots politics.[40] In 1985, they formed Citizens for a Sound Economy, recast in 2004 as Americans for Prosperity, "to recruit, educate, and mobilize citizens in support of the policies and goals of a free society at the local, state, and federal level." In the early 1990s, Koch financing helped spawn state-level, free-market think tanks modeled after CATO across the country. The Kansas version, formed in 1996, was initially called the Kansas Public Policy Institute and later the Kansas Policy Institute (KPI), "a think tank guided by the constitutional principles of limited government and personal freedom." Charles Koch also provided financial support to the American Legislative Exchange Council (ALEC), an association of state legislators and corporate officials dedicated to "the principles of free-market enterprise, limited government, and federalism at the state level."[41]

On a parallel path but distinct from that of the Kochs, thirty-year-old economist Arthur Laffer emerged in the 1970s as an advocate of tax cuts to stimulate economic growth. After a stint as a professor at the University of Chicago, Laffer joined George Shultz, former dean of the university, head of the Office of Management and Budget (OMB) at the time, and later secretary of the treasury, as the OMB's first chief economist in 1970. Laffer famously sketched his tax-cutting scheme on a napkin while attending a dinner with top officials in the Ford White House in 1974. *Wall Street Journal* editor Jude Wanniski was present and dubbed Laffer's idea the "Laffer curve" in articles and later in a book.⁴² Wanniski wrote in 1978, "Politicians who understand the curve will find that they can defeat politicians who do not, other things being equal."⁴³

The idea of cutting taxes to stimulate economic growth gained attention in the late 1970s through articles in the *Wall Street Journal* and the neoconservative journal the *Public Interest*. This publicity drew the interest of Congressman Jack Kemp, who engaged Laffer as an informal adviser and became a leading advocate of across-the-board tax cuts at the national level. Kemp's tax initiatives came up short during the Carter administration but spread as gospel among a growing number of Republicans at the national level; subsequently, Reagan made Laffer-like tax cuts a core element of his 1980 campaign for the presidency.⁴⁴ Laffer joined President Reagan's Economic Policy Advisory Board, and in August 1981, Reagan would sign the Economic Recovery Tax Act, which slashed income tax rates by 25 percent across the board.

The Laffer curve, supply-side economics, and Reaganomics became part of the political language of Republicans throughout the 1980s. In 1999, *Time* recognized Laffer as one of the great minds of the twentieth century and the Laffer curve as one of "a few advances that powered" the century. In 2008, Laffer became affiliated with the Koch-sponsored ALEC as the leading tax-cut guru for state governments. He coauthored *Rich States, Poor States: ALEC-Laffer State Economic Competitiveness Index*, which advocated the reduction and elimination of state income taxes as a stimulus for economic growth. Updated every year by ALEC, the volume became the tax-cut gospel for states. Laffer continued to preach his gospel and appeared in Kansas in 2011 when Governor Sam Brownback hired him as a consultant to provide a blueprint for eliminating state income taxes.

Aligning Social Order and Economic Liberty: The 1994 Elections

Reagan gave voice to the alignment of social order and economic liberty, and the 1994 elections would demonstrate the potency of this opportunistic alliance both nationally and in Kansas. At both levels, Republican politics was transformed not only through dramatic electoral success but also through the increase in partisan polarization. Kansas would become a national laboratory for this transformation over the next twenty years.

President Bill Clinton's first midterm election took place in 1994, and Democrats expected to lose some congressional seats. Instead, voters thoroughly thrashed the president and congressional Democrats across the nation. Clinton's presidency had begun with Democratic majorities in Congress—a twelve-seat margin in the Senate and an eighty-two-seat advantage in the House. Voters obliterated those numbers, converting both chambers from blue to red. Democrats lost fifty-four seats in the House and ten in the Senate. Newt Gingrich, who nationalized congressional elections in 1994 with his Contract for America, was elevated to Speaker of the House. Kansas's own Bob Dole returned to his position as Senate majority leader, which he had surrendered in 1987.

Kansas voters contributed to this red revolution, as Democrats lost their two congressional seats. Upstart state senator Todd Tiahrt surprisingly defeated nine-term congressman Dan Glickman in the Fourth District, centered in Wichita. Six-term congressman Jim Slattery gave up his Second District eastern Kansas seat to run in an open race for governor. Republican Sam Brownback, a former state secretary of agriculture, entered electoral politics for the first time in 1994 and won that open seat. The Kansas congressional delegation thus went from two Republicans and two Democrats to all Republicans.

At the state level, the political alliance of economic liberty and social order was gaining steam as a growing number of Republican activists embraced these opposing cultural forces during the Finney transition. Their influence helped turn back Governor Hayden's reelection bid in 1990. Republicans stirred by taxes, abortion, or both peeled away from the incumbent governor and supported his challengers in the primary and Finney in the general election. This budding party faction "espoused freedom from governmental intervention on economic matters such as taxing, spending, and regulation while demanding governmental intervention in social matters such as abortion, marriage, and gambling."[45] This "polar" alliance divided Republican voters and began a transformation of Republican Party politics in Kansas.

This faction of the Republican Party did not enjoy immediate success at the ballot box. A few stepped up to challenge incumbent officeholders in 1992, but with limited success; in the 1994 statewide elections, centrist Republicans continued their domination. Republican primary voters advanced Bill Graves for governor, Carla Stovall for attorney general, and Ron Thornburgh for secretary of state, and all three won by huge margins. But state legislative elections were a different matter.

Democrats had taken over the governor's office with Finney's win in 1990, and for only the third time in state history, they captured the Kansas House by the thinnest margin, 63–62. Their success was short-lived, however. Democrats lost four house seats in 1992 and another fourteen seats in 1994—reducing their numbers from sixty-three in 1991 to forty-five in 1995. Thirteen house incumbents, including speaker Barkis, were defeated in this period. Four senate seats were lost as well. While the new crop of state legislators did not uniformly align with one faction or the other, a majority of newly elected house Republicans immediately dumped Robert Miller, the moderate speaker of the house. Tim Shallenburger, the newly elected speaker, issued a "Declaration for Change" to "find ways to cut government . . . put money back in the pockets of taxpayers . . . less government intervention."[46]

These new partisans also took control of the state Republican Party organization in 1994. They quietly ran candidates for party offices at the precinct level in the August primaries and then threw long-standing Republicans out of county and district party offices. Early in 1995, they elected state representative David Miller, a legislative renegade, as state party chair. Miller thanked "almighty God" for his victory, and the Sedgwick County party chair declared a "clean sweep. Absolutely. Spic-and-span . . . pro-lifers have taken over the Republican Party." A stunned state senator responded in disbelief: "The thing that bothers me is the fact that a good share of these people I haven't ever heard of before, and they haven't been in the party that long. I'm basically pro-life. But I'm not a single-issue person. If these people have just one mission in mind, it will be the demise of the Republican Party."[47]

In the wake of the 1994 elections, the Kansas Republican Party had clearly split into two camps. A faction energized by the alliance of economic liberty and social order controlled the party organization and the Republican caucus of the Kansas House. Centrist Republicans held on to key statewide offices, most importantly the governorship, and maintained control of the Republican caucus of the Kansas Senate. Passionately motivated polar alliance Republicans would align with groups that demanded loyalty through litmus tests on abortion or pledges on taxes. Centrists would espouse mainstream pragmatism and show a willingness to compromise to achieve results. This polarization would reshape Kansas politics for the next twenty-five years.

Notes

1. Roger Meyer, "Joan Finney, the Feisty Populist Who Switched Political Parties and Went on to Become the First Female Governor of Kansas," *Topeka Capital-Journal*, July 29, 2001.
2. "Joan Finney—The People's Governor," *Topeka Capital-Journal*, July 31, 2001.
3. Warren B. Armstrong and Dee A. Harris, eds., *Populism Revived: The Selected Records of Governor Joan Finney, 1991–1995* (Wichita: Hugo Wall School of Urban and Public Affairs, Wichita State University, 1998), 1, 579.
4. Meyer, "Joan Finney."
5. Meyer; Armstrong and Harris, *Populism Revived*, 16–17.
6. Michael Johnston interview, January 6, 2017.
7. Armstrong and Harris, *Populism Revived*, 119.
8. Rochelle Chronister interview, January 11, 2017.
9. Armstrong and Harris, *Populism Revived*, 514.
10. Dennis McKinney interview, January 6, 2017; Armstrong and Harris, *Populism Revived*, 516–517.
11. Armstrong and Harris, *Populism Revived*, 522–523.
12. Armstrong and Harris, 414.
13. Marvin Barkis, telephone interview, February 22, 2017. See also H. Edward Flentje, oral history interview with Marvin Barkis, October 27, 2017, https://www.kshs.org/km/items/view/474327.
14. William O. Wagnon Jr., "In the Service of the Queen of Hearts: A Memoir of an Education Advisor to a New Governor of Kansas," May 19–31, 1991, 44.
15. H. Edward Flentje, oral history interview with Donna Whiteman, January 19, 2018, https://www.kshs.org/km/items/view/455235.
16. Armstrong and Harris, *Populism Revived*, 528, 591–593; H. Edward Flentje and Joseph A. Aistrup, *Kansas Politics and Government: The Clash of Political Cultures* (Lincoln: University of Nebraska Press, 2010), 102; James W. Drury, *The Government of Kansas* (Lawrence: KU Capitol Center, University of Kansas, 1997), 102.
17. See Mark Tallman, "The 1992 Kansas School Finance Act: A Political and Legislative History" (paper submitted in partial fulfillment of master of public administration degree, University of Kansas, December 1993).
18. Tallman, 60.
19. Barkis discusses his role in agenda setting in H. Edward Flentje, oral history

interview with Marvin Barkis, October 27, 2017, https://www.kshs.org/km/items/view/474327.

20. See Nancy McCarthy Snyder, "Reform of Children and Family Services: A Case Study of Kansas" (paper presented to the annual research meeting of the Association for Public Policy Analysis and Management, Washington, DC, October 29, 1993).

21. John Hanna, "Joan Finney Left Legacy of Legalized Executions," *Lawrence Journal-World*, December 5, 2000.

22. Johnston interview. See also Armstrong and Harris, *Populism Revived*, 527; Whiteman oral history interview; Wagnon, "In the Service of the Queen of Hearts," 28–45.

23. John Hanna, "Kansas Gov. Joan Finney Reckons with Administrative Revolving Door," Associated Press, August 8, 1992.

24. Armstrong and Harris, *Populism Revived*, 527.

25. Armstrong and Harris, 437, 507–511; Johnston interview.

26. Mary Holiday, telephone interview, February 17, 2017.

27. See Flentje and Aistrup, *Kansas Politics and Government*, 13–29; Robert Smith Bader, *Prohibition in Kansas* (Lawrence: University Press of Kansas, 1986).

28. Elizabeth Kolbert, "Abortion, Dole's Sword in '74, Returns to Confront Him in '96," *New York Times*, July 8, 1996. See also Robert Wuthnow, *Red State Religion: Faith and Politics in America's Heartland* (Princeton, NJ: Princeton University Press, 2012), 274–275.

29. Wuthnow, *Red State Religion*, 275, 282–283.

30. Wuthnow, 283–284.

31. Wuthnow, chap. 6.

32. David Shribman, "Upside Down Kansas Gubernatorial Race Offers Voters Choice between 2 Unpopular Candidates," *Wall Street Journal*, October 9, 1990; Wuthnow, *Red State Religion*, 288.

33. Wuthnow, *Red State Religion*, 287–294. See also Isabel Wilkerson, "Drive against Abortion Finds a Symbol: Wichita," *New York Times*, August 4, 1991.

34. "Bill Limiting Access to Abortion Is Signed by Governor of Kansas," *New York Times*, April 24, 1992.

35. Quoted in Wuthnow, *Red State Religion*, 301.

36. Flentje and Aistrup, *Kansas Politics and Government*, 8.

37. Flentje and Aistrup, 8–29.

38. Daniel Schulman, *Sons of Wichita: How the Koch Brothers Became America's Most Powerful and Private Dynasty* (New York: Grand Central Publishing, 2014), 89–105.

39. Charles Koch, "The Business Community: Resisting Regulation," *Libertarian Review* 7, 7 (August 1978): 31, 32.

40. Schulman, *Sons of Wichita*, 263–264, 266–276.

41. Charles Koch, speech at the Institute for Humane Studies Research Colloquium, January 11, 1997.

42. See Jude Wanniski, "The Mundell-Laffer Hypothesis—A New View of the World Economy," *Public Interest* (Spring 1975); Jude Wanniski, "Taxes, Revenues, and the 'Laffer Curve,'" *Public Interest* (Winter 1978); Jude Wanniski, *The Way the World Works* (Morristown, NJ: Polyconomics, 1978).

43. Wanniski, "Taxes, Revenues, and the 'Laffer Curve,'" 16.

44. Geoffrey Kabaservice, *Rule and Ruin: The Downfall of Moderation and the Destruction of the Republican Party, from Eisenhower to the Tea Party* (New York: Oxford University Press, 2012), 350–355.

45. Flentje and Aistrup, *Kansas Politics and Government*, 24.

46. Flentje and Aistrup, 26.

47. Flentje and Aistrup, 26–27.

CHAPTER FIVE

Contentious Republicans
The Graves Years

Michael A. Smith

The Graves-Sebelius-Parkinson era, 1994–2010, was marked by an increasing cleavage between moderate Republicans and Democrats, on the one hand, and conservative Republicans, on the other. The bipartisan coalition focused on workhorse state issues. Bill Graves emphasized highway construction and maintenance, Kathleen Sebelius argued for education and health care reform, and Mark Parkinson pushed for compromise between economic development and environmentalism. These issues reflect the less ideological and more pragmatic policymaking that epitomized both parties for much of the state's history.

The new breed of conservative Republicans continued their ascent during this time. The issues they emphasized differed dramatically from those of the three governors: sharp restrictions on access to abortion, tax cuts, gun rights, and even a challenge to recommended state science education standards that embraced evolution. The moderate Republicans and Democrats were not always allies—the latter were particularly critical of the former's embrace of regressive sales taxes to fund state operations—but they shared a generally centrist outlook that focused on the nuts and bolts of state government. The rising stars of the Right, by contrast, emphasized tax cuts and hot-button, sharply divisive social issues that received substantial media publicity—first abortion rights, and then gun rights.

Background

In *Time, Politics, and Policies,* Burdett Loomis argued that political processes relate to their particular interacting concepts of time. Trends (long term and occurring apart from the political process), cycles (regular and recurring), and deadlines (fixed or set by one-time actions such as court rulings) all combine to create a sense of what Loomis called "political time."[1]

Loomis observed the 1989 Kansas legislative session and found it to be a highly productive one that resulted in a host of policy changes, including a major highway bill, relief of prison overcrowding, and funding for a water plan. But numerous other issues were not acted on, such as tort reform and a property tax overhaul. Each issue had its own unique combination of trends, cycles, and deadlines, as well as varying roles for policy entrepreneurs. Not all issues had such champions, but those individuals who took on the entrepreneurial role accepted responsibility as advocates for policy change.

In addition, Loomis noted that state legislators—particularly house members, who had two-year election cycles—had shorter time horizons than governors did. "Presidents and governors," he wrote, "are supposed to be able to take longer, more comprehensive views of politics and policymaking." He added that Kansas's part-time legislature was (and still is) in session only about four months per year, shifting even more responsibility to the full-time governor.

Finally, Loomis observed the legislature at a time when the divisions within the Kansas Republican Party were intensifying. He referred to the emerging dissident Republicans, whose leaders included Representative David Miller, as "rebels." According to Loomis, the rebels tended to be confrontational toward leadership, pushed for more conservative approaches to taxes and abortion rights, and were generally out to disrupt the status quo in which the Kansas Republicans had become, in Loomis's words, "the party of government."

In the 1990s and early 2000s, many of the long-term trends present in Kansas politics continued those documented by Loomis. For example, the state's population increased slowly, as another phenomenon grew in significance: immigration, which kept the state's population growing rather than declining but also produced a backlash led by activist Kris Kobach. The rural-to-suburban population shifts continued, with Johnson County alone capturing 20 percent of the state's population, two of its largest cities, and 25 percent of its gross domestic product (GDP) by 2010. In addition, Johnson County experienced many of the shifts occurring in other American suburbs, as documented by Myron Orfield.[2] Older suburbs in northeastern Johnson County became increasingly diverse, with many migrants from Wyandotte County and Kansas City, Missouri. Suburb-to-suburb migration resulted in people who had grown up in those areas raising their own families in exurban communities such as De Soto, Gardner, and Spring Hill, which remained heavily white and Republican. In addition, many migrants to Johnson County's exurbs had never lived in the Kansas Cities or the inner-ring suburbs at all—they had come from rural areas or other metropolitan regions.

In rural Kansas, depletion of the Ogallala (or High Plains) Aquifer continued, mitigated only in part by state water plans. Native Kansans—particularly college-educated young people—continued to migrate to metropolitan areas or to other states, replaced in some cases by immigrants. An aging population put more pressure on the state's social services, and medical costs continued to rise faster than inflation, affecting small rural hospitals. Nevertheless, the political culture remained, as always, sharply individualistic on issues such as guns and property rights.

Wichita's dependence on the volatile aerospace industry continued as well, making that city prone to boom-and-bust cycles based on a single sector of its economy. Another issue confronting the relatively dry city at this time was its dependence on just two sources for its water supply. Topeka's economy remained split between state government and blue-collar work, with city and county politics often falling into dysfunction and adopting a not in my backyard (NIMBY) attitude.

Loomis's book focused primarily on a single legislative session, although he extended his findings to the intermediate-term changes occurring in Kansas. By contrast, Ed Flentje and Joseph Aistrup took a wide-angle perspective, analyzing the dominant themes driving the state's political culture starting before statehood.[3] They posited that the shifting tension among three different cultural strands forms Kansas political culture: individualism (a highly libertarian approach advocating sharply limited government), egalitarianism (particularly noticeable during the Populist Era of the late nineteenth and early twentieth centuries), and order (for example, the state's long embrace of Prohibition). According to the authors, the relative salience of each strain in the state's political culture shifts over time, but all three are always present. Kansas Democrats tend to embrace a combination of individualism and egalitarianism, while the usually dominant GOP combines individualism and order. Since the moderate-conservative (rebel) split that Loomis observed starting in the 1980s, the Republicans have been unable to agree among themselves about the appropriate balance of egalitarianism, individualism, and order.

The Graves, Sebelius, and Parkinson governorships all contended with this Republican split, which Flentje and Aistrup called a "polar alliance" of convenience between conservatives and moderates. Graves became the clear leader of the moderate GOP faction, preferring individualism and a bit of egalitarianism, as manifested by his support for the funding of education and social services. The pro-order conservatives opposed him bitterly, to the point that Miller resigned his post as GOP chair to run against Governor Graves in the 1998 primary election; this unprecedented move resulted in an overwhelming victory for the incumbent.

During this same period, Sebelius embraced egalitarianism as insurance commissioner, fighting premium increases and health care company mergers that she considered threats to Kansas consumers. Finally, and most importantly, at the end of virtually every legislative session, the moderate Republican–Democratic alliance passed the omnibus bills that funded Kansas government.

According to Flentje and Aistrup, the emerging—and imperfect—moderate Republican–Democratic alliance represented a blend of individualism and equality. Its members took pro-choice stands on abortion rights and generally opposed the Religious Right, showing their preference for individualism over order. One exception should be noted: Graves signed an anti–same-sex marriage bill, albeit one considered routine at the time. Regarding egalitarianism, moderate Republicans generally defended funding for social services and education, while conservatives moved to cut or even do away with the K–12 base state aid formula, which accounted for more than half the state budget. Democrats joined moderates in funding the school formula, but there were occasional squabbles. In addition, Sebelius fought for health care reforms to expand insurance coverage, as did state senator and later insurance commissioner Sandy Praeger, a moderate Republican—again showing a preference for egalitarianism across the imperfect but relatively stable alliance.

The conservative Republicans, in contrast, balanced a preference for individualism with a preference for order. Their three signature issues were taxes, gun rights, and opposition to abortion. They took pro-individualism stands on taxes and gun rights, strongly favoring tax cuts and concealed-carry permits. The conservatives were sharply opposed to abortion and often sought to pass laws restricting it. Shortly before this era, the 1991 Summer of Mercy antiabortion protests in Wichita added fuel to a conservative movement that had already started to gain ground. Graves resisted most attempts to tighten the abortion laws, but abortion rights remained a potent political issue, as did guns and taxes.

The Graves Governorship

Bill Graves's victory in the 1994 gubernatorial race reflected the politics of the time. *USA Today*'s brief write-up of the final election result is full of references from a bygone era. Leo Mullen noted that Democratic gubernatorial candidate Jim Slattery, a six-term congressman, derided Graves's experience as Kansas secretary of state, calling it a "minor state office." This is the same office that Kris Kobach later turned into an aggressive pursuer of alleged voter fraud, rivaling the attorney general as the second most powerful executive post. Mullen also commented that "Kansas newspapers dubbed the [gubernatorial] race lackluster, calling the candidates more similar than different on most issues."[4] Mullen found only one issue on which the candidates differed: Slattery favored adopting the petition initiative in Kansas, while Graves opposed it. Otherwise, the campaign focused on the things that are often emphasized when the candidates agree on the issues: experience, endorsements (both pro and con), and the sources of campaign contributions. Graves also tied Slattery to the US House banking scandal that had taken down many of his congressional colleagues from both parties. The House seat Slattery vacated was narrowly won by former Kansas agriculture secretary Sam Brownback, who began his political career as a moderate but quickly and definitively moved right as a member of Congress.

In the presence of a strong Republican wave, Graves's party affiliation gave him a decided edge in a red state. Nor did it hurt that Graves enjoyed statewide name recognition, not only from his former post as secretary of state but also from his position as the scion of a Salina-based trucking company. For years, the name "Graves" appeared on hundreds of eighteen-wheelers rumbling across Kansas and neighboring states. Slattery's name recognition was largely limited to his Second Congressional District. Finally, outgoing governor Joan Finney's quirky, one-term governorship did little to help the Democratic "brand" in Kansas; after suffering dozens of veto overrides, she chose not to seek a second term. In the end, Graves won easily as part of a nationwide GOP sweep. Kansas Democrats had a rough year, losing fifteen state house seats. The party ratio shifted from 69–59 to 81–44, which weakened their role in any partnership with moderate Republicans.[5] The Kansas Senate was not on the ballot that year. Kansas is one of the only states that do not stagger their four-year senate terms—all senate seats are contested in presidential election years.

Graves had been a traditional, nonpartisan secretary of state, performing the tasks of overseeing elections and licensing businesses with little fuss and taking pride in a competent administration, which culminated in a 1991 award from the International Association of Corporation Administrators for effective service to business. His successor, Ron Thornburgh, would continue that no-fuss tradition for four more terms in the pre-Kobach era.

Graves tried to be friendly to everyone, staying highly visible and avoiding unnecessary controversy. His cabinet was composed of competent people who won their appointments for their expertise rather than their political connections. *Kansas City Star* reporter John Dvorak contrasted Graves's cabinet with the appointees of former governor Finney, some of whom "turned into embarrassments."[6]

In his first State of the State address, Graves made some major promises, including a cap on state spending, a moratorium on new regulations, and a general assertion that "there will be realigning, reinventing, and results." However, the cap on spending was tied to economic growth—the budget could still increase, within limits. The cap did not pass the legislature, but if it had, the $1.6 million increase from fiscal year 1995 to fiscal year 1996 would not have violated those limits. Likewise, the regulation freeze was not overly onerous, featuring a loophole and an expiration date. In the end, analyses of the 1995 legislative session found little in the way of major reform. The signature act of the first legislative session under Graves's governorship was to cut the personal property tax on automobiles by 7.1 percent, with larger cuts set for future years, much like a proposal offered the previous year by Democrats.

While Graves did not bring revolutionary change, he received highly positive press coverage about his relationships with legislators, reporters, and residents. He was friendly to reporters and even staffed the phones at a Kansas Public Radio fund-raiser. Perhaps most startling was the praise he earned from Democrats. He invited every legislator to a dinner he hosted at Cedar Crest (the governor's mansion). Lawrence Democrat Barbara Ballard told a reporter, "He is accessible," and Kansas City's David Haley said, "He has put people at ease." Moderate Republican Tom Sloan contrasted Graves with Finney, noting that Graves "interacted better with members of both parties," whereas Finney would "dabble" with the legislature. According to Sloan, "Finney would suddenly appear in a committee and want to testify on a bill."[7]

Finney was the perfect foil for Graves. Contrasted with her four tumultuous years, his managerial competence, vaguely conservative rhetoric, and don't-rock-the-boat proposals led to high approval ratings for most of his governorship. He also benefited from some windfalls. For example, Finney's governorship had culminated in passage of a new base funding formula for schools that remained intact for two decades. Graves and legislative leaders only needed to tweak it at the margins and provide funding. For his first several years in office, the latter task was made much easier by the era's economic growth. In future years, lawmakers would face the "problem" of having *more* money than they knew how to spend.

Editorialists and legislators (especially Democrats) offered some rare criticism when they noted that the governor often took credit for the accomplishments of others or hung back and let others do the work, then offered his own position at the end of the process. As an example, they pointed to the 1999 highway bill: Graves did little until the wrap-up session (officially known as the veto session) was about to start and then claimed credit when the bill passed. But even these critics gave Graves high marks for being flexible and adapting to circumstances. Pundits compared him to a magician and dubbed his leadership style the "rabbit from a hat," pulling out victory at the end of the legislative session. Like Sebelius, Graves understood that in end-of-session votes, he could generally rely on his moderate-conservative coalition to back legislation he supported, even if he did not initiate it.

Each year, Graves would start strong, remain aloof mid-session, then re-engage at the end to achieve his legislative victories.[8] In terms of budgeting, the overriding issue most years was funding the annual per-pupil increases in the base state aid formula. The relatively modest recession of 2000–2002 ended Graves's passive approach, as the governor became more hands-on and issued more vetoes and veto threats.[9] For example, Graves issued twenty-two line-item vetoes in 2001, versus no line-item vetoes and only two vetoes in 1997.[10]

On the Roads Again

One high priority for Governor Graves was roads—hardly a surprise for someone who cut his teeth in the trucking business. In his 1995 State of the State speech, Graves made roads a priority, not only for convenience and safety but also as an economic development tool. Motor fuel taxes were notably higher in Kansas than in neighboring states, and motorists along one of the state's most well-traveled routes had to pay turnpike fees, but Graves and his legislative allies argued that this money was well spent. The generous state funding of highways leveraged plenty of federal matching support as well. The centerpiece of these efforts was a $13 billion transportation bill that Graves signed in 1999. Similar to a 1989 highway bill, the politics of transforming two-lane rural roads into divided four-lane highways required assembling enough votes in the legislature to pass the bill. Legislative leaders cobbled together enough road projects and combined them with highway maintenance funding until the requisite number of votes was reached in each chamber. Legislative leaders made it clear to anti-tax conservatives that they were welcome to vote against the new taxes to fund the bill, but if they did, they could say good-bye to any new four-lane roads in their districts.[11] The politics of Graves and his allies may have been centrist and consensus oriented, but this did not preclude the use of strong-arm tactics when a major policy priority was at stake.

Graves's stalwart defense of highway spending was bolstered by an unlikely source: the rapid deterioration of highways in neighboring Missouri. Many Kansans lived close to the Missouri border and experienced firsthand the stark difference in road quality on their daily commutes. Missouri had failed to plan for road maintenance, and it had one of the highest percentages of highways and bridges rated "fair" or "poor" in the nation. Lower motor fuel taxes and no turnpikes left the Show Me State in the lurch for matching federal funds. Wichita sits near the Oklahoma border, another state with far more roads rated "fair" or "poor" than Kansas. As these neighboring states considered and rejected extreme solutions such as using general sales taxes to fund road building, adding a lane to I-70 across Missouri over twenty years at a cost of billions, and converting heavily traveled freeways into fee-funded turnpikes, Graves benefited from the comparisons.

As the 2002 election approached, Graves accepted, a year in advance, an offer to head the American Trucking Association in Washington, DC.[12] Given his administrative experience and family background, this was a natural move for him. At the same time, a national recession caused an economic slowdown in Kansas, and Graves left office with general goodwill but amid criticism that he had encouraged too many tax cuts, leaving the state in a precarious fiscal condition. This provided an opening for Democrats in the 2002 election.

Funding the Schools

Debates over the local option budget (LOB), allowing extra taxes to be levied, were part of a larger, ongoing policy issue: funding the K–12 state aid formula passed during the Finney administration. Beginning in 1996, House Taxation Committee chair Phill Kline pushed hard for elimination of the state-mandated, 35-mill property tax levy that provided the local base for the formula.[13] Graves vowed he would "not allow schoolchildren to be held hostage to election-year politics." Conservative house speaker Tim Shallenburger personally supported Kline's move but announced, "I don't want to vote on things that aren't going to go anywhere."[14] Some house Republicans were so angry that they ran a cable TV commercial criticizing the governor on the property tax bill.[15] In 1997, economic growth made it possible to enact some tax cuts, with a final number in between the governor's priorities and Kline's.[16] Another modest property tax decrease came in 1998. Despite these cuts, strong revenue collection allowed base per-pupil state aid to rise during each year of Graves's first term.[17] Otherwise, most haggling concerned the LOB (discussed again later).

Later in Graves's governorship, Kansas became increasingly dependent on accounting maneuvers and federal money, along with trust fund diversions.[18] Furthermore, the school aid formula ran up against a combination of declining enrollment (the formula was per pupil) and rising costs, so that even a small annual increase would fall short of the amount needed to continue services at their current level in the coming year.[19] Even so, the legislature was in no mood for tax increases.[20] School aid had become the largest item in the state budget, and other spending had to take a hit.[21] For example, a trust fund had been established for the money obtained from the settlement of tobacco lawsuits, but much of it was later diverted to cover budget shortfalls.[22]

Health and Justice

While school funding, taxes, abortion, and highways were the dominant issues during the Graves years, health care and the justice system were notable as well. Kansas implemented the federal State Children's Health Insurance Program (SCHIP) in 1998 with a program called HealthWave.[23] Insurance coverage for mental health was also on the agenda. Senator Sandy Praeger, who would become insurance commissioner in 2003, spent several years advocating for mental health parity in health insurance plans and was successful in 2001.[24] Finally, skyrocketing Medicaid costs threatened to bust the budget in future years, but the legislature enacted no major reforms during this period.[25] In general, more funding went to health care and other social services in the Graves years, but not enough to keep up with the growing demand.[26]

The biggest changes to the justice system concerned juvenile offenders. In this "tough on crime" era, they faced longer sentences, expanded detention facilities, and a new system of administration.[27] Overcrowded adult prisons also gained funding for a time, but these monies were later trimmed due to budget shortfalls.[28]

The Wrap-up Session

Kansas's is considered a citizen legislature, with relatively short sessions, minimal staff, and low pay.[29] Yet the pressures of governing an increasingly complicated society fall to the legislature, regardless of its makeup, just as they would to a more professional body. As a result, the Kansas legislature needed to get more creative in the use of its time. Particularly notable was the transformation of the constitutionally mandated veto session. According to the state constitution, legislative sessions are limited to ninety days, with a short break and then a reconvening to consider the governor's vetoes (including line-item vetoes). Yet the legislature had ceased to function this way long ago. Even the term "veto session" became obsolete during the Graves years, with legislators and journalists increasingly using the term "wrap-up session" instead. In addition to vetoes, other crucial items, including the state budget, often came up for final action in these sessions, which often lasted more than the ninety days mandated in the state constitution. One legislator even suggested that the session be divided into two halves with a break in between—a sort of spring break for legislators—perhaps leading to a more balanced use of time, rather than leaving everything until the end.[30]

Everything's Up to Date in Johnson County

One of the long-standing cleavages bedeviling policymakers was the split between Johnson County and rural communities. A case in point was a failed 1995 tax-shift proposal that would have dramatically increased taxes on Johnson County's higher-income constituents while benefiting rural Kansans.[31] Haggling was also intense over changes to the local option budget—that portion of the base funding formula that allowed school districts to raise additional monies from local sources, which was much easier to do where property values were higher. Johnson County legislators pushed hard for changes that made it easier for school districts to retain LOB levies, and these were passed despite resistance from other parts of the state.[32]

Several legislative leaders hailed from Johnson County, with Senator Dick Bond being the most powerful. Bond began serving as senate majority leader before Graves became governor and continued in that role until 2000. Bond was well regarded by capitol insiders, and *Governing* magazine honored him in 2000 for "leaving the state capital in much better shape than he found it."[33] Known for his patient listening style and close relationship with Graves, Bond functioned as a powerful ally and astute vote counter. Bond encountered some controversy related to his presence on the board of Kaw Valley Services, the major foster-care contractor for eastern Kansas. An exposé in the *Lawrence Journal-World* accused the state foster-care system—and Kaw Valley in particular—of driving away social workers and mistreating children.[34] However, the controversy did little to harm Bond or his close ally Graves.

Like the governor, Bond's strongest criticism came from legislative conservatives. For example, House Budget Committee chair (and future speaker) Robin Jennison told a reporter, "It's not the governors who bust the budget. The legislature busts the budget."[35] Bond was also an ally of Senator Praeger, a Lawrence moderate who used her committee chair role to scuttle antiabortion legislation (see later).

Johnson County–rural conflicts were typically about school funding and taxes, but occasionally a grab bag of other issues—often dubbed "rats and cats" by legislators—would arise. One example concerned driver's licenses.

In rural communities, learner's permits at age fifteen and unrestricted access to licenses at age sixteen are viewed as critical for traveling long distances and accomplishing farmwork. In urban areas, the number of teenagers dying in traffic accidents led to a push to restrict driver's licenses for sixteen- and seventeen-year olds.[36] The Farm Bureau took a strong stand in favor of the rural view, and attempts by Johnson County legislators to restrict driver's licenses were foiled in 1998.[37]

In addition to the rivalry with rural communities, the Johnson County delegation tangled with its neighbors from Wyandotte County. While Johnson County was mostly middle class and suburban, Wyandotte was more diverse, more urban, and less wealthy. Bond's actions sometimes reflected his affinity for power. For example, he strongly supported a city-county merger between Kansas City, Kansas, and Wyandotte County, which was ultimately enacted.[38]

The Mod[erate] Squad

As governor, Graves epitomized Kansas's moderate Republicanism. His first State of the State address set the tone in 1995. He opened by stressing individualistic Kansan and Republican themes, such as self-reliance and a heritage of frontier ideals. When Graves got down to business, he emphasized competent administration, not conservative revolution. He praised the state's recently enacted school aid funding formula, celebrating the fact that it settled lawsuits and allowed for additional funding. Graves set the standard, and the per-pupil base of the formula continued to grow throughout the Graves and Sebelius administrations, with a few hitches, until the Great Recession of 2008 cratered the state's tax revenue. The legislature focused on funding and tweaking the formula, with squabbles often breaking out over its complicated LOB formula. The LOB limited the ability of wealthier districts to allocate property tax revenue to their own schools, making it unpopular in Johnson County. Still, most Johnson County legislators were willing to live with the formula, which promised stable school funding but redistributed some of suburban Kansas City's wealth to the rest of the state. Indeed, Johnson County's sales and income taxes have long provided a disproportionate amount of revenue to fund statewide governmental functions.

The 1995 State of the State address prioritized the same competent administration that had defined Graves's service as secretary of state. He sought performance-based budgeting and an end to the "use it or lose it" rule that led to careless last-minute spending by state agencies. He sought to end off-budget state spending and increase year-end reserves. Graves advocated an end to the state property tax lid, arguing that local governments and voters could decide tax rates for themselves. Even a seemingly red-meat conservative initiative, a moratorium on new state rules and regulations, contained moderating influences. Graves proposed a loophole that would allow new regulations if they were approved by him personally. He also set the moratorium to expire after only six months.

Tellingly, Graves's inaugural State of the State address contained no references at all to hot-button social issues. The governor was quietly pro-choice but had not campaigned on the issue of abortion rights. The preference for order was not reflected in this governor's stated priorities.

The Conservative Challenge

The Kansas Senate remained in moderate hands during the Graves years, but the Kansas House switched back and forth between moderates and conservatives. However, both chambers remained solidly under GOP control throughout his tenure. Speaker Tim Shallenburger (1995–98) was considered a conservative.[39] Kent Glasscock (2001–3) was a moderate and close Graves ally.[40] In between these two, both chronologically and ideologically, was Robin Jennison (1999–2000).[41] House-senate and moderate-conservative fights were common during this time. One dispute even led to a shouting match in the capitol men's room.[42]

Along with taxes, the signature issue for conservatives during this time was abortion rights (gun rights would grow in prominence during the Sebelius years). Graves considered himself pro-choice and vetoed an antiabortion bill in 1996 and a "Choose Life" vanity license plate in 2002.[43] He signed a ban on so-called partial-birth abortion, but critics still assailed him on the mental health exception, which they derided as a loophole.[44] Many other antiabortion bills never made it to Graves's desk, thanks to the decisive leadership of Senator Praeger, who chaired the committee that considered most of these bills. She made sure they never came up for a vote.[45]

Frustrated with moderates like Graves and Praeger, conservatives lashed out on other issues, but sometimes their priorities seemed a bit random. For example, the issue of gun rights was only sporadically contested back then, but conservatives spent a great deal of time in 2001 trying to prevent local governments from using eminent domain against shooting ranges, even as a budget shortfall loomed.[46] Another point of contention was a proposed registry of people living in disaster-prone areas, intended to be used for evacuation and relief efforts, should they become necessary. Conservative talk-show hosts feared the invasion of personal privacy, and the legislature scuttled the plan.[47] Similar privacy concerns delayed legislation implementing new federal guidelines regarding child-support enforcement.[48] Later, the legislature attempted to defund conservation and restoration efforts for the Equus Beds Aquifer, which is critical to Wichita's water supply.[49] Graves restored the money at the last minute by executive action.[50]

All these issues—gun rights, personal privacy, spending limits—are consistent with conservative ideology, but the priority legislators placed on them, along with the timing, often had editorialists scratching their heads. Still, few observers could deny that conservatives' signature issues at this time were cutting taxes and restricting abortion. Gun rights also grew in importance, involving not only the shooting-range controversy but also a concealed-carry bill that Graves vetoed in 1997.[51]

Brownback Enters the Senate

Graves remained popular throughout his governorship, but he often failed to prevail in interparty splits. The biggest defeat of his governorship occurred when his handpicked successor to Bob Dole lost a special primary election to Sam Brownback. Upon becoming the 1996 Republican nominee for president, Dole resigned his US Senate seat to campaign full time. Graves appointed Lieutenant Governor Sheila Frahm to fill his seat until an election could be held. In addition, Senator Nancy Kassebaum had announced her retirement, putting Kansas in the unusual position of having two Senate seats on the ballot in the same year. Big First District congressman Pat Roberts was a shoo-in to win Kassebaum's seat, and all attention focused on the competition to fill the two-year balance of Dole's term.

Frahm picked up a primary challenger almost as soon as Governor Graves appointed her. As a member of the US House, Sam Brownback had not aggressively sought the conservative label—at first. After serving as agriculture secretary under moderate governor Mike Hayden, Brownback became one of only three Republicans elected to the House in 1994 who refused to sign Newt Gingrich's Contract with America. Brownback argued that he could not support the contract's provisions regarding public welfare programs. Later, he redefined himself as a strong conservative, especially on social issues. Brownback ignored a call from Graves to stay out of the Senate race and chose to challenge Frahm from the right. For her part, Frahm had voted with Senate Republicans more than 90 percent of the time during her brief service in that chamber, but she also campaigned on the themes of pragmatism and building consensus. Closely associated with Graves as a moderate, she had compiled a relatively centrist record in the state senate before becoming lieutenant governor. Brownback called for antiabortion legislation and the elimination of four federal departments, including the Department of Education, a popular conservative target. Stressing social conservatism and the traditional family, Brownback organized many of his supporters through churches. Conservative turnout surpassed that of moderates in the primary, and Brownback won convincingly, 55 to 42 percent. In a personal interview, Graves said his greatest regret as governor was that he did not better prepare Frahm for her primary challenge.[52]

Brownback's opponent in the general election was Democrat Jill Docking, who had married into a well-known Kansas political family. Docking tried to take on the mantle of a pragmatic moderate, calling for tax cuts and other Republican-friendly policies, while stressing compromise and pragmatism, much like Frahm. It was not enough in a state that had not elected a Democrat to the US Senate since 1932. Brownback defeated Docking by a 54 percent–43 percent margin and began his career in the Senate, where he would carve out a role as a strong social conservative.

Senator Brownback stressed conservative themes, such as opposing abortion, but he also cut a path of his own on issues that fit with his religious faith, if not the views of other Senate conservatives. Brownback and Ted Kennedy and their respective staffs were hard at work on a bipartisan immigration reform bill when the September 11, 2001, attacks moved immigration reform off the country's political agenda. Brownback was an outspoken advocate of the United States taking strong action to oppose genocide, particularly in Darfur, Sudan. He also sponsored anti–human-trafficking legislation.[53] Brownback even participated in an event with Senator Barack Obama designed to raise HIV awareness among populations that shied away from being tested. Hosted by Pastor Rick Warren's Saddleback Church in California, the event targeted evangelical Christians and African Americans, two populations that tended to avoid HIV testing. At the event, both Brownback and Obama volunteered to be tested themselves.

Brownback could surprise on occasion, but he generally stressed the conventional social conservative themes such as opposition to abortion and same-sex marriage, support for homeschooling, and a refusal to confirm moderate judges. In particular, Brownback led the fight against the Senate confirmation of Harriet Miers, White House counsel to George W. Bush, whom Bush had nominated to the Supreme Court. Brownback's ostensible rationale was Miers's lack of judicial experience. However, the underlying issue was a concern that she might not vote to overturn the 1973 *Roe v. Wade* decision legalizing abortion. Brownback and his allies prevailed, President Bush withdrew Miers's nomination, and the conservative, presumably antiabortion Samuel Alito subsequently won nomination and confirmation.

Overall, it was an agenda that Brownback labeled pro-family. He met regularly in Washington with socially conservative groups such as the Family Research Council and mobilized his base by stressing those issues at home. A convert from Methodism to Catholicism, Brownback was not shy about discussing his religious faith and campaigning to conservative faith-based groups. Like all Kansas Republican senators, Brownback's seat was safe, and he served for one partial and two full Senate terms before seeking the governorship in 2010. In his three Senate elections, Brownback proved a formidable electoral force, encountering no serious opposition after his initial victories over moderates Sheila Frahm and Jill Docking. He had little reason to believe that such results would change when he ran for governor.

A Reelection Challenge

Graves stood for reelection in 1998, and the Republican Party split along moderate-conservative lines, as party chairman David Miller resigned to oppose Graves in the primary. Miller had been influential in helping conservatives win other primary fights, including Todd Tiahrt's victory in the contest for the Wichita-area congressional seat and Brownback's 1996 victory over Graves ally Frahm.[54] Despite strong support from the Reverend James Dobson and his Focus on the Family organization, Miller was soundly defeated by Graves, 73 to 27 percent.[55] Even so, Miller ally Steve Abrams, who initially planned to oppose Graves himself, secured the post of state Republican Party chair, maintaining conservative opposition to Graves.[56]

On the Democratic side, Representative Tom Sawyer entered the primary at the last minute, and he did so only to prevent the controversial Westboro Baptist Church pastor Fred Phelps from running unopposed for the party's nomination.[57] Sawyer was outspent in the general election by the popular Graves, who won another huge victory, 73 to 23 percent. Graves's double landslides against Miller and Sawyer left him and his allies riding high, but at the grass roots, conservatives continued to organize and build unabated.[58] In a 2016 interview, Graves spoke highly of Sawyer while condemning Miller as divisive and unprofessional. Graves said, "I think Tom [Sawyer] is a fine public official and I consider him to be a friend."[59]

Evolution and Devolution

A major but mostly symbolic setback for Graves occurred in 1999, when the elected Kansas School Board voted six to four to remove certain teachings about evolution from the state's science curriculum for public schools. Some observers connected this to the outrageous behavior of the Westboro Baptist Church, which consisted largely of the extremist Reverend Fred Phelps and his family. Protesting funerals of LGBTQ individuals and even military veterans with signs reading "God Hates Fags," Westboro became an international embarrassment for Kansas. TV comedy writers quickly made Kansas the butt of national jokes, and cars in liberal Lawrence sprouted bumper stickers that read, "Welcome to Kansas: Turn Your Clock Back 100 Years." Graves was horrified, worrying that the evolution controversy would hurt Kansas's pro-business climate. Both sides of the ensuing controversy mobilized. Some Democrats strategically re-registered as Republicans to influence the partisan Board of Education elections. Kansas Board of Education districts are based on the map used for the state senate's districts. In this heavily GOP, closed-primary state, Republicans often had contested primaries, whereas Democrats did not. By registering as Republicans, Democrats could participate in that party's primaries, where moderates and conservatives often squared off, without forfeiting their right to vote as they chose in the general election. Republicans, especially conservatives, took a dim view of such tactics, but there was little evidence that they succeeded.

At any rate, pro-evolution advocates captured two more state school board seats in the 2000 election and quickly passed new standards endorsing evolution. Over the coming years, the board's majority would flip back and forth—sometimes pro-evolution, sometimes not. Local school districts and teachers remained the final arbiters of classroom content, but the initial vote signaled that a rightward push was afoot in Kansas. Still, it would be almost a decade before the moderate-conservative dominance would face an effective challenge. In the interim, Kansas would elect a Democratic governor, and the moderate majority, though frayed, would hold.

Notes

1. Burdett Loomis, *Time, Politics, and Policies: A Legislative Year* (Lawrence: University Press of Kansas, 1994).

2. Myron Orfield, *Metropolitics* (Washington, DC: Brookings Institution Press, 1997).

3. H. Edward Flentje and Joseph Aistrup, *Kansas Politics and Government: The Clash of Political Cultures* (Lincoln: University of Nebraska Press, 2010).

4. Leo Mullen, "Meet the USA's New Governors and Senators," *USA Today*, November 11, 1994.

5. Dave Toplikar, "Hefty Agenda Awaits State GOP: Widening the Gap," *Lawrence Journal-World*, November 13, 1994.

6. John Dvorak, "A Good Start in Giving Good Will—But so Far, Graves Has Done Little to Overhaul Government," *Kansas City Star*, April 19, 1995.

7. All quoted in Dave Toplikar, "Governor Learns Role," *Lawrence Journal-World*, April 30, 1995.

8. John Petterson, "Graves' Agenda Shaped Outcome of Legislature as Session Ended, Governor Mobilized for His Moderate Viewpoint," *Kansas City Star*, May 4, 1996.

9. Randy Brown, "A Legislative Session that Would Not Die," *Wichita Eagle*, May 10, 2001.

10. John Milburn, "Graves Signs Final Budget Bill for 2002," *Wichita Eagle*, May 26,

2001; editorial, "Legislature Comes to Final, Uneventful End," *Wichita Eagle*, May 28, 1997.

11. Robert Tomlinson, "Remarks to Michael Smith's State and Local Government Class," Emporia State University, October 2010.

12. Miriam Pepper, "Bullied Graves Is Quite Ready to Move On," *Kansas City Star*, December 22, 2002.

13. Petterson, "Graves' Agenda Shaped Outcome of Legislature."

14. John A. Dvorak, "Shift to Right Stalls in Kansas," *Kansas City Star*, April 2, 1996.

15. Editorial, "House GOP Goes Public in Tax Fight with Graves," *Wichita Eagle*, May 9, 1996.

16. John A. Dvorak and John Petterson, "Conservative Lawmakers Advance Agenda by 'Baby Steps': Their Road to Power in Kansas Legislature Has Many Detours," *Kansas City Star*, April 14, 1997.

17. Steve Painter, "The Governor Got His Way: For the Most Part, Bill Graves Fended off Legislation He Didn't Want to See on His Desk," *Wichita Eagle*, May 7, 1997; Jim Sullinger, "School Bill Is Signed in Kansas: State Spending per Pupil Will Rise by $50, Thanks to Growth of Economy," *Kansas City Star*, April 21, 1998.

18. Phillip Brownlee, "In Praise of State's Accounting Tricks," *Wichita Eagle*, April 29, 2000; editorial, "What They Didn't Do," *Lawrence Journal-World*, May 4, 2000; Steve Painter, "Graves Says He'll Veto Budget—The Governor Calls a Preliminary Bill that Passed the House by Voice Vote 'Complete[ly] Unacceptable and Fiscally Irresponsible,'" *Wichita Eagle*, April 27, 2001.

19. Laura Scott, "When the End Isn't in Sight," *Kansas City Star*, May 17, 2001.

20. John L. Petterson, "Graves Gives Session 'Incomplete' Grade," *Kansas City Star*, May 10, 2001.

21. Painter, "Graves Says He'll Veto Budget."

22. Scott Rothschild and Steve Painter, "Legislature's Victories Are Debatable as Lawmakers Head Back to Their Districts: The Victors and the Vanquished Offer Dueling Assessments of the Session," *Wichita Eagle*, May 5, 1999; Jim Sullinger, "Tax, Budget Issues Pressured Lawmakers: Funding Shortfall Brought Tough Decisions that Were Likely to Be Unpopular," *Kansas City Star*, May 29, 2002.

23. John Petterson, "Graves Signs Bill Expanding Children's Health Insurance," *Kansas City Star*, April 22, 1998.

24. Scott Rothschild, "Governor Gets Mental Health Parity Proposal," *Lawrence Journal-World*, May 6, 2001.

25. David Broder, "Congress Ignoring Woes of States Such as Kansas," *Wichita Eagle*, May 23, 2002.

26. Dave Ranney, "SRS Chief Eyes Waiting List," *Lawrence Journal-World*, April 12, 2000.

27. Editorial, "Graves Signs Budget, Tax Lid into Law," *Wichita Eagle*, April 29,

1997; editorial, "Omnibus Bill Passes in Closing Hours," *Manhattan Mercury*, May 3, 1999; Phillip Brownlee, "JJA Chief Defends Agency, Style," *Wichita Eagle*, April 15, 2000.

28. Painter, "Governor Got His Way"; Jim Sullinger, "Lawmakers Slice Funding at Local Level," *Kansas City Star*, May 2, 2000; Painter, "Graves Says He'll Veto Budget."

29. "Full- and Part-Time Legislatures," National Conference of State Legislatures, 2017, https://www.ncsl.org/research/about-state-legislatures/full-and-part-time-legislatures.aspx.

30. Scott, "When the End Isn't in Sight."

31. Julie Wright, "Graves and Both Parties Agree on Car Tax-Cut Plan," *Wichita Eagle*, April 26, 1995.

32. John Petterson, Jim Sullinger, and John A. Dvorak, "Legislature Adjourns, but Big Issues Remain, among Them: Juvenile Justice Reform, School Finance," *Kansas City Star*, April 12, 1997.

33. Alan Greenblatt, "Public Officials of the Year: Dick Bond, 2000 Honoree, President, Kansas Senate," *Governing*, 2000.

34. Mike Shields, "Kansas Foster Care," *Lawrence Journal-World*, April 26, 1998.

35. John A. Dvorak, "Budget Bulks up with 'Cut'—Increase of $1.6 Million Is Result Despite Plan to Drop $100 Million," *Kansas City Star*, April 9, 1995.

36. John Petterson, John A. Dvorak, and Jim Sullinger, "Driving Restrictions Unchanged: Kansas Lawmakers, Near Adjournment, Don't Toughen Rules for 15-Year-Olds," *Kansas City Star*, May 4, 1998.

37. Robert P. Sigman, "Farm Lobby Kills Needed Driver Reforms," *Kansas City Star*, May 5, 1998.

38. Rick Alm, "Choices Show Mark of Bond," *Kansas City Star*, May 23, 1996.

39. Dvorak, "Shift to Right Stalls in Kansas."

40. John Hanna, "Glasscock Determined to Run for Governor, Spokesman Says," *Wichita Eagle*, April 23, 2002.

41. Rothschild and Painter, "Legislature's Victories Are Debatable."

42. Jim Sullinger, John A. Dvorak, and John L. Petterson, "Toplikar, House Speaker Clash," *Kansas City Star*, April 3, 1999.

43. John A. Dvorak, "Graves Target for Hot Issue: Calls, Letters Flood Kansas Governor with Advice on Abortion," *Kansas City Star*, May 15, 1996; Joshua Akers, "'Choose Life' Tags Vetoed for Being Overtly Political," *Wichita Eagle*, April 19, 2002.

44. John Petterson, "Graves Approves Abortion Limits: Politics Had No Role in Decision to Ban Late-Term Methods, He Says," *Kansas City Star*, April 28, 1998.

45. Dvorak, "Shift to Right Stalls in Kansas."

46. Phillip Brownlee and Rhonda Holman, "Editorials in Brief," *Wichita Eagle*, May 18, 2001.

47. Julie Wright, "'Hidden Agenda' Kills Interstate Pact: Concerns in House about

Ulterior Motives behind Emergency Management Idea May Have Contributed," *Wichita Eagle*, April 5, 1996.

48. Painter, "Governor Got His Way."

49. Steve Painter, "Budget Proposal Nearing Final Vote," *Wichita Eagle*, May 8, 2001.

50. John Milburn, "Graves Signs Final Budget Bill for 2002," *Wichita Eagle*, May 26, 2001.

51. Dvorak and Petterson, "Conservative Lawmakers Advance Agenda by 'Baby Steps.'"

52. Bill Graves, personal interview with Michael A. Smith, video recording, September 23, 2016.

53. Sam Brownback, *From Power to Purpose: A Remarkable Journey of Faith and Compassion* (Nashville: Thomas Nelson, 2007).

54. Steve Kraske, "Is Factional Fracas Ahead for Kansas GOP Leaders?" *Kansas City Star*, April 10, 1998.

55. John A. Dvorak and John Petterson, "Bill Graves Takes Huge Triumph: Vote Margin over Tom Sawyer Could Be Biggest in History," *Kansas City Star*, November 4, 1998.

56. Colleen McCain, "Abrams Elected Kansas Republican Chairman," *Wichita Eagle*, May 31, 1998.

57. Editorial, "Democrats Scramble for Candidate with the Filing Deadline Approaching Next Week, Kansas Democrats Are Short on Options for the Governor's Race," *Wichita Eagle*, June 4, 1998.

58. Dvorak and Petterson, "Bill Graves Takes Huge Triumph"; John A. Dvorak, "Expect Trench Warfare in Battle for Governor: Kansas Primary Is Shaping up as a Real Race to Get out the Vote," *Kansas City Star*, May 23, 1998.

59. Graves interview.

CHAPTER SIX

Democratic Rule in Red-State Kansas
The Sebelius-Parkinson Years

Michael A. Smith

Democrat Kathleen Sebelius embraced egalitarianism as insurance commissioner, fighting premium increases and health care company mergers that she considered threats to Kansas consumers. Later, as governor, Sebelius lacked the legislative majorities needed to pass bills, so she depended heavily on an on-again, off-again moderate Republican–Democratic alliance to move major legislation forward. The results were mixed: Sebelius attained passage of part of her health care agenda and support for casinos but was overridden by the legislature on concealed-carry permits for handguns. She also won a major increase in school funding that conservative Republicans strongly opposed. Moreover, at the end of virtually every legislative session, the moderate Republican–Democratic alliance prevailed in passing the omnibus bills funding the state government.

Sebelius's successor, Mark Parkinson, may have embodied the state of politics in Kansas even more than Governors Graves and Sebelius did. A former chair of the state Republican Party, Parkinson switched parties to be Sebelius's running mate in 2006, then ascended to the governorship when she became secretary of the Department of Health and Human Services in the Obama administration. Parkinson governed a bit to the right of Sebelius on most issues. His most notable accomplishment was to broker a compromise over the proposed Sunflower coal-fired electric plant. He gained a host of green energy provisions in exchange for granting the plant's permit, but Parkinson later stated that he never expected it to be built. In fact, it almost certainly will not be constructed. However, the environmentally friendly alternative energy provisions have been fully and successfully implemented, making Kansas a leader in wind energy. Beyond that, Parkinson's governorship was defined by the budgetary crises caused by the early years of the Great Recession. Critics assailed Parkinson's decision not to seek a full term in 2010, arguing that he was leaving the field wide open for conservative US senator Sam Brownback.

Perhaps most divisive of all was the dispute over abortion rights. It hit a particularly violent point in 2009, when an antiabortion activist shot and killed Dr. George Tiller of Wichita, one of the only doctors in the United States who performed late-term abortions. Kansans for Life immediately denounced the shooting. Abortion rights opponents continued to push for restrictions in every legislative session.

Redefining the Insurance Commissioner's Office

While Bill Graves was residing in the governor's mansion, Kathleen Sebelius was remaking the insurance commissioner's office. Kansas is one of a handful of states with a directly elected insurance commissioner, but traditionally the job had gone to low-key officeholders who worked closely with the industry they regulated. Often, endorsements from insurance companies were the fastest route to capturing the office. Ambitious politicians did not see it as a springboard to the governorship or to other higher posts. In this pro-business state, previous commissioners had not been aggressive regulators. Sebelius set out to change that.

Sebelius was the daughter of a Democratic governor of Ohio, and her father-in-law, Keith Sebelius, had served as a Republican congressman from western Kansas. As a state legislator from Topeka, Sebelius had a hand in writing the base funding formula for schools in 1992 and advocated sentencing reform to reduce prison overcrowding. She sought the insurance commissioner's office at a time when insurance was becoming increasingly controversial. For example, a panel chaired by First Lady Hillary Clinton had proposed a major overhaul of health insurance. Although that proposal bogged down in Congress, it was part of a larger debate about rising health care costs and insurance premiums, an aging population, and the fear of health care "rationing," whether by government or by private companies that denied coverage, such as that era's cost-containing health maintenance organizations (HMOs). The stage was set for a candidate who promised to transform the insurance commissioner's office into an aggressive regulator instead of a rubber stamp. First, however, Sebelius needed to overcome the Republican wave of 1994. As luck would have it, her opponent was embroiled in a personal injury scandal. Sebelius, with substantial political skills and a great western Kansas last name, prevailed against a powerful Republican tide and a flawed Republican incumbent.

Sebelius leaped into her work as commissioner and was much more likely than her predecessor to deny applications for insurance premium increases. Perhaps most dramatically, in 2002 her office rejected the proposed takeover of Blue Cross and Blue Shield (BCBS) of Kansas by Anthem, an out-of-state company.[1] At the time, BCBS of Kansas had a market share approaching a monopoly in the state (and it still does today). Sebelius faced several court challenges over her decision. The plaintiffs argued that she had exceeded the authority of her office when she cited the impact on premiums as justification for rejecting the merger. In the end, Sebelius prevailed. She also promoted a patients' bill of rights and maternity leave, among other legislation. Sebelius made the office a storehouse of information for consumers and became chair of the National Association of Insurance Commissioners. All this, plus a reputation for managing her staff efficiently, led to her recognition as one of *Governing* magazine's 2001 Administrators of the Year.[2]

When Conservatives Run, Democrats Win

Sebelius's victory occurred at a time when a clear, pronounced trend was emerging among Kansas voters. When moderates like Graves and attorney general Carla Stovall won the Republican primaries, they were untouchable in the general election. For example, Graves obtained 74 percent of the vote against Tom Sawyer, even though the latter was a respected, credible (if grossly underfunded) Democratic challenger with a memorable name. Even Graves liked his opponent. Furthermore, until Brownback's victory, Kansas had not seen a competitive US Senate race in twenty years, with senior senator Bob Dole leading the Republicans in that chamber. Dole gained a national reputation worthy of satire and even appeared on *Saturday Night Live*, and he was the GOP's presidential nominee in 1996. Nancy Landon Kassebaum was another experienced, respected voice in the US Senate, famously coining the phrase "a bad idea whose time has come" to describe a proposed balanced-budget amendment to the US Constitution. Kassebaum's approach was a good fit with the Kansas Republican Party when she was elected in 1978. She was fiscally conservative and pro-choice. With regard to other polar alliance issues such as gun rights, she typically did not emphasize them. Moreover, she consistently ranked as one of the most popular Kansas politicians of any era.

The Kansas Republican Party had long harbored a strain of conservatism, but it typically did not emphasize divisive social issues. One notable exception was Senator Dole, who narrowly defeated opponent Bill Roy in 1974 by attacking him on abortion. Roy was pro-choice in deed as well as in spirit; as a doctor, he had performed abortions. Dole made it an issue and mobilized church congregations, especially in Catholic areas. Only one year after *Roe v. Wade*, this was one of the earliest examples of abortion coming to the fore as a national political wedge issue. Dole won in 1974, but afterward he focused on fiscal conservatism and national security, rather than the much wider array of polar alliance issues such as gun rights. Dole was content to chip away at abortion rights primarily by supporting conservative Supreme Court appointments and denying federal funding for the procedure.

At the state level, Kansans displayed a marked preference for Republicans who stayed away from these issues altogether. Governors Mike Hayden and Bill Graves, for example, were pro-choice, but they did not make abortion a campaign issue. The Kansas City area's Third District was (and is) the most metropolitan in the state, and its politics do not always translate statewide. Still, the perception that some Republicans were too extreme apparently influenced other elections, such as the hard-right Phill Kline's surprisingly narrow victory (0.5 percent) over Chris Biggs for attorney general in 2002. Biggs did well in the race, despite having the triple drawbacks of the Democratic label, less name recognition than Kline, and far less campaign money.[3]

This dynamic also affected Kansas House races. Four years before Sebelius won the governorship, Democrat Dennis Moore captured the seat representing Kansas City's Third Congressional District in 1998. When moderate Republican Jan Myers had retired two years earlier, conservative Newt Gingrich ally Vince Snowbarger was elected to fill her seat. Although both Myers and Snowbarger were Republicans, the latter's election represented a switch from pro-choice to pro-life on the issue of abortion rights. Even so, the seat did not look like a good prospect for Democrats in 1998, having been held by Republicans for nearly forty years. Wealthy, suburban Johnson County, which anchored the district, had not voted for a Democratic presidential candidate since 1912, even sticking with GOP dark horses like Wendell Willkie, Kansas's own Alf Landon (Kassebaum's father), and Barry Goldwater.[4] But this did not deter Moore, the county's former district attorney, from taking on Snowbarger, who had won by less than five percentage points in 1996.[5] Moore came across as a fiscal moderate and pounded Snowbarger on his conservative social positions, tying him to the outspoken Gingrich and arguing that he was too extreme for a moderate Republican district.

Snowbarger was also criticized for supporting conceal-and-carry gun legislation as a state legislator—not a popular stand in the soccer-mom suburbs. National Democrats declared the seat winnable and helped Moore raise money, although the candidate's team did the heavy lifting. In the end, Moore pulled off the upset and then served six terms, surviving a GOP-led redistricting plan in 2002 that moved half of college-town Lawrence into the Second District and made the Third more Republican. Moore mastered retail politics and built name recognition. In his later races, he won Johnson County outright, no longer depending on supporters in smaller, more Democratic Wyandotte and Douglas Counties to give him the margin he needed. Moore worked the constituency, becoming a regular presence at meetings, ribbon cuttings, and barbecues throughout his district. His staff even aided Kansas City, Missouri, congressman Emmanuel Cleaver's staff with constituent requests—a rarity for a metro area long accustomed to a deep split along the state line.

When Kansas Republicans nominated Far Right candidates like Snowbarger or Kline, Democrats found they could compete and win. Indeed, Democrats controlled the governorship for the eight years of the Sebelius-Parkinson era, as well as winning the attorney general's office when Paul Morrison defeated Kline in 2006.

The State of the Woman

Sebelius may have benefited from Kansas's propensity to elect women to public office. Kassebaum was, for a time, the only woman in the US Senate. Joan Finney's 1990 election made Kansas the first state in the nation to simultaneously have a woman in the governor's office, in the US House (Myers), and in the US Senate (Kassebaum). In 1994, Carla Stovall would capture the powerful post of state attorney general. Lana Oleen served as majority leader in the Kansas Senate. Except for Finney, who was a difficult-to-categorize Democrat, these women were all political moderates; their politics were defined far more by pragmatism than by ideology, and their political stands balanced individualism and egalitarianism, despite their different parties. Within this context, Sebelius fit right in to the tradition of pragmatic, moderate Kansas women.

Building on her work as insurance commissioner and her name recognition, Sebelius secured the Democratic nomination for the governorship in 2002. Her opponent, former house speaker Tim Shallenburger, claimed that schools could make do "with 1, 2, or 3% less funding," in an effort to avoid any tax increases. Sebelius countered by calling for an audit of state government and saying that tax increases were a last resort. Sebelius showcased her political skills when she quickly apologized after making a significant gaffe during the campaign—stating that she was more afraid for her life when driving on Missouri roads than she had been on 9/11. She put the matter behind her and suffered little long-term political damage.

In the end, Sebelius won by a 53 percent–45 percent margin. The 2002 election was hardly an electoral mandate for any party or coalition, however. Hard-charging, highly conservative antiabortion activist Phill Kline narrowly won the race for attorney general on the same ballot, and Senator Pat Roberts won a crushing reelection victory, garnering more than 80 percent of the vote against a Libertarian opponent in a race in which no Democrat ran. In a 2016 interview, Sebelius expressed bafflement that Kansas voters had elected her and Kline on the same ballot, but the result demonstrated the continuing tension between the Republican Far Right and moderates in the state.[6]

The Sebelius Years

As governor, Sebelius had an off-and-on reputation for working with Republican leaders in the legislature. It did not hurt that the state senate was solidly in moderate hands, led by majority leader Steve Morris from western Kansas. The house was a different story. The ascension of suburban Topeka's Doug Mays to the speakership marked a victory for conservatives, who claimed Mays as one of their own. In contrast, his predecessor Kent Glasscock was a close Graves ally and a clear moderate. Yet the blunt-spoken Mays was also a political animal who could work with house Democratic leaders and liked to get things done.

Sebelius carried through on her promise to initiate an audit. The results produced some modest reorganizations and improvements in efficiency, but not enough to make a major dent in the state budget. Her other priorities revolved around some of the same health care issues she had tackled as insurance commissioner. She was successful in getting Kansas into a multistate consortium that ordered prescription drugs from Canada and other countries to lower costs, as well as persuading the legislature to expand HealthWave, Kansas's implementation of the federal State Children's Health Insurance Program (SCHIP). Her push for a cigarette tax hike to fund expanded medical coverage proved less successful, as GOP legislators were not interested in a tax increase. The school aid formula continued, and its per-pupil funding increased in most years, including a sharp spike in 2005, when Sebelius and the moderate Republican–Democratic coalition in the legislature responded to the Supreme Court ruling in the *Montoy* cases. The court ordered the legislature to fund higher-quality education in all schools across the state. Kansas schools continued to be weaned off their heavy dependence on local property taxes, demonstrating that when push came to shove, the bipartisan moderate-conservative alliance had the votes to prevail on major issues.

Sebelius remained relatively popular with both Kansas voters and legislators. In early 2006, Emporia state senator Jim Barnett, once considered a moderate, appeared to be moving right to position himself for a run against Sebelius. The strategy paid off in the primary, when he won a six-person contest for the Republican nomination. Barnett's winning streak ended in November, however, when Sebelius defeated him easily, 58 percent to 40 percent.[7] He even lost in his home county.[8] Fund-raising was lopsided: Sebelius raised over $5 million, Barnett about one-fifth that amount.[9] A minor flap about a campaign finance law violation—Sebelius had sent fund-raising letters to registered lobbyists—resulted in a small fine of $1,500 and no lasting political damage.[10] The opposition had accused Sebelius of taking credit for school funding plans that her office did not write, but the criticism was ineffective. Indeed, governors ordinarily receive credit or blame for whatever happens on their watch. In this case, reaching a deal on school funding, as well as governing competently, served the governor well.

As the nation's economy collapsed in 2008, Sebelius confronted some hard choices. She had to balance the budget in the face of declining revenue and without any significant new tax increases. She chose to support the base funding formula for schools as much as possible, allowing many of the cuts to fall on the state's colleges and universities. The legislature pushed back, favoring deeper K–12 cuts and fewer reductions to higher education.

For most of the Graves and Sebelius administrations, the Kansas economy had made governing feasible, if not simple. But the Great Recession of 2008 dictated cutbacks rather than enhanced programs; K–12 education suffered the most, and the state would once again face lawsuits arguing that it had unconstitutionally underfunded public education.

As governor, Sebelius continued her reputation as an effective administrator. She was given high marks for her first year in office, not only from editorialists but also from legislative leaders, particularly speaker Doug Mays. Sebelius was less close to senate president Dave Kerr. One consistent theme in comments about her leadership was that Sebelius was more "hands-on" than Graves, taking an active role in negotiations with the legislature throughout the process.[11] She also reorganized state bureaucracies; for example, all the agencies concerning water quality and use were placed under the direction of former governor Mike Hayden, whom she appointed wildlife and parks secretary.[12] Later, when there was concern that Base Realignment and Closure (BRAC) would shutter a military base in Kansas, she commissioned a report from a Washington, DC, firm and presented it to BRAC. All the state's military facilities stayed open.[13]

Not all issues fell along the state's usual political cleavages. Some activists were so extreme—most notably, Fred Phelps Sr.'s Westboro Baptist Church of Topeka—that they brought Democrats, moderates, and conservatives together to denounce them. On May 4, 2007, while the legislature was still in session, an F4 tornado hit Greensburg in western Kansas, destroying 95 percent of the city and killing eleven people. House minority leader Dennis McKinney, who hailed from Greensburg, became a visible public face of the disaster as the legislature quickly appropriated $32 million in relief.[14] Meanwhile, a bill to ban any type of protest within 150 feet of a funeral—directed at the Westboro Baptist Church—was pending court rulings when Phelps and others appeared near Greensburg to protest the legislation at the funeral of a tornado victim who was also a veteran. Notably, the "buffer zone" legislation had been sponsored by a Democrat, Raj Goyle of Wichita.[15] Volunteers—many on motorcycles—arrived to show support for the victim's mourners and create a barrier between the Westboro protesters and the funeral attendees.

Health Care

Sebelius continued her strong interest in health care throughout her governorship. In 2004, she and insurance commissioner Sandy Praeger, a moderate Republican, declared the creation of Uninsured Awareness Week.[16] This may have helped prompt the legislature to pass a new hospital tax to fund higher reimbursement rates for Medicaid, which had not been increased substantially since 1976.[17]

One of Sebelius's top priorities combined her strong interests in administration and health care. She backed a 2005 bill creating a new Kansas Health Authority to coordinate health care policies among state agencies. The legislature initially rejected her proposal, then passed a similar bill that gave the legislature a bigger role in naming and confirming the authority's members. Legislators also passed tax credits for small businesses to provide employee health care and expanded prescription drug coverage for the poor. However, the governor was not always successful. Sebelius's proposed cigarette tax increase to expand health care coverage was rejected.[18]

By 2007, Sebelius had acquired a surprising ally: Dr. Jim Barnett, her Republican opponent from the previous year. Barnett and Sebelius teamed up to support a bill providing insurance premium assistance for low-income Kansans, loans to small businesses that pooled their insurance liability, additional assistance to free health clinics, and a new state inspector general to investigate Medicaid fraud.[19]

Finally, Sebelius's time in office saw the creation of an investment vehicle, the Kansas Bioscience Authority, as well as a bistate, Kansas City–area research triangle that included the University of Kansas Hospitals.[20]

School Funding

By the time Sebelius took office, school funding was well established as the largest item in the state budget. School funding could not be determined separately from larger budget issues, and court rulings raised the stakes further. In 2003, the private firm Augenblick & Myers produced a report recommending that substantially more money be added to the school aid formula to meet the adequate-education standard set forth in the state constitution. Lawsuits had been initiated on behalf of minority and disabled students, arguing that the formula's preference for small school districts discriminated against the larger ones that educated most of the disabled and minorities. These lawsuits were grouped together and were known collectively as the *Montoy* cases.

District court judge Terry Bullock lowered the boom in 2004 when he ruled that the current formula was unconstitutional because it short-changed lower-income and special-needs students.[21] Bullock called for more funding and took aim at the formula's preference for low-enrollment districts. He also ordered that schools be closed unless the formula was fixed and new funding approved by June 30, a move opposed by Sebelius and the legislators. The Kansas Supreme Court later overturned this deadline.[22]

The legislature formed a bipartisan interim committee to review alternatives in June 2004, but this was overshadowed by the national publicity surrounding the fiftieth anniversary of *Brown v. Board of Education of Topeka* in May.[23] President George W. Bush, Senator John Kerry, Supreme Court justices, members of Congress, NAACP leaders, and the national news media all descended on Topeka. Sebelius tied the commemoration to the current debate, arguing that there was still work to be done to improve Kansas schools.[24]

The legislature responded in 2005 with a bill that increased funding by $142 million, enticing votes from Johnson County legislators with a new "super" local option budget (LOB) that allowed more local money in certain districts.[25] The bill passed, but the courts rejected the super LOB and found that the amount allocated was inadequate.[26] The result was a raucous special session called by Sebelius in June 2005. Protesters on both sides (anti-tax advocates versus the National Education Association) made an appearance.[27] Democrats walked out of a committee meeting at one point, and there was a major house-senate split. The house fought hard to send voters a constitutional amendment prohibiting courts from closing schools.[28] Finally, an additional $148 million was allocated to the schools, funded by enhanced tax revenue that had exceeded projections. The house amendment regarding the courts was placed in a separate bill to be taken up in January, but it never passed.[29]

Things settled down a bit from 2006 through 2008. The legislature passed and funded a three-year package to increase school funding.[30] The only major flap concerned a meeting between Kansas Supreme Court justice Lawton Nuss and two moderate Republican senators. The incident, nicknamed the "Nuss fuss," culminated in the judge recusing himself from an upcoming ruling on school funding.[31]

The Great Recession cratered the state's revenue collections beginning in 2008. The legislature had to cut the current year's budget by 5.25 percent and accept federal stimulus money just to survive fiscal year 2009. The budget for fiscal year 2010 called for $138 million in cuts, despite a sales tax increase. Every attempt was made to spare K–12 spending, and the final decrease was limited to less than 3 percent. Higher education, government administration, and city and county assistance took deeper cuts.[32]

The higher sales tax and intensified collection efforts paid off in fiscal year 2010. Despite the expiration of more than $170 million in federal stimulus money, per-pupil school funding remained at the previous year's level.[33] Still, a price had been extracted. For one thing, the sales tax increase was later made permanent. In addition, city and county assistance was slashed, as was funding for higher education, and money was transferred from fee funds. Rainy-day funds were gone too. At the end of fiscal year 2009, the balance was a tiny $17,000.[34]

Taking a Gamble

Sebelius supported the expansion of casino gambling and was able to overcome substantial opposition in the legislature—including from house leadership—to get bills passed that authorized new casinos. In a strange twist, casinos not on Native American reservations would be owned by the state, due to a quirk in the 1986 constitutional amendment authorizing the state lottery.[35] Passed over the opposition of house speaker Melvin Neufeld, a 2007 bill allowed the establishment of state-owned casinos at four sites: in Kansas City, Kansas; near Wichita; in southeastern Kansas; and in Dodge City. Native American tribes opposed these casinos, as the new facilities would compete with their existing ones. Sebelius also agreed to support a large Native American–owned casino in Park City if the community wanted it. The project near Wichita was financed by a consortium of tribes that hired former Wichita mayor Bob Knight as their lobbyist.[36] However, the proposal encountered numerous hurdles before it was completed.

Pro-Order Phill Kline

At the same time Kansans were first electing Sebelius governor, they also handed victory to a staunchly pro-order conservative. In 2002, former state legislator Phill Kline eked out a victory over the lesser-known and underfunded Chris Biggs for attorney general. Kline's four years in that post were a harbinger of things to come. As House Taxation Committee chair, Kline had taken a strong stand in favor of spending cuts, and he occasionally worked with Democrats to isolate Graves and other Republican moderates. As attorney general, Kline repeatedly demanded medical records from the state's abortion clinics, claiming that he needed the records to ascertain whether the clinics were violating state law by performing the procedure on minors without parental consent. The clinics fought back, arguing that releasing patients' private medical records would violate the federal Health Insurance Portability and Accountability Act (HIPAA). Kline was so determined that he continued the quest even after leaving office and remained embroiled in the controversy for years. His behavior toward abortion clinics led to the revocation of his license to practice law and numerous lawsuits. Documents in one court case revealed that Kline had kept private medical records from abortion clinics in a plastic container at an employee's apartment.[37]

Kline also made national headlines when he prosecuted a nineteen-year-old man for having sexual relations with a fourteen-year-old boy. Both lived in an assisted-care facility. Under Kansas's "Romeo and Juliet" law passed a few years earlier, this type of statutory offense would have resulted in a greatly reduced sentence if the couple involved had been heterosexual teenagers. However, Kline argued that it did not apply to same-sex relations. He prosecuted, and the defendant was found guilty and sentenced to seventeen years in prison. The Kansas Supreme Court overturned the conviction.[38]

Kline's tenure in office was short, but he represented a new breed of Kansas Republican—ideologically on the right, uninterested in compromise, and willing to sacrifice moderate votes in pursuit of his agenda. Kline's role as forerunner of a new Kansas politics would be captured several years later by a yard sign that popped up around Johnson County with the message: "Remember Phill Kline? Then you'll love Kris Kobach!"

Kline's signature issue was opposition to abortion, while Kobach's were anti-immigration and tightened voting laws, but both shared an uncompromising conservatism and love of the limelight. They transformed workhorse state executive offices into a base to advocate for strongly right-wing policies in Kansas and nationwide. But they also faced many court challenges (and defeats) stemming from their advocacy.

After four years of outspoken and sometimes eccentric antiabortion and anti-LGBT actions from Kline, Kansans replaced him with Johnson County district attorney Paul Morrison, who had switched parties to gain the Democratic nomination. A tough prosecutor, Morrison ran hard, raised a lot of money, and soundly defeated Kline in 2006. However, a sex scandal limited Morrison's tenure to only about a year in office. After his resignation, the Democrats appointed Stephen Six, who earned bipartisan accolades for administering the office quietly and competently. However, this was not enough to save Six, a moderate Democrat, from a sound defeat in the powerful red wave of 2010.

Nor was Kline willing to give up so easily. Morrison had vacated his position as Johnson County district attorney to run against Kline. Because Morrison had been a Republican when he was elected DA, county Republicans had the power under Kansas law to appoint his replacement, and they appointed Kline. Thus, the two officeholders switched places, giving Kline a platform to continue his antiabortion work in the state's most populous county. An employee who worked for both Morrison and Kline was at the center of the sex scandal that brought down Morrison.

Abortion Rights and the Tiller Murder

In June 2009, Dr. George Tiller was shot and killed by an antiabortion extremist while serving as an usher at his church. Several years before, Tiller had been shot in both arms, and since then, he had maintained a low public profile. Antiabortion groups moved quickly to distance themselves from the shooter, claiming that he was not a member or a supporter and stating that they did not condone his actions.[39]

As one of the only doctors in the United States who performed elective late-term abortions, Tiller had been a longtime focal point of the antiabortion movement. His practice in Wichita was a major reason that city had been chosen for the Summer of Mercy protests in 1991.[40] Tiller's murder raised the already high profile of this most divisive of polar alliance issues.

The pro-choice Sebelius had left office shortly before Tiller was killed, but she had vetoed antiabortion laws in 2004 and 2008, with the senate sustaining her vetoes in both years.[41] The 2008 bill was particularly remarkable, for two reasons. First, it would have allowed private citizens to sue to stop abortions, and second, Sebelius's veto drew a sharp rebuke from Archbishop Joseph F. Naumann, who requested that she not present herself for communion. But Sebelius, a Catholic, did not change her position on the issue.[42] However, she did sign a 2007 bill with potential antiabortion implications. Called Alexa's Law, the bill made it a crime to harm a fetus. Pro-choice groups worried about the law's implications, but proponents noted that the law exempted voluntary abortion.[43]

Governor Mark Parkinson saw less abortion politicking during his short time in office. His two years encompassed the highly publicized killing of Tiller, the coal plant compromise, and an economic recession. Amidst all this, the antiabortion movement kept a low profile, but it would be back.

Other Hard-Right Issues

The push for order had other aspects besides abortion rights. For example, a major spat between Senator Susan Wagle and the University of Kansas erupted in 2003 over a sex education class taught by Dr. Dennis Dailey. Wagle's college intern found the class offensive, and the dispute was featured in several episodes of TV's *The O'Reilly Factor*.[44] Wagle's attempt to sanction the university with a $3.1 million funding cut "if the materials were found to be obscene" passed in the legislature but was vetoed by Sebelius. Compromise language was later approved that required all state universities to adopt policies for sex education classes and make those policies public. During the fracas, many students, administrators, and professors defended Dailey, and he even won a teaching award at the time.

The same-sex marriage issue arose too. Graves had signed a law—but not a constitutional amendment—stating that same-sex marriages from other states would not be recognized in Kansas. Conservative church leaders wanted more and vowed to make same-sex marriage a major issue in 2004 and register more church members to vote.[45] The Democrats lost a few seats in the legislature that year.

Immigration began to emerge as a wedge issue, in large part due to the efforts of Kris Kobach. The legislature had approved in-state college tuition for undocumented immigrants who had been brought to the United States as children and graduated from Kansas schools in good standing.[46] Kobach, then a candidate for Congress, announced his strong opposition and argued that it violated federal law.[47] FAIR, a national anti–illegal immigration group, threatened a lawsuit.[48]

Finally, the bipartisan team of Republican senator Phil Journey and Democratic representative Candy Ruff proved to be Sebelius's undoing on the issue of concealed-carry permits. Although Graves's vetoes of the proposal had been sustained, Journey and Ruff put together enough votes to override Sebelius's veto in 2006.[49] The two legislators staged a repeat performance in 2008, passing a law giving Kansans the right to own automatic weapons if they registered them and followed federal regulations. This time, Sebelius signed the bill.[50]

The Second Congressional District: Unintended Consequences

This was an era of unusual political combinations and surprising coalitions, as illustrated in Kansas's Second Congressional District. Combining Topeka and southeastern Kansas, the Second was one of the state's most Democrat-friendly districts. Topeka is a small metropolitan area with many of the characteristics of larger cities—urban poverty, pockets of gentrification, suburban wealth, white flight to outlying school districts, and a significant African American population. As such, Topeka included many central-city areas inclined to vote Democratic, offset by outlying suburbs that trended Republican plus some "swing" districts in between. Sharing that district was southeastern Kansas, once a thriving mining and farming area that attracted immigrants from southern and eastern Europe. These immigrants were likely to be Catholic, and historically, they and their descendants were more likely to be Democrats than their counterparts in other rural parts of the state (though this was no longer true as of 2022).[51] Representing these disparate elements in the Second District was Democrat Jim Slattery, before his unsuccessful run for governor in 1994. Still, based on party registration, the district remained Republican, and Sam Brownback captured the seat in 1994 before winning a US Senate seat in 1996. Succeeding Brownback in the Second District was Jim Ryan, a prominent social conservative. Ryan was (and is) a Kansas sports icon: a track star in high school, at the University of Kansas, and in the 1964, 1968, and 1972 Olympics. His campaign slogan was inevitable—"Run with Ryan"—and his name recognition carried him to an easy victory. However, his political record proved more vulnerable than his performance on the track.

In Kansas, the redistricting process employs no nonpartisan commissions, advisory committees, or any of the other methods used in other states to make the process more professional and less partisan. After each decennial census, the Sunflower State's legislative maps move through the legislature just like other bills, except for the creation of special reapportionment committees in each chamber that seek citizen input around the state and help draw the initial maps. The house ordinarily defers to the senate on senate districts, and the senate reciprocates for house districts, essentially giving the majority coalition in each body the power to draw their own districts (an exception was the 2012 redistricting process). On the US congressional map, however, each of the two state bodies insisted on having their say.

By the early 2000s, Republican legislators had grown accustomed to splitting deeply into moderate and conservative factions, but the one thing they agreed on was the need to rebalance eastward population shifts by moving western Lawrence from the Third District into the Second District with Topeka. This move seemed to be a clear attempt to make the state's lone Democrat in Congress, Dennis Moore, more vulnerable, since college-town Lawrence was one of two heavily Democratic areas in the Third District. The revised district left Moore with a shrunken Democratic base consisting of only eastern Lawrence and Wyandotte County. The latter is the site of Kansas City, Kansas, a diverse, mostly lower-income urban satellite; its relationship to Kansas City, Missouri, is like that between East St. Louis, Illinois, and St. Louis, Missouri. Nevertheless, by this time, Moore's constituency-based representation and moderate record had been so successful that he was winning Republican Johnson County outright, with the district's two remaining Democratic areas only adding to his vote totals.

In contrast, dividing Lawrence by redistricting in 2002 resulted in significant blowback for Kansas Republicans in the Second District. Moving west Lawrence into the Second District made that district more Democratic, setting the stage for populist Democrat Nancy Boyda to challenge Jim Ryan. In 2004, a presidential election year, Boyda ran against Ryan—an uphill battle in a red state—and Ryan won. However, two years later, the presence of popular Governor Sebelius at the top of the Democratic ticket and the lower turnout of a midterm election were just what Boyda needed. She highlighted a minor scandal involving Ryan's purchase of a Washington, DC, townhouse from a conservative interest group for a price below market value—an apparent gift. Although the incident had occurred back in 2000, Boyda managed to use it to her advantage, portraying Ryan as being out of touch with constituents. She won the seat in 2006.

As a congresswoman, Boyda earned a reputation for doing things her own way. For instance, she particularly liked advertising in small-town newspapers. Two year later, the Democratic National Committee (DNC) saw Kansas's Second District as vulnerable and worth targeting for assistance. In a quirky if ideologically consistent move, Boyda denounced the DNC for helping her. She had been sharply critical of "independent expenditures"—that is, parties and interest groups spending large amounts of their own money on races and not coordinating with the candidates' campaigns. A supporter of campaign finance reform that would rein in such spending, Boyda thought it would be hypocritical to accept the DNC's independent expenditures on her behalf in 2008, and she publicly told the Democrats to "stay out of my race." Her opponent, state treasurer Lynn Jenkins, enjoyed pointing out the irony in the hopes of hurting Boyda's chances. Boyda also genuinely disliked the DNC's focus on big television ads, which diverged from her small-town, small-media approach.

In 2008, Jenkins won back the seat for Republicans. Boyda was the only incumbent Democrat to lose across the nation. Jenkins rose quickly in the House leadership, serving as vice chair of its Republican Caucus, only to decide not to seek reelection in 2018.

Still, it is remarkable that for two years in the early 2000s, this reddest of red states had a US House delegation that was split: two Democrats and two Republicans. Despite its deeply Republican history, Kansas Democrats have regularly made inroads in gubernatorial and congressional elections.

Sebelius Accepts a New Job

In 2009, Barack Obama became the forty-fourth president of the United States, but without Kansas's electoral votes. Kansans voted Republican, as they had in every presidential election since 1964. Obama's mother had been born in Wichita and lived there as a young child, and Obama frequently mentioned his "mother from Kansas" on the campaign trail.

Noting Sebelius's strengths in the areas of bipartisan negotiations and health care policy, Obama offered her the job of secretary of the Department of Health and Human Services (HHS) after his initial choice, former senator Tom Daschle, withdrew from consideration. Ironically, Sebelius not only joined the administration of a president who did not win Kansas but also, as HHS secretary, was charged with implementing the Affordable Care and Patient Protection Act (ACA), popularly known as Obamacare, which most Kansas politicians opposed. Sebelius oversaw the first several years of ACA expansion, resigning in 2014 amidst controversies regarding the slow rollout of the internet-based health insurance exchanges. Governor Brownback and the Kansas legislature resisted creating a state exchange (despite the offer of $31 million to do so); nor did they expand Medicaid.

Sebelius had endorsed Obama shortly after giving the Democratic response to President Bush's last State of the Union address in 2008. She had even been vetted as a possible vice-presidential pick.[52] During her confirmation hearings for the HHS post, she vowed to crack down on fraud, saying, "There's a new sheriff in town." Kansas Republicans like Barnett were skeptical, arguing that Medicaid fraud had continued during her governorship and she had not been aggressive enough about enforcement.[53] However, Sebelius had a reputation for managerial competence and a passion for health care. Obama was convinced, and a Democratic Senate easily confirmed her.

Governor Parkinson

During this period, Democrats increasingly found themselves grouped with moderate Republicans. Thus, it was only fitting that a former state Republican chair would ascend to the governorship—as a Democrat. Lieutenant Governor Mark Parkinson assumed the office after Sebelius departed for the HHS job. A former moderate Republican, he had been elected with Sebelius on the 2006 Democratic ticket, having abandoned the increasingly conservative Republican Party. As governor, Parkinson was saddled with a particularly rough job, overseeing budget cuts during the Great Recession and dealing with a state legislature that was generally disinclined to fill budget holes through tax increases. The legislature did give Parkinson a temporary 1 percent sales tax increase, which somewhat eased the pain of the budget cuts (it would later become permanent during the Brownback administration). Still, Parkinson and the legislators were forced to make tough choices. With the base funding formula for schools now the largest item in the budget, it was inevitable that it would take a hit, and it did. Parkinson and the legislature left the basic formula intact, but for the first time since 1992, they cut the base per-pupil amount that determined school districts' allocations. Funds for prisons, higher education, and social services were also cut. Parkinson declined to seek election to a full term as governor, choosing instead to become head of a home health care industry group in Washington, DC. Parkinson, like Graves before him, left the state in the midst of fiscal challenges.

In 2008, Kansas politics were dominated by the debate over the licensing of two new coal-fired electric power plants near Holcomb. The plants would be constructed by Sunflower Electric, adjacent to an existing one. Sebelius's secretary of health and environment, Roderick Bremby, denied the permits in 2007, citing emergency authority and the role of coal in the release of greenhouse gases. Critics claimed that this was a misuse of the emergency power.[54] Mays had stepped aside by then, and new house speaker Melvin Neufeld was determined to override Bremby's decision. Sebelius offered a compromise of licensing one smaller plant, and Neufeld countered by demanding two smaller plants. He attempted to drive the legislation through by adding unrelated perks for Johnson and Shawnee Counties, hoping to entice more votes to override Sebelius's veto. It failed, leading to speculation that Neufeld was an ineffective leader.[55] Sebelius told reporters she disliked Neufeld's "attitude of ultimatum." He had lost an earlier battle with the governor over casinos in 2007, his first year as speaker.

As governor, Parkinson moved immediately to negotiate a compromise of the Sunflower Energy coal plant.[56] He proposed, and Republican legislative leaders accepted, one slightly larger plant than the one Sebelius had offered the previous year. Mandated renewable energy portfolios were part of the deal, but so was a reduction in the Department of Commerce's regulatory power.[57] The Sierra Club and liberal editorialists quickly pounced on the deal. Unhappy with the coal deal, Mike Hendricks of the *Kansas City Star* also argued that Parkinson should not have pledged not to seek reelection. With

Democrats having no other heir apparent, Hendricks predicted that the GOP would easily win the governor's race next year and mentioned Brownback as a likely candidate. Hendricks claimed that Parkinson was still a Republican.[58]

In contrast, senate majority leader Steve Morris and many other editorialists were ecstatic, noting that this was the most environmentally friendly coal plant ever approved and praising Parkinson's can-do attitude.[59] Parkinson later stated that he thought the Sunflower plant would never be built, and to date, it has not been. Meanwhile, the alternative energy and environmental provisions have had a major impact on Kansas's movement away from fossil fuels, with a particular emphasis on wind energy.

Conclusion

Prognostications about Kansas's future were notable. Professor Joe Aistrup editorialized that the moderate Republican–Democratic coalition should savor its victories now because the front-runner in the governor's race in 2010, Senator Sam Brownback, was likely to pursue an aggressive, conservative agenda, including tax cuts, less support for public schools, and antiabortion legislation.[60] In addition, a Koch-supported group, the Kansas Policy Institute (KPI), published reports claiming that data on the state budget shortfall were inaccurate. The KPI claimed the shortage was actually much smaller, but it had created its own numbers by ignoring the loss of federal stimulus money and by counting contributions to KPERS (the state's deferred compensation plan) as on-budget items. The *Wichita Eagle* harshly criticized the KPI's budget calculations in an editorial, but this was a harbinger of things to come over the next decade.[61]

Despite two turnovers of the governor's office and one party switch, the policies of the Graves-Sebelius-Parkinson era did not differ sharply across administrations. All three governors were part of the moderate Republican–Democratic alliance that struggled to balance individualism and equality. They were strongly opposed by a growing conservative movement that favored equilibrium between individualism and order. School funding was a priority for all three governors. Graves also emphasized funding roads and other infrastructure, while Sebelius's focus was health care, both as insurance commissioner and as governor. Sebelius also helped expand casino gambling.

Senate leadership remained relatively moderate during this time, but the house switched back and forth between moderate and conservative leadership. The moderate Republican–Democratic alliance was not seamless. Certain issues tended to splinter the alliance, including LOB caps in the school funding formula—strongly opposed by Johnson County moderates but supported by Democrats—and a sales tax on groceries, which the moderates tended to favor and the Democrats opposed. Overall, though, they often had to work together to withstand the increasingly intense battering from conservative challengers. For their part, conservatives stayed true to their three core issues of lower taxes, restrictions on abortion, and gun rights, varying their political tactics as necessary to maximize effectiveness against the alliance. Those tactics paid off. Brownback's 2010 victory would make him the state's first Far Right governor, perhaps bringing to fruition the trend begun by the legislative rebels in 1989. Order and a particular view of individualism were both on the rise.

Notes

1. Anna Jaffe, "Sebelius Rejects Takeover of Blue Cross and Blue Shield," *Kansas City Business Journal*, February 11, 2002.

2. Rob Gurwitt, "Public Officials of the Year, Kathleen Sebelius, 2001 Honoree, Insurance Commissioner, State of Kansas," *Governing*, 2001.

3. Steve Kraske, "Secretary of State Race Like a Repeat of 2002," *Wichita Eagle*, August 19, 2010.

4. Neal R. Pearce and Jerry Hagstrom, "Kansas," in *The Book of America: Inside the 50 States Today* (New York: Warner, 1983), 585–592.

5. Burdett Loomis, "The Kansas 3rd District: The 'Pros from Dover' Set up Shop," in *The Battle for Congress*, ed. James Thurber (Washington, DC: Brookings Institution Press, 2001).

6. Kathleen Sebelius, interview with Bob Beatty, digital audio recording, Topeka, KS, September 22, 2016.

7. Barbara Hollingsworth, "Sebelius Wins Second Term," *Topeka Capital-Journal*, November 8, 2006.

8. Office of the Secretary of State of Kansas, "2006 General Election," https://www.sos.ks.gov/elections/06elec/2006GeneralElectionOfficialResults.pdf.

9. Laura Bauer, "Sebelius Scores a First by Winning Second Term: State Has Never Re-elected a Woman Governor before, but Heavily Funded Campaign Leads to Success This Time," *Kansas City Star*, November 8, 2006.

10. Chris Moon, "Economy, Education to Be Touted," *Topeka Capital-Journal*, May 27, 2006.

11. Steve Painter, "Sebelius' Agenda Survives Session," *Wichita Eagle*, May 8, 2003.

12. Editorial, "Team Presents United Front on Water Issues Affecting State," *Lawrence Journal-World*, May 18, 2003.

13. Chris Moon, "Base Realignment and Closure," *Topeka Capital-Journal*, March 30, 2005; Chris Moon, "Surviving Once Again: Forbes Field Escapes BRAC List; Homeland Security Mission on Hold," *Topeka Capital-Journal*, May 22, 2005.

14. Jim Sullinger, "The Greensburg Tornado—Kansas Session in Topeka Takes Action: Legislature Approves $32 Million Package—Lawmaker Is Cheered by State's Help for the Devastated Community," *Kansas City Star*, May 23, 2007.

15. Tim Potter, "Church Protests Storm Victim's Funeral," *Wichita Eagle*, May 18, 2007.

16. Chris Moon, "Legislators to Tackle Homework," *Topeka Capital-Journal*, May 26, 2004.

17. Jim Sullinger, "New Hospital Tax Will Allow Kansas to Mend Medicaid," *Kansas City Star*, April 10, 2004.

18. Melodee Hall Blobaum, "Sebelius Signs Health Measure at Ceremony in KCK," *Kansas City Star*, May 11, 2005; Rhonda Holman, "Judgment—Sebelius Used Veto Pen Wisely," *Wichita Eagle*, May 20, 2008.

19. Dion Lefler, "Legislators Did Little for Average Kansans—Business Owners, the Elderly and the Poor Will See Tax Savings, but Lawmakers Admit the Middle Class Hasn't Been a Priority," *Wichita Eagle*, May 27, 2007.

20. Editorial, "Just the Beginning: Legislation to Be Signed Monday Is Just the First Step in the State's Effort to Become a Major Player in the Field of Biosciences," *Lawrence Journal-World*, April 18, 2004; editorial, "What Was Approved by the Kansas Legislature," *Kansas City Star*, May 3, 2007.

21. Scott Rothschild, "State's Financing Formula Contested; School-Funding Lawsuits Allege Inequalities," *Lawrence Journal-World*, May 12, 2003.

22. John L. Petterson, "Court Keeps Schools Open—Kansas Judge's Order Is Blocked," *Kansas City Star*, May 20, 2004.

23. Moon, "Legislators to Tackle Homework."

24. Steve Kraske, "'That Was a Day of Justice'—But Anniversary Recalls Promise Unmet," *Kansas City Star*, May 18, 2004.

25. Scott Rochat, "Rating the Session: Emporia Area Cast Long Shadow over the 2005 Legislature," *Emporia Gazette*, May 28, 2005.

26. Jim Sullinger, Melodee Hall Blobaum, and Laura Bauer, "More for Schools, Court Says: Ruling Rejects Local Option Budget Increases, Sets July 1 Deadline," *Kansas City Star*, June 4, 2005.

27. Melodee Hall Blobaum, "Shouting Replaces Placards at Rally: Capitol Bans Signs at Rotunda Protest," *Kansas City Star*, June 23, 2005.

28. Steve Painter and Fred Mann, "Funding Showdown: House Slashes School Bill, Democrats Walk out of the Committee Meeting Where the Senate's Proposal Is Sharply Reduced," *Wichita Eagle*, June 24, 2005.

29. David Klepper and Jim Sullinger, "$148 Million School Fund Plan Passes—Bipartisan Effort a Key in Solving Dilemma," *Kansas City Star*, July 7, 2005.

30. Editorial, "What Was Approved by the Kansas Legislature."

31. Tim Carpenter, "Session Marked by Little Progress," *Topeka Capital-Journal*, May 9, 2008.

32. Tim Carpenter, "Budgets and Coal," *Topeka Capital-Journal*, May 10, 2009.

33. Editorial, "Reviewing the Legislative Session in Kansas," *Kansas City Star*, May 13, 2010.

34. Carpenter, "Budgets and Coal."

35. David Klepper, "Governor Signs Kansas Casino and Slot Law," *Kansas City Star*, April 12, 2007.

36. Bob Knight, "Casino in Park City Is Only Game in Town," *Wichita Eagle*, May 8, 2005.

37. Tony Rizzo, "Kansas Supreme Court Indefinitely Suspends Phill Kline's State Law License," *Wichita Eagle*, October 18, 2013.

38. In overturning the conviction 6–0, the Kansas Supreme Court noted that *Bowers* had recently been overturned in *Lawrence v. Texas*, 539 U.S. 558 (2003). Editorial, "Kansas Strikes Down Same-Sex Rape Law," *Washington Post*, October 22, 2005.

39. Dion Lefler, "Shooting Could Alter Debate over Abortion," *Wichita Eagle*, June 1, 2009.

40. Jim McLean, "My Fellow Kansans: The Summer of Mercy," KCUR, September 24, 2018, https://www.kcur.org/politics-elections-and-government/2018-09-24/my-fellow-kansans-the-summer-of-mercy.

41. John L. Petterson, "Sebelius' Vetoes Stand," *Kansas City Star*, May 28, 2004; James Carlson, "Governor's Abortion Veto Barely Survives," *Topeka Capital-Journal*, May 1, 2008.

42. Bill Blankenship, "Catholic Leader Explains Decision," *Topeka Capital-Journal*, May 24, 2008.

43. Dion Lefler, "Sebelius Signs Alexa's Law," *Wichita Eagle*, May 10, 2007.

44. Editorial, "KU Sex Ed Class Once Again to Be Topic on 'O'Reilly Factor,'" *Lawrence Journal-World*, May 7, 2003.

45. Steve Painter, "Legislature Locks with Governor in Budget Showdown—The Statehouse Sends on a Budget that Sebelius Says She'll Strike Down, Lawmakers Aren't Warming to Her Proposal, Either," *Wichita Eagle*, May 2, 2003.

46. Editorial, "Immigrant Tuition to Face Challenge: KU, K-State Students Recruited to Join Group's Class-Action Suit," *Lawrence Journal-World*, May 25, 2004.

47. Kris W. Kobach, "Immigrants' Tuition," letter to the editor, *Kansas City Star*, May 21, 2004.

48. Editorial, "Immigrant Tuition to Face Challenge."

49. Editorial, "Kansas Legislative Scorecard—A Look at the Key Issues and Players from the 2006 Session," *Kansas City Star*, May 11, 2006.

50. James Carlson, "Sebelius Signs Gun Bill into Law," *Topeka Capital-Journal*, April 22, 2008.

51. Pearce and Hagstrom, "Kansas."

52. Sebelius interview.

53. Tim Carpenter, "Kansas Republicans Doubt Sebelius Claims: HHS Nominee Vows to Monitor Health Care Dollars," *Topeka Capital-Journal*, April 2, 2009.

54. Jim Sullinger, "Kansas Coal Plant Dust Settles, but There's More Debate Ahead," *Kansas City Star*, May 22, 2008.

55. Tim Carpenter, "Drama, Defeats Mark Tenure," *Topeka Capital-Journal*, May 18, 2008.

56. Editorial, "Intense Views, Immense Sums," *Manhattan Mercury*, April 16, 2008.

57. Deb Gruver, "Success No Surprise to Colleagues," *Wichita Eagle*, May 10, 2009.

58. Mike Hendricks, "It Didn't Take Long for Parkinson to Sell out to GOP," *Kansas City Star*, May 9, 2009.

59. Gruver, "Success No Surprise to Colleagues."

60. Joseph A. Aistrup, "Moderates May Want to Savor Success," *Manhattan Mercury*, May 12, 2010.

61. Phillip Brownlee, "State Budget Solutions Aren't Simple," *Wichita Eagle*, April 7, 2010.

CHAPTER SEVEN

Political Strategy Shifts Rightward
The Brownback Years

Chapman Rackaway

State-level political parties are, at their cores, electioneering entities.[1] The measure of a state party organization's strength lies less in its partisans than in its ability to recruit, support, and elect candidates for office.[2] When a party organization struggles to support candidates, the entire party becomes weaker.

Republicans in Kansas experienced a dark time between 2006 and 2009. Given the state's history as a bastion of GOP control, the fact that the state Republican Party organization was in shambles may seem shocking. However, the party was in a difficult position. Dominant parties sometimes struggle. Blue states elect Republican governors, and states as deep red as Kansas elect Democrats. Often these cross-party elections are signs of weakness in the losing party, and the Sebelius era represented a low period for Kansas Republicans.

To understand the state of the Kansas GOP in the late 2000s, we must revisit the election (2002) and reelection (2006) of Kathleen Sebelius. Years of division within the state Republican Party, dating back to 1989–90, emerged in the wake of Sebelius's election.

The Kansas Republican Party was a small operation in 2003 with only one full-time staff member, executive director Scott Poor. The state party was divided between two factions: the conservative "polar alliance" wing and the more moderate center-right coalition.[3] Factionalism is a common element of dominant state parties, but Kansas's GOP had become so divided that observers claimed the factions constituted two separate parties.[4]

The division between the two factions led the state GOP to act as an observer rather than a participatory coordinating body for campaigns, which had become the norm for federal party committees between the 1980s and the 2000s.[5] Any support a candidate received from the state GOP was commonly seen as a sign of the party's allegiance to one faction, leading to recriminations and accusations of bias. Ironically, the state GOP became so ineffective that individual members felt free to make their own decisions about which candidate to support, leading some center-right Republicans to go so far as to support Democratic candidates over right-wing members of their own party.

The Democratic Party of Kansas appeared strong, notably because of Sebelius's electoral fortunes and her success in convincing moderate Republicans to change parties and run for statewide office. These included lieutenant governor candidates John Moore and Mark Parkinson, along with successful attorney general candidate Paul Morrison. As the state's governing became more sophisticated, the governorship evolved into a more modern likeness of its peers in other states. Governors were committed to full-time engagement, becoming more involved in their party's election apparatus and highly engaged in party building and succession planning.[6]

After Sebelius's election, longtime GOP chair Parkinson left his position and later crossed party lines to run as lieutenant governor in 2006. Parkinson subsequently became governor when Sebelius accepted an offer from President Obama to become secretary of the Department of Health and Human Services (HHS) in 2009.

Despite Kansas's reputation as a solidly red state, the Sebelius era demonstrated the GOP's electoral vulnerability. Moreover, it did not respond well in organizational terms, with a series of weak chairs. Most notably, right-wing activist Kris Kobach took over the party's reins in 2007. Despite experiencing a series of electoral defeats, Kobach was viewed as a promising young politico. Indeed, he was already a well-known figure in the Kansas political world, having run unsuccessfully for Congress against incumbent Democrat Dennis Moore in 2004 and establishing himself as an articulate but firebrand conservative. With his hard-line stance on illegal immigration, Kobach gained notoriety on the issue and received just 43 percent of the vote against the incumbent, the worst performance by a Republican in Moore's six races. Kobach had never run for elective office before, but as a Harvard-educated attorney and with his issue stances, he was soon celebrated among conservatives.

Three years after Kobach ran for Congress, he became state party chair. His attempts to revitalize a moribund state party committee were unsuccessful; in fact, his actions only exacerbated the problems the GOP had experienced prior to his chairmanship. In his two years as state party chair, Kobach was responsible for three decisions that made things worse for the Republicans:

the loyalty committee, involvement in primaries, and bad fund-raising and accounting practices.

Kobach brought in a familiar face as the party's executive director: Christian Morgan, who had worked on Kobach's 2004 congressional campaign. Morgan and Kobach would lead the Kansas Republican Party into disaster. First, Kobach wanted to unify the party. This was a strategically sound decision, but efforts to unify two mutually distrustful factions would prove impossible. Kobach's efforts focused on creating a so-called loyalty committee that would sanction elected Republicans for supporting non-Republican candidates by stripping them of seniority or committee and leadership assignments.[7]

The loyalty committee was poorly received, especially by center-right Republicans. In some areas, such as Hays in northwestern Kansas, center-right Republicans and Democrats worked as a local coalition. For example, Republican Dan Johnson from the 110th House District rode in parades with Democrat Eber Phelps from the 111th House District and Democrat Janis Lee from the 29th Senate District; the three also met regularly and voted together. Johnson was chair of the House Education Committee, but his support for Lee and Phelps cost him that position under Kobach's loyalty regime. Johnson was so frustrated that he retired from the legislature the following term.

Kobach decided the party should stop being a spectator and become more actively involved in electioneering efforts, especially among candidates for the state legislature. Kobach and Morgan became much more aggressive about fund-raising, but they encountered challenges because of the party's internal divisions. The state GOP would overreport the amount it raised over the next two years, perhaps to build enthusiasm for a revived party organization.

The Republican Party seemed to have trouble accounting for its money—both the amount it took in and the amount it spent. A Federal Election Commission (FEC) investigation found that the state party organization had failed to pay rent for four months; nor could it account for significant amounts of money allegedly flowing into the organization. While internal reports claimed that inadequate staffing was a core problem, inadequate supervision was also cited as a reason for the FEC's investigation and punitive action.[8]

Despite its longtime fund-raising advantage over Democrats, Kansas's Republican Party was unsuccessful in attracting adequate funds. Even with the party's historical strength in Kansas, Republicans from 2000 to 2010 raised significantly less money than their Democratic counterparts (table 7.1). Beginning

Table 7.1. Kansas Political Party Fundraising, 2002–12

	2002	2004	2006	2008	2010	2012
Democrat	$1,030,800	$813,791	$1,148,533	$893,710	$823,037	$1,050,341
Republican	$409,545	$78,948	$389,287	$250,869	$330,530	$856,904
Total	$17,511,822	$10,298,044	$21,500,560	$12,981,873	$39,803,650	$22,361,265

Source: Follow the Money, https://www.followthemoney.org/tools/election-overview/
Note: Total represents the combined fundraising of all candidates for state legislative and statewide offices from individuals, parties, corporations, unions, and interest groups.

with Sebelius's first campaign for governor in 2002 and lasting until the 2010 election, the Kansas Democratic Party's fund-raising total was more than triple that of the Kansas Republican Party. Sebelius's leadership had transformed the electioneering capabilities of Kansas Democrats, both directly through the party and through her Blue Stem political action committee.[9]

During the 2004 cycle, Republican fund-raising plumbed new depths. With no statewide offices contested, fund-raising was generally down. However, Kansas Democrats dropped from their $1 million-plus in 2002 to $813,000 in 2004, while Kansas Republicans dropped from just over $400,000 in 2002 to a mere $78,000 in 2004. The Kobach-Morgan tenure did not result in a significant increase in fund-raising either. In 2006, which did feature some statewide contests, the Republicans raised $389,000, slightly less than their 2002 total. By comparison, Democrats increased their fund-raising success by nearly 10 percent between 2002 and 2006, raising more than $1.1 million for the 2006 campaign, which featured both Sebelius and the ultimately successful attorney general candidate Paul Morrison.

Kansas was not the only state where party organizations were struggling. Although, for the most part, the GOP had successfully transformed itself at the national level into a strong electioneering organization, its state counterparts had struggled.[10] The growing Democratic fund-raising and electoral support mechanisms sent a warning to the Kansas GOP that it needed to catch up.

Republicans began to show signs of progress in 2008, after Kobach and Morgan had departed from their state GOP leadership posts. The $250,000 raised that year was far behind the nearly $900,000 brought in by the Democrats, but it was close to two-thirds the 2006 total and three times the amount raised in 2004. However, the party's record keeping and supervision were both highly suspect, as evidenced by the FEC's investigation and the eventual fine it levied against the party. The result of the Kobach era was a state Republican organization in shambles. Candidates under the GOP's banner basically ran on their own. There was little coordination between the state party and candidates running in general elections. The Republican Party of Kansas lacked a clear message or vision; moreover, its communications capacity was modest at best. Even so, Republicans retained nominal control of both legislative chambers, although Democratic governors could work with a coalition of their fellow partisans and moderate Republicans.

Kobach's tenure poorly prepared the state GOP to resuscitate its moribund campaign apparatus. His departure, though, would allow new leadership to rebuild the party organization and help elevate a key figure to the governor's mansion: Sam Brownback. Moreover, a national red wave was approaching, which would propel the Republicans into a formidable governing force.

Sam Brownback and David Kensinger

Samuel Dale Brownback is not a conventional Kansas political figure. While he may check many of the boxes used to describe a typical Kansas politico, he is different. To understand Kansas politics from 2010 forward, it is vital to get to know its most pivotal player.

Born in 1956 in the eastern Kansas town of Garnett, Brownback had a normal childhood, growing up on the family farm in nearby Parker. Agriculture, the cornerstone of much of Kansas's history, ran in Brownback's blood. He was a member of the Future Farmers of America (FFA), including serving as local and state chapter president before becoming the organization's national vice president while a student at Kansas State University. Brownback's ambition led him to attend law school at the University of Kansas, and he returned to Manhattan, Kansas, to work as an attorney in 1982. Four years later, Brownback was named secretary of agriculture by Democratic governor John Carlin. Brownback served in that post, except for a brief stint in the US Trade Representative's office, until 1994, when he won a seat in the US House of Representatives. In 1996, when US senator Bob Dole resigned his seat to campaign for president, Governor Bill Graves appointed his lieutenant governor, Sheila Frahm, to replace him, but Frahm would have to face the electorate in November. Without hesitation, Brownback jumped into the race, running an aggressive campaign against the more moderate Frahm. His victory illustrated the changing nature of Kansas Republicanism.

By age forty, Brownback had become a US senator, and he established a unique portfolio in that chamber. Staunchly Republican and culturally conservative on most major issues, Brownback took great interest in Africa and was a champion of causes that led to greater aid to African nations. He was also focused on issues related to human trafficking. At the same time, he authored no major legislation and stood outside the ranks of influential Senate insiders. After twelve years in the Senate, Brownback sought the Republican nomination for president in 2008. His campaign rhetoric and strategy placed him among the most conservative individuals seeking the nomination. He had strong conservative credentials, and some predicted he would perform very well in the nomination process. However, after Brownback finished third in an Iowa straw poll six months before the caucuses, his success in fund-raising and his ability to attract media attention stalled.[11] After a poor debate performance, Brownback lost financial support, which stalled the campaign and eventually led to his withdrawal in October 2007.[12] In the end, Brownback's low-key style simply did not work well in the presidential arena. Still, he did not abandon his presidential aspirations. Brownback probably would have continued to win reelection to the Senate had he returned to that chamber after his withdrawal, but his eyes remained firmly on the White House. At the time, with two consecutive presidents (Bush and Clinton) being former governors, conventional wisdom suggested that winning the governorship represented an attractive path to the presidency. Such conventional wisdom may have encouraged Brownback to leave the Senate and seek the Kansas governor's mansion, known as Cedar Crest.

At the time, pursuing the governorship of Kansas must have seemed like a difficult task. With the weakness of the state Republican Party organization in the wake of Kobach's tenure, there was precious little institutional support for an ambitious statewide campaign. Brownback had the advantage of an established organizational presence from his prior senatorial campaigns. Most notably, he had a powerful strategic actor on his side: David Kensinger.

Brownback's story is intertwined with that of Kensinger. Shortly after graduating from college with a bachelor's degree, Kensinger went to work for Brownback's Senate office. He left in 1998 to chair GOPAC, the Republican congressional campaign juggernaut that was the backbone of the GOP's successful efforts to wrest majority control of Congress from the Democrats in 1994. In 2001, Kensinger returned to Brownback's staff, where he served as chief of staff and managed his boss's 2008 presidential bid to its conclusion in 2007. Kensinger then managed the reelection campaign of Senator Pat Roberts in 2008, in preparation for the campaign that would define both Kensinger and Brownback: the 2010 run for governor.

During the 2008 campaign, Kensinger would sharpen his focus for 2010. Roberts was already a popular elected official and a strong favorite to win re-election. Democrat Jim Slattery, Roberts's competition, was never a strong challenger; he failed to attract support beyond his partisan base, raised less than $2 million (a third of Roberts's take), and won less than 40 percent of the statewide vote. Meanwhile, Kensinger was looking forward to 2010 and laying the groundwork to revive the Kansas GOP and catapult Brownback into Cedar Crest.

The Context of 2010

To understand the election of 2010, it is important to understand the significant change it represented. The entire country was undergoing a rightward shift. Two years after Barack Obama's election unified Democratic control of the executive and legislative branches of the federal government, Democrats would lose majority control of both chambers of Congress to Republicans. Opposition to Obama's signature program, the Affordable Care Act (commonly referred to as Obamacare), solidified support behind Republican candidates. Anti-tax advocates, rallying nationwide behind the loosely organized Tea Party movement, were gathering support for Republicans across the nation.

Deep-red Kansas had experienced two consecutive terms of a Democratic governor and a moderate Republican–Democratic policymaking coalition in the legislature. However, polar alliance Republicans swiftly moved to a dominant place in Kansas politics. This move was centered around the state GOP's revival and an important strategic ally that distinguished Kansas from other states. Kansas has long been a one-party state, and although the minority party occasionally disrupts the status quo, the Republican Party inexorably returns to power, consistent with other states where one party is dominant.[13]

Brownback and his allies received assistance from an unexpected source:

Table 7.2. Party Composition of the Kansas House of Representatives, 2002–16

	2002	2004	2006	2008	2010	2012	2014	2016
Republican	79	80	83	77	76	92	92	85
Democrat	46	45	42	48	49	33	33	40
Independent	0	0	0	0	0	0	0	0
Vacant	0	0	0	0	0	0	0	0

Source: http://www.ncsl.org/research/about-state-legislatures/partisan-composition.aspx

Kansas Democrats. Kansas was well established as a Republican state, but Sebelius's time in the governor's office saw a significant downturn in Republican power. Majority control of both chambers of the Kansas legislature has been in Republican hands almost exclusively for decades, but majority control alone does not tell the story of the 2000s for Kansas's elected Republicans.

Republicans did not have the bully pulpit of the governor's office, and although they maintained majority control of the legislature, that majority was split between center-right moderates and a conservative Far Right wing. Republicans were used to having strong control of the legislature, holding no less than 60 percent of seats in the state house since Sebelius's election in 2002 (table 7.2). However, the 2002–10 reign of Democrats in Cedar Crest led to some of the largest numbers of Democrats in the Kansas House over the past thirty years, with the exception of the high point of 1991–92, when 63 Democrats served in the 125-member house. By the 2010 election, forty-nine Democrats served in the house, a slight increase from the forty-six they had eight years earlier. If not for their internecine factional divisions, Republicans would have been able to make almost all policy decisions without Democratic involvement at all.

The story was similar in the Kansas Senate (table 7.3), with the GOP in majority power but the intraparty division evident. This division meant that the Democrats, under the aegis of Governor Sebelius, could selectively collaborate

Table 7.3. Party Composition of the Kansas Senate, 2004–16

	2004	2008	2012	2016
Republican	27	30	32	31
Democrat	13	10	8	9
Independent	0	0	0	0
Vacant	0	0	0	0

Source: http://www.ncsl.org/research/about-state-legislatures/partisan-composition.aspx

with either of the two Republican factions and be a regular player in public policy. Democrats worked with the center-right wing on school funding and then worked against that coalition by joining forces with the polar alliance on redistricting.[14]

Because of term limits, Sebelius would be out of office after 2010, and she set about creating a "farm team" of new Democratic leaders to step into campaigns for the legislature and statewide constitutional offices. Lieutenant Governor John Moore chose not to run in 2006, creating a significant opportunity for the party. To succeed Moore, Sebelius recruited a former state Republican Party chair, Mark Parkinson, and convinced him to switch parties. Parkinson's selection was largely a risk-versus-reward gamble. If he could establish his legitimacy with Democrats, he could continue building the centrist coalition begun by Sebelius and her team. To do so, though, Parkinson would have to endear himself to Kansas Democrats, who looked at party-switching Republicans with disdain and distrust.

To support the next generation of Democratic candidates, Democrats would need to win Republican-held seats in constitutional offices, just as Sebelius had done as insurance commissioner before becoming governor. Democrats found one potential winner in Overland Park prosecuting attorney Paul Morrison. Morrison had been a Republican until 2005 and had switched parties to run against the incumbent Republican attorney general Phill Kline. During his term as state attorney general, Kline generated national publicity by successfully defending the state's death penalty statute in the US Supreme Court, as well as aggressively prosecuting Wichita abortion provider Dr. George Tiller. Kline's fixation on social issues made him a popular target among Democrats, and Morrison unseated him in 2006. With both Morrison and Parkinson in statewide office, it appeared that Democrats had recruited a strong team of future candidates.

Other Democrats, such as young Lindsborg state representative Joshua Svaty, were rising through the ranks. The success was short-lived, however. Morrison, a likely shoo-in for the nomination for governor in 2010, was exposed for having an extramarital affair; he resigned from office in early 2008. The election of Barack Obama in 2008 led to Sebelius's appointment as HHS secretary and Svaty's selection as an Environmental Protection Agency administrator. Parkinson decided not to run for governor, breaking a promise he had made when running for lieutenant governor.

Rise of the Tea Party

Obama's election created a variety of reactions, but the most salient was the response to his economic policies and his push to create a new health care program funded partially by the government. Supporters of Ron Paul's candidacy for the Republican nomination in 2008 began a protest on April 15, 2009, under the banner "Taxed Enough Already" (TEA).[15] From a small number of seemingly disconnected protests across the country, the movement spread quickly. Disparate groups began to use the "Taxed Enough Already" slogan as part of their names, and the movement quickly became known as the Tea Party. Though not a party in the traditional sense, the name evoked not only the Tax Day protests of Paul's Libertarian supporters but also the revolutionary ethics of the War for Independence.

As President Obama's supporters advanced the Affordable Care Act, Tea Party organizations gathered strength. These groups, all economically conservative but diverse across the social spectrum of the conservative movement, presented a simultaneous opportunity and challenge for Republicans. Some of the groups were extremely conservative and run by individuals with unpalatable agendas. Most of their representatives were amateurs and not particularly strategic in their public statements and efforts. Republican Party organizations saw the Tea Party as a threat to their hegemony over conservative voters and sought to marginalize the upstart groups.[16]

In Kansas, the story was different, partly because the upstarts had taken over day-to-day management of the state GOP. Whereas Republican establishment political figures saw the Tea Party as a threat, nonestablishment leaders may have seen it as an opportunity for co-optation. Such was the case when Kensinger brought in Amanda Adkins as chair of the Republican Party of Kansas in 2008. The party was still reeling from the FEC investigation and fine and the relative chaos of the Kobach-Morgan era, and Adkins's job was to rebuild the organizational capacity of the state GOP to assist Brownback's 2010 campaign for governor.

Adkins had help from several rising stars in the Kansas Republican firmament. Ashley McMillan and Clayton Barker immediately began to build the state GOP's electoral capacity. McMillan's role was primarily to enhance grassroots strength, while Barker's was to develop a modern data operation. They had all been active Republicans, but none of them had worked for the state GOP or had statewide experience. The Kansas Republican Party needed a fresh start, and Adkins and Kensinger trusted that McMillan and Barker could build a party organization largely from the ground up.

Barker's role was particularly important because Kensinger had watched the 2008 elections carefully and knew that the Obama campaign's success derived from a data-driven decision-making process. While social media was the campaign's attention-getting strategic element, mining data from social media interactions gave the campaign a better ability to predict voting preferences and the likelihood of voting.[17] Using the Obama model, Colorado Democrats reversed a trend toward Republican ascendance in that state. A well-developed data collection and analysis strategy fueled what the Democrats did, with help from the national database developed by the Obama campaign. Barker realized that a rich database of individual characteristics could predict who would vote, which voters would be more receptive to Republican candidates, and what messages would resonate best with them.[18]

With new leadership at the Kansas GOP came an openness to new ideas, such as the voter database. This new vision also meant that the GOP leadership did not fear the insurgent Tea Party groups. In fact, they saw opportunity in the Tea Party. Barker had noticed many active Republicans side by side with Tea Party protesters at Democrats' town hall meetings, such as those held by Congressman Dennis Moore. First Congressional District hopeful Tim Huelskamp readily embraced the Tea Party movement and succeeded with that strategy, winning the Republican nomination in a crowded seven-candidate field (a virtual guarantee of general election victory in the district with the state's highest percentage of registered Republican voters).

Barker recognized that the overlap between active Kansas Republicans and Tea Party protesters was significant. Therefore, he believed the Tea Party should be regarded not as a threat but as a powerful ally whose involvement with the state GOP apparatus could be mutually beneficial.[19]

The Road Map to Cedar Crest

Sam Brownback's campaign team had a plan. Kansas's population had been increasing slowly but steadily; however, the western part of the state was depopulating, and overall, Kansas was not growing as fast as other states. The incremental changes put forward by prior governors and legislatures had done little to spur faster population growth. Brownback had a vision for Kansas that would require significant change. For some time, he had looked to Texas as an example of how to grow as a state. His affinity for the Texas model came partly from the American Legislative Exchange Council (ALEC), a network of conservative state legislators funded at least partially by Wichita-based Koch Industries. Brownback also had a close personal friendship with then–Texas governor Rick Perry, and they both had another ideologically aligned friend in Louisiana governor Bobby Jindal. Both Jindal and Brownback were enamored of the ALEC-supported zero-income-tax model in Texas and believed that the state's growth over the past twenty years was a direct result of that business-friendly approach.[20]

The Brownback plan was relatively simple: invigorate the Kansas economy and thus promote population growth.[21] Conventional wisdom held that Kansas was losing population because there were relatively few jobs in the state, forcing Kansans to move elsewhere. The trend was especially pronounced in the western half of the state, where the predominant industries were oil and agriculture. While oil jobs had been relatively stable for some time, agricultural jobs had declined substantially. Young people, even those who stayed in the state, were abandoning western Kansas at a significant rate. Brownback wanted to keep out-migrating Kansans at home and find a way to increase the population faster. Citing Texas's explosive population growth and ascribing it to entities seeking low taxes, Brownback planned to replicate Texas's zero-tax plan for individuals and limited liability corporations (LLCs).

The moderate Republican–Democratic coalition that had largely governed the state for forty years would be Brownback's biggest roadblock. Tax rates in Kansas ranked near the median among states, according to the Tax Foundation's annual tax burden survey, which compares state tax rates with real per capita income.[22] In 1996, Kansas had the sixteenth highest tax rates among the fifty states, and by 2006, it had dropped to twenty-eighth highest. In other words, Kansas was not an especially high-tax state. Its typical per capita tax burden was marginally higher than that of the other forty-nine states, but not appreciably so (figure 7.1). In real dollars, Kansans paid less in taxes than the average taxpayer in the United States (figure 7.2). Selling the idea of a complete elimination of income and LLC taxes was going to be a difficult proposition because taxes were already relatively low.

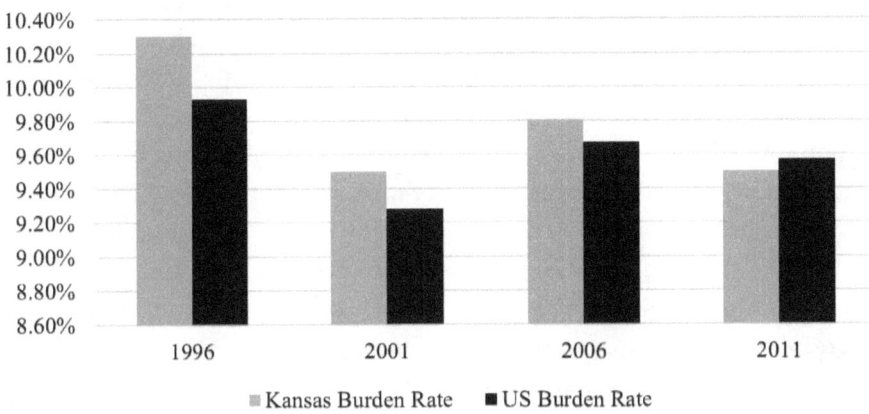

Figure 7.1. Kansas's Tax Burden Relative to All States, 1996–2011

Kansas's school spending prior to Brownback's arrival was consistent with the "austere but adequate" philosophy. In 2009, the National Education Association ranked Kansas twenty-second nationally in public school revenue per student.[23] Like many other states, Kansas's budgetary priorities had expanded

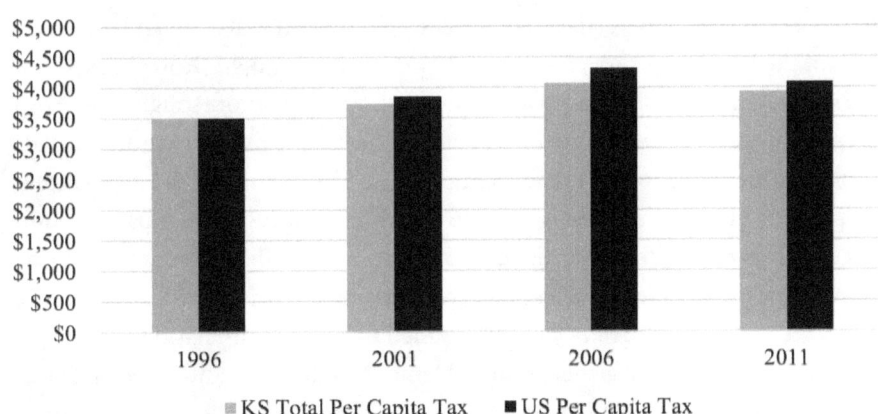

Figure 7.2. Kansas's per Capita Tax Burden Relative to All States, 1996–2011

since the 1970s, but revenue had not increased commensurately. The result in Kansas and elsewhere was a reduction in spending on education relative to other budget items.[24] After more than a decade of litigation, the US Supreme Court's 2005 *Montoy* decision directed the legislature to address the court's finding that K–12 public schools in Kansas were significantly underfunded and in violation of the state constitutional mandate to provide an adequate education for the state's children. Thus, there was little will among legislators to cut the budget; nor did they believe there was any room to do so. This made it harder for them to justify a tax cut that would, in the short run, significantly reduce the state's revenue. Nevertheless, Governor Sebelius and the moderate-conservative legislature responded to the court's ruling and substantially increased funding for education. Subsequently, with the Great Recession of 2008–9, state funding dropped again as the 2010 election approached.

If Brownback were to burnish his resumé for another run for the White House by winning the governorship, he would need the tax-cut plan to pass and succeed. After consulting pro–tax-cut economist Arthur Laffer, who received $75,000 for his advice, Brownback concluded that the tax cut would have a significant positive impact on the Kansas economy. The challenge would be convincing the state legislature to pass such legislation. If the incumbent moderate Republican–Democratic coalition was not interested in approving the tax cut, Brownback and his team would have to change the composition of the legislature.

The 2010 campaign cycle was a good one for a prospective governor hoping to change the makeup of the Kansas legislature. New competitors for Brownback's Senate seat emerged, causing a cascade of open seats. When two members of the US House (Jerry Moran and Todd Tiahrt) sought Brownback's Senate seat in the Republican primary, numerous state legislators sought their congressional seats. The resulting open seats in the state legislature would provide opportunities for Brownback to handpick recruits to run for those positions, giving him a built-in support system to get his tax-cutting agenda passed. Kansas elections had not been particularly volatile historically, but 2010 introduced more legislative change than had been seen for more than a decade. At the same time, the anti-Obama "red wave" that rolled over the entire nation had a huge impact in Kansas. Across the country, Democrats lost seven hundred state legislative seats. Brownback played a role, to be sure, but he also came to power with a lower house dominated by polar alliance Republicans.[25]

In the Kansas House, typically more than a third of races in the general election were unopposed, and in 2010, thirty-seven incumbents, or 32 percent of the chamber, faced no opposition, including twenty-three Republicans. In the primaries, four conservative challengers, recruited by Brownback and his allies, defeated their incumbent moderate Republican opponents. Additionally, six of the ten open seats were won by conservative Brownback supporters.

The 2010 Elections

The rise of the Tea Party nationally and its dissatisfaction with President Obama provided strong indications that the 2010 elections would go well for Republicans generally and for Sam Brownback specifically.[26] With a cadre of allies running for the Kansas House (there were no Kansas Senate races that year), Brownback had a plan in place to pass his agenda once he was elected governor. His path to the nomination was reasonably direct. After Ron Thornburgh suspended his candidacy, Brownback trounced Joan Heffington by more than 60 percent in the primary. His opponent in the general election, state senator Tom Holland, could not compete. Holland lacked statewide campaign experience and had minimal support from the Democratic Party, which was still reeling from Sebelius's departure. With Parkinson declining to run and the disgraced Morrison out of office, Kansas Democrats had reached out to native Kansan and national news personality Bill Kurtis and encouraged him to run in 2010, but he declined.[27] The general election results were nearly as lopsided as those in the primary, as Brownback defeated Holland 63 percent to 32 percent. Brownback had been confident he would win and looked forward to working with the most conservative legislature in the modern (post-1970) era of Kansas politics.

The Kansas House added more than twenty new Republican representatives, most of whom Brownback and the Kansas Chamber of Commerce had supported. The chamber's involvement became an issue during the general election campaign when Holland claimed that Brownback's willingness to involve business leaders in setting the state's policy agenda was a sign of his inability to lead.[28] In reality, the Chamber of Commerce had become one arm of the Far Right alliance that would dominate Kansas politics for the next six years.

The Republican presence in the Kansas House increased from 76 representatives in the 125-member chamber to 92 after the 2010 elections. The character of those Republicans changed significantly as well. Many moderate Republicans retired, sought other offices, or lost to pro-Brownback Republicans. Brownback thus had one chamber on his side. Since the state senate elections in 2008 had occurred before the state GOP became Brownback-friendly, a moderate Republican–Democratic coalition still controlled that chamber. To implement his agenda, Brownback would have to either get a bill through the moderate-controlled senate or remake that chamber, just as he had done in the house.

Brownback Takes Office

Despite campaigning on a center-right platform, Brownback's conservative leanings became apparent immediately after he was sworn in as governor. One of his first acts was to eliminate the Kansas Arts Commission, which had been receiving roughly $700,000 a year from the state budget. This state funding allowed the commission to seek federal grants approaching $1.3 million annually. Brownback's action eliminated the state's ability to apply for these grants, angering arts advocates and setting the tone for a contentious relationship throughout Brownback's tenure.[29] Brownback also advanced other legislation consistent with a turn to the right, such as expanded restrictions on the availability of abortion after the twenty-first week of pregnancy.[30] More generally, however, Brownback did not need to set the agenda on social issues, as the Far Right house now routinely sent such bills to a senate that was fearful of primary challenges in 2012, assured that the governor would sign them. Brownback could turn his attention to the economy and taxes.

Later that year, Brownback would unveil his signature plan. During a swing across the western half of the state in December 2011, Brownback claimed that Kansas was losing taxpayers, citing its higher income, corporate, and sales tax rates than in neighboring states.[31] Brownback's justification for saying that Kansas's taxes were prohibitively higher than those of its neighbors was unclear. Tax Foundation data from 2011 showed that Kansas's overall tax burden, per capita taxes paid, and per capita incomes all fell roughly in the middle of the five states immediately surrounding it (table 7.4).

Table 7.4. 2011 Tax Rates in Kansas and Neighboring States

	Burden Rate	Income per Capita	Taxes Paid to State per Capita	Taxes Paid to Other States per Capita	Total Taxes Paid per Capita
Arkansas	10.40%	$33,147.74	$2,507.31	$953.77	$3,461.08
Colorado	9.00%	$46,412.35	$2,870.77	$1,312.30	$4,183.07
Kansas	9.50%	$41,564.02	$2,632.47	$1,299.93	$3,932.40
Missouri	9.20%	$37,586.40	$2,346.88	$1,092.39	$3,439.26
Nebraska	9.60%	$43,071.52	$2,880.48	$1,262.48	$4,142.96
Oklahoma	8.70%	$38,187.19	$2,240.93	$1,079.68	$3,320.61

Source: https://taxfoundation.org/state-and-local-tax-burdens-historic-data/

Governor Brownback introduced his tax-cut package to the state legislature on its opening day in 2012. At that time, Kansas had two personal income tax rates: 3.5 percent for income below $15,000 per year, and 6.4 percent for income above that threshold. Brownback's plan—known as the Glide Path to Zero—would shrink those rates to 3.0 percent and 4.9 percent, respectively, ratcheted down over five years to zero. Immediately, taxes on LLCs and other independent business entities would be eliminated. Roughly twenty tax deductions faced elimination. The state sales tax, previously set at 6.2 percent, would decrease to 5.3 percent.[32]

To help sell the plan to voters and skeptical legislators—especially more moderate-leaning senators—Brownback hired a consultant. Arthur Laffer, known as one of the architects of Ronald Reagan's 1981 tax reform package, helped make the case that the tax cuts would spur enough economic growth to compensate for the reduction in state tax revenue.[33] Brownback's budget director, Steven Anderson, produced an unprecedented five-year budget projection that predicted an increase in state revenue from $6 billion to $6.9 billion by 2018, even with the tax cuts factored in.[34]

The tax-reduction plan went to the legislature, where both Democrats and Republicans immediately pushed back. Democrats pointed to a $466 million state treasury surplus that would be eliminated over two years, countering the governor's and the budget director's predictions. The moderate Republican–Democratic coalition steering senate action claimed that spending on public education, social services, and highways would be gutted by adopting the Brownback plan.[35] Republicans, especially moderates led by senate president Steve Morris of Hugoton, suggested that their constituents wanted tax cuts but favored reductions in the sales tax on food or lower property taxes rather than the income tax cuts advocated by Brownback and his allies.[36]

The house advanced the governor's proposal to reduce taxes without significant fanfare or dissent, but a fight occurred in the still-moderate senate. Initially, the senate rejected the bill by a tie vote on March 20, 2012. However, the next day the senate reversed course and brought the bill forward for reconsideration. The primary issue was how to deal with an estimated $800 million annual reduction in the state treasury resulting from the tax cuts. The polar alliance house majority was willing to make significant spending cuts to accommodate the reduction, but the senate did not concur. The initial vote to reject the budget was based primarily on a concern for public education. But by keeping the sales tax at its prior rate, the senate was able to offset any projected cuts to education spending while accommodating the governor's desired cuts to income and LLC taxes.[37]

Brownback had promised the senate leadership that if that chamber passed the tax-cut bill, he would negotiate with both chambers and come up with compromise legislation. As talks proceeded, however, they produced no package that could pass both the conservative house, elected in 2010, and the more centrist senate, elected in 2008. Faced with the possibility of losing on his signature policy issue, Brownback chose to sign the original bill, with its substantial income tax cuts and its removal of at least 330,000 independent businesses from the state's tax rolls.

Brownback did not get everything he wanted. For example, he favored changing the method of distributing K–12 public school funding. He advocated moving from a formula system of allocation to a block grant system, in which every district or county would get an amount determined by the state's Department of Education. The block grant plan also would have limited local school boards' ability to raise property taxes, a tacit admission that the governor planned to reduce state funding to schools, despite clear and consistent decisions by the Kansas Supreme Court that school funding was barely adequate at best. The senate rejected the governor's proposal to strip local governments of the power to adjust property tax rates and included increased funding for K–12 schools, although critics expressed concern that the combination of increased spending and reduced taxes would not be sustainable by the state government.[38]

The bruising 2012 session left both the Brownback team and the moderate

Republican–Democratic coalition with hurt feelings. Many in the senate coalition felt that Brownback had lied to them and that the governor's allies had tricked the senate into passing a budgetary time bomb. The legislative solution based on Brownback's optimistic surplus projections encouraged equally optimistic planning in the legislature, thus increasing spending while cutting taxes.

Brownback immediately went into campaign mode after the legislature adjourned. The Kansas Chamber of Commerce, always an ally of the governor, had been recruiting new candidates for the senate just as it had for the house two years earlier. Prior to the August primaries, Brownback released an op-ed to the statewide *Wichita Eagle* claiming that the tax cuts would serve as a "shot of adrenaline to the heart of the Kansas economy."[39] While the effect on the economy would not be nearly that strong, the electoral benefits to Brownback's team would be very much like an adrenaline shot. Moreover, despite his initial reluctance to support the senate bill, Governor Brownback fully embraced it and made it completely his own.

The 2012 Landslide

If the 2010 campaign was a win for Brownback and his team, 2012 was a landslide. A few important factors contributed to the complete takeover of the state's executive and legislative branches. The first was redistricting. Kansas's redistricting fight was a lengthy, pitched battle that lasted well over a year. It was the last state in the union to complete its remapping process. In Kansas, remapping is a four-tiered process, with the legislature having primary responsibility for redrawing the maps for Congress, the state Board of Education, and both chambers of the legislature. Each of the four maps would be a unique challenge, with the courts eventually drawing the congressional map. Most significant for the electoral fortunes of Brownback and his team was the state legislative remap. Typically, each chamber drew its own map, but 2012 would be different. With the state senate firmly in the sights of Brownback's team, the practice of in-chamber deference would be violated, beginning a fight that would spill into different venues for at least five years.

Kansas received its federal census reallocation allotment in June 2011, with no change in the state's federal representation. This officially began the process, although the work would not start in earnest until the new legislative session opened in January 2012. Kansas House speaker Mike O'Neal initiated the remapping process with the first of many unprecedented maneuvers—appointing himself chair of the redistricting committee in his chamber.[40] Population growth in Kansas had occurred exclusively in the eastern part of the state, so western (mostly conservative and libertarian) interests were keen to minimize the damage to their representation caused by that demographic shift since 2000. Over the 2000–2010 span, Johnson County, in the Kansas City suburbs, had overtaken Wichita's Sedgwick County as the state's most populous.[41]

The O'Neal-led house committee released its first map in early 2012, shifting three state house seats to the Kansas City area. Quickly, the house approved the plan, which largely protected incumbents of both parties, and O'Neal announced the house's intention to review and perhaps edit the senate map, which it had previously rubber-stamped. O'Neal's move to review the senate map led state senators, especially moderate Republicans, to believe that they were about to be targeted. They were.[42]

The senate took until late April to approve its own map and a revised house map as well. The house responded in May by passing an alternative version of the senate map. With the legislature constitutionally mandated to complete the redistricting process during the ninety-day legislative session, the feud over district lines would spill over the time limit and prompt the filing of a lawsuit.[43]

On May 3, a Kansas Republican precinct committeewoman filed a federal lawsuit over the legislature's failure to complete redistricting during the session. The lawsuit contended that operating under the 2010 map violated her right to equal representation. Robyn Essex of Olathe (in the Kansas City area) sought relief by requesting that the court use maps drafted by Brownback's house allies early in the legislative session. Essex was represented by O'Neal's former chief of staff.[44]

During the trial, Kansas secretary of state Kris Kobach intervened and advised the court to complete its deliberations and issue a decision by the June 20 filing deadline to run in the primary election, scheduled for August 7. Any delay in the court's decision would force a delay of the primary. In essence, the legislature's indecision meant that a three-judge federal panel would draw the maps. The judges completed the congressional map very quickly and then, acting like a nonpartisan redistricting commission, redrew the senate map. Given the prior house agreement on its map, many observers assumed the judges would simply adopt those districts, but that would not be the case.

The federal court finalized plans for all four maps on June 7, and none of the interested parties in Kansas expressed pleasure with them. The judges' maps moved forty-eight representatives and six senators into districts where incumbents would have to face other incumbents. Based on the candidates who had already filed, twenty-six Republicans and four Democrats in the house alone would have primary challengers. Dealing a small blow to Brownback's plans to dominate the senate, three conservative challengers to moderate incumbents were removed from the districts in which they had planned to run.[45]

With the new maps in place, a scramble began among candidates seeking to file before June 20, leaving just six weeks to campaign for the August primary. Thirty-three members of the house, a full third of the chamber, did not seek reelection in 2012. Some of those candidates ran for senate seats, but many moderates saw the wave of Chamber of Commerce– and Brownback-supported conservative challengers coming and decided to retire rather than face an expensive and brutal reelection campaign. Ten moderate legislators who did run lost to conservative challengers, solidifying Brownback's hold on the state house.[46]

The Kansas Senate stood as the true epicenter of the Brownback push to consolidate power over the legislature, even though it had already passed his signature tax plan. Four of the forty senators retired prior to the election—a 10 percent turnover. The Chamber of Commerce targeted eight moderate Republicans for defeat. Prominent moderates Terrie Huntington and John Vratil retired; Tim Owens, Pete Brungardt, Jean Schodorf, and senate president Steve Morris were all defeated in their primaries. Only Carolyn McGinn and Vicki Schmidt survived the conservative purge of the primaries.

In both chambers, the aggregate number of members from each party stayed roughly the same. The house remained at ninety-two Republicans and thirty-three Democrats. The senate lost one Republican seat in the general election, ending with thirty-one Republicans and nine Democrats. Most important was the shift within the Republican Party in both chambers. A new cadre of conservatives that included Larry Powell, Greg Smith, and Jake LaTurner had replaced old-line moderates Melvin Neufeld, Dan Johnson, and Jean Schodorf.

With the victory of conservative challengers in the 2012 primaries, the shift would be complete in Kansas. The moderate Republican–Democratic governing coalition, which had been under threat since Brownback's victory in 2010, ceased to exist. Enough conservatives populated both the house and the senate to make Brownback allies the leaders in both chambers. With polar alliance majorities in both chambers, Brownback would have no more barriers to implementing the rest of his agenda. At the same time, the night of the 2012 elections would prove to be the political high point of the Brownback years.

The Election of 2014: To the Brink

Brownback would stand for reelection in 2014 in one of the most pivotal races in the state's history. The election would be a referendum on Brownback, his Glide Path to Zero, the hostile takeover of the state legislature, and executive-dominated lawmaking. Brownback was facing a consistent drumbeat of negative news about his governing style and extreme policies. Moderate Republicans wanted to take back their place as the central body in Kansas's governing coalition, and Democrats saw the heated conflict between factions within the Republican Party as an opportunity to retake the governor's mansion and reboot their efforts to establish a stronger Kansas Democratic Party.

Incumbents always have a substantial advantage when running for reelection, regardless of the level of government or the particular seat.[47] Voters in gubernatorial elections tend to base their decisions on party identification, economic conditions, and the executive's job performance. Referendum effects have been identified at other levels,[48] but voters with a favorable image of the incumbent governor are likely to reelect him or her.[49] Gubernatorial elections thus often function as referenda on the incumbent, who, for better or worse, is held responsible for the state's fortunes.

Initially, Brownback seemed to be in a very strong position as a Republican governor in a Republican state. Still, Mike Hayden had lost his bid for reelection in 1990, largely due to property tax concerns. Early on, despite moderate Republican disdain for Brownback, voters generally regarded him positively. Especially among Republicans who were thankful to have retaken Cedar Crest, Brownback was the man responsible for assembling the GOP team that completely dominated state government.

Early in his term, Brownback's approval ratings were in the midrange for Kansas elected officials. Though not reaching the high levels of the most popular elected official in the state (Senator Pat Roberts at 62 percent), Brownback's approval rating in 2011 was a respectable 56 percent. However, as more of Brownback's agenda emerged, his support began to drop. In 2012, Brownback's approval rating slipped to 51 percent, and it would never exceed 50 percent for the remainder of his governorship.[50] At that time, all Kansas elected officials saw a drop in their approval ratings. By 2014, the most popular state officeholder was Senator Jerry Moran, whose approval rating was well below 50 percent. Brownback's rating had dropped into the high-30s to mid-40s, indicating serious reelection problems.

All Kansas elected officials were viewed less favorably during the 2010s, and Brownback was partly responsible. The governor had pushed through a controversial and unpopular tax plan, purged the legislature of dissent, and apparently ignored public antipathy toward his agenda. Since Republicans held all state constitutional offices, made up the entire congressional delegation, and accounted for more than 70 percent of the state legislature, the public came to distrust Brownback's administration and Republicans in general. Plummeting state revenue and declining contributions to education, social services, and other priorities ran contrary to Brownback's public promises that tax cuts would not necessitate a significant decline in state spending.

Brownback would face primary opposition once again, but as in 2010, he would have little to worry about. Jennifer Winn, a Wichita executive whose son had been charged with first-degree murder in the aftermath of a failed drug deal, used her campaign to highlight cultural and law enforcement issues.[51] Winn was a marginal candidate with no experience, meager funds, and a small staff. However, she had name recognition due to her son's high-profile case, and she used that to her advantage in populous Sedgwick County, which constitutes Wichita's metropolitan area. Early polls had Brownback winning the primary handily, but Winn actually polled ahead of him in Sedgwick County. She leveraged her Wichita notoriety and Brownback's growing unpopularity among Republicans to garner 36.7 percent of the GOP primary vote in August. Despite her loss, Winn's shoestring campaign greatly outperformed expectations, and the fact that many Republicans chose Winn over the incumbent governor suggested Brownback's electoral weakness. If a Democratic candidate could convince many of those same Republicans, along with many of the moderate Republicans who had stayed home during the primary, to cross party lines in November, Brownback might be vulnerable.

Democrats did not have a contested primary, as they continued to find it difficult to attract a candidate. A number of relatively high-profile Democrats considered entering the race or were actively recruited by state Democratic leaders but opted not to run against Brownback. Wichita mayor Carl Brewer, former Kansas City mayor Joe Reardon, former US Senate candidate Jill Docking, and former transportation secretary Deb Miller all declined to run. Likewise, several notable Republicans or ex-Republicans were approached, including former state party chair and already converted Democrat Mark Parkinson and former insurance commissioner Sandy Praeger.

All these potential candidates eventually decided not to contest the election. The only Democrat to run was Paul Davis, the house minority leader. Davis started campaigning early and worked assiduously to win the nomination. Although he lacked the statewide profile possessed by other potential candidates, he could focus his attention for more than a year on the general election against an incumbent with a highly negative reputation. The 2014 election would be a referendum on Sam Brownback, but other factors would come into play as well.

Senator Roberts and the Orman Disruption

The other high-profile Kansas campaign in 2014 should have been a runaway. Pat Roberts, a US senator since 1996, had considered retiring after his 2008 reelection to a third term, but he decided to run again in 2014. Roberts was seventy-eight years old when his reelection campaign began, and his age meant fewer trips back to Kansas to interact with constituents. Roberts's absence from the state was highlighted by his junior colleague in the Senate, Jerry Moran, who had honed his particular style of constituent service during his years as the First District's representative in the House and continued it after moving to the Senate. Moran become a ubiquitous presence throughout the state, making Roberts's absence more notable. Exacerbating the problem was the fact that although Roberts's Kansas address was in Dodge City, he owned no property there. Roberts's approval ratings declined accordingly. In a January 2014 poll conducted by the Tarrance Group, Roberts held a

69 percent–15 percent advantage over his main primary opponent, Dr. Milton Wolf. By July, that advantage had shrunk to 42 percent–30 percent in a poll from GEB International.

A Tea Party devotee and cousin of President Barack Obama, Wolf attacked Roberts from the right. Two others, D. J. Smith and Alvin Zahnter, also entered the primary, but Wolf represented the greatest threat to Roberts's reelection. Well funded by his medical practice in the Kansas City area, Wolf attacked Roberts fiercely, adopting an aggressive strategy against a politician who, until recently, had been the most popular elected official in the state. Wolf ran an ad on statewide television that depicted Roberts as out of touch with his home state and featured an empty recliner as Roberts's Kansas "residence." The relentless attacks in a quarter-million-dollar advertising campaign helped Wolf edge closer to Roberts, leading observers to wonder whether Roberts would be defeated in the primary. Roberts held on and defeated Wolf by about seven percentage points—48.1 to 40.8 percent. Going into the general election, Roberts looked vulnerable, and his possible defeat meant that Republicans might be unable to capture the Senate. Suddenly, the Roberts seat became the focal point of national politics. Given Brownback's troubles, the two top candidates on the Republican ticket in Kansas both appeared weak enough to lose in the general election.

Two Democrats, Patrick Wiesner and Chad Taylor, entered the primary for the opportunity to face Roberts in the general election. Taylor had a slight advantage as the district attorney in Topeka's Shawnee County, and he won the primary by the unexpectedly narrow margin of 53.3 to 46.7 percent. Despite Roberts's problems, Democrats expressed little enthusiasm. With a weak putative Democratic nominee, Roberts's path to reelection seemed set.

The two major parties dominate American politics, making the likelihood of an independent candidate succeeding nearly nil.[52] When voters perceive one or both major parties as failing, however, independents or third-party candidates can prosper, exemplified by Ross Perot's role in the 1992 presidential campaign.[53] The major disruption in the 2014 US Senate race came from independent candidate Greg Orman. A self-made millionaire, Orman returned to Kansas (where he grew up) from Minnesota and prepared to run for office. He had previously made some tentative efforts, but in 2014, with a significant paid media presence and other media interest based on his novelty as a nonpartisan candidate, Orman rapidly ascended into contention. One week after the early August primary, a Public Policy Polling survey reported a close race, with Roberts at 32 percent, Taylor at 25 percent, and Orman at 23 percent. Orman's sudden rise led Kansas Democrats to worry that he would take votes away from Taylor and hand Roberts the win. *Hays Daily News* editor and publisher Patrick Lowry wrote an editorial calling for Taylor to withdraw, as he saw Orman as the only chance to unseat Roberts.

On September 3, Taylor abruptly announced, without explanation, that he was withdrawing from the race. Speculation at the time was that Taylor knew he could not compete with Roberts and Orman in terms of funding and campaign infrastructure, so he withdrew to give Orman a better chance at unseating Roberts. However, withdrawing from a race is not as simple as notifying the state's chief elections officer. Kansas law requires withdrawing candidates to provide a reason why they could not assume the duties of office if elected, which Taylor failed to do. Secretary of state Kris Kobach, an ambitious Republican, notified Taylor that his name would remain on the ballot. Taylor appealed and had his name removed. Kobach then notified the state Democratic Party that it would have to nominate a replacement candidate by September 26 to allow time for ballots to be printed. Kansas Democrat David Orel filed suit to force the party to nominate a replacement, but it was not resolved in a timely fashion, leaving just Orman and Roberts on the ballot, with no Democratic challenger.

Taylor's absence immediately shifted Democratic support to Orman, who led by the slightest of margins—37 to 36 percent, with 11 percent of voters still undecided—in the September 4 SurveyUSA poll. Media coverage fueled much of Orman's ascent. He had spent $1.3 million on advertising by September, but Roberts had more than $3 million to spend, which allowed his campaign to buy substantial advertising time. Moreover, millions of dollars was flowing into the state to support the Republican incumbent. Orman was in a difficult position because his stance against the evils of interested money in politics limited his fund-raising options. When wealthy donors such as investment moguls Peter Ackerman and John Burbank learned of Orman's predicament, they infused his campaign with cash, allowing Orman to compete again on the airwaves. Nevertheless, with control of the US Senate possibly at stake, Republican money poured into the Roberts campaign, and by the end of the race, he had outspent Orman by $1 million. Still, these amounts paled in comparison to the outside, unreported funds that supported Roberts.[54]

The Orman campaign invited the possibility that moderate Republicans, fed up with Governor Brownback, might take their anger out on Roberts. Even though conservatives had led the revolt against Roberts in the primary, he appeared vulnerable on both sides as the general election neared. Polls showed that the race was tight, too close to call, and various surveys showed wildly different results. Orman led Roberts 48 percent–38 percent in a late September poll, but Roberts led Orman 49 percent–48 percent during the first week of October, just eight days later. Different pollsters made varying predictions, but in the last five weeks of the campaign, no survey gave either candidate an advantage outside the margin of error. The race would draw some attention away from Brownback and Davis; more important, it would indirectly but powerfully nationalize the gubernatorial race, which would ultimately benefit Brownback as the Republican candidate.

The 2014 General Election

Paul Davis chose Jill Docking, heir to a Kansas political dynasty, as his lieutenant governor nominee. Docking's great-grandfather-in-law George Docking served as Kansas governor from 1957 to 1961, and her grandfather-in-law Robert Docking served four two-year terms as governor from 1967 to 1975; her husband Thomas was lieutenant governor during the Carlin administration from 1979 to 1987, and he ran unsuccessfully for governor in 1986. The Docking family is such an iconic Kansas political brand that the state's main governmental services building bears the Docking name.

Jill Docking contributed the family's name and extensive fund-raising potential, as well as a history of opposition to Sam Brownback, to the race. When Bob Dole retired from the Senate to pursue the presidency in 1996, Docking was the Democratic candidate who ran against Brownback. In 2014, Davis and Docking's principal strategy was to highlight Brownback's negatives, most notably the state's ongoing budgetary ills resulting from his tax plan. The governor's approval rating had sagged going into his 2014 reelection bid—37 percent favorable versus 52 percent unfavorable—suggesting that Brownback was vulnerable.[55]

Since the Davis-Brownback matchup was set early in 2014, pollsters had many opportunities to measure public perception of the race (table 7.5). In

Table 7.5. 2014 Kansas Gubernatorial Polls, Rolling Averages

		Party (% Polled)			Republican Brownback	Democrat Davis	
Poll	Date	Republican	Democrat	Independent			Spread
Insight Kansas average	10/20–10/31	50.6	28	21.6	43.6	47.8	Davis +4.2
PPP	10/30–10/31	53	31	16	44	48	Davis +4.0
Fox News	10/28–10/30	47	30	22	42	48	Davis +6.0
SurveyUSA	10/22–10/26	49	29	24	43	46	Davis +3.0
Marist	10/18–10/21	49	25	26	44	45	Davis +1.0
Rasmussen	10/20–10/21	55	25	20	45	52	Davis +7.0
Gravis	10/21	54	25	21	44	49	Davis +5.0
Monmouth	10/16–10/19	60	25	15	45	50	Davis +5.0
Remington	10/9–10/12	55	28	17	48	45	Brownback +3.0
PPP	10/9–10/12	52	28	20	42	42	Tie
Fox News	10/4–10/7	47	28	22	46	40	Brownback +6.0
SurveyUSA	10/2–10/5	50	29	20	42	47	Davis +5.0
Gravis	9/30–10/1	54	25	21	40	48	Davis +8.0
Fort Hays State University	9/10–9/27	48	33	19	36.5	38.8	Davis +2.3
Rasmussen	9/16–9/17	55	25	20	43	47	Davis +4.0
Fox News	9/14–9/16	49	28	20	41	45	Davis +4.0
PPP	9/11–9/14	51	26	22	38	42	Davis +4.0
SurveyUSA	9/4–9/7	50	30	17	40	47	Davis +7.0
SurveyUSA	8/20–8/23	46	32	18	40	48	Davis +8.0

PPP	8/14–8/17	50	30	20	37	39	Davis +2.0
Rasmussen	8/6–8/7	55	25	20	41	51	Davis +10.0
SurveyUSA	7/17–7/22	56	26	18	40	48	Davis +8.0
SurveyUSA	6/19–6/23	26	28	16	41	47	Davis +6.0
Rasmussen	4/16–4/17	51	25	24	47	40	Brownback +7.0
PPP	4/1–4/2	52	30	18	41	45	Davis +4.0
PPP	2/18–2/20	47	28	25	40	42	Davis +2.0

Source: insightkansas.wordpress.com

Note: Polling data were aggregated by the Insight Kansas consortium throughout the 2014 Kansas gubernatorial election cycle, and Insight Kansas writers calculated an average. The first polls, conducted in February and April 2014 by Public Policy Polling (PPP), showed Democrat Paul Davis with a lead of two to four points over incumbent Republican Sam Brownback. An April poll by Rasmussen showed Brownback with a seven-point lead over Davis, but this was only one of three polls suggesting that Brownback would win, as he eventually did. From June through the election in November, all polls—except for the three predicting a Brownback victory and one predicting a tie—had Davis with a one- to ten-point lead. The final calculation by Insight Kansas suggested that Davis would win by a margin of 4.2 points.

February, Public Policy Polling (PPP) conducted a survey and concluded that Davis narrowly led Brownback. Davis's two-point lead was within the margin of error, but it was enough to sound the alarm that Brownback was vulnerable. A second PPP poll in April showed that Davis had increased his lead to four points, just outside the margin of error but suggesting Davis's strength and an increasing likelihood that he could win. However, just two weeks later, a Rasmussen poll showed that Brownback was up seven points. These polls demonstrated a close race throughout the year, with no clear favorite. Momentum and public perception were on Davis's side, however. Reelections are usually referenda on the job performance of the incumbent, and Kansas is a Republican state, so anything less than a twelve-point lead suggested that Brownback's reelection chances were less than they should have been.

Davis continued his attacks on Brownback through the summer, even during the primary. Running ads for the general election so far out, rather than focusing on building his name recognition and positive image among voters, was a risky political strategy. Name recognition and credibility are important factors in establishing a candidate's subsequent ability to go negative.[56] These early attacks could therefore be a significant miscalculation that might hinder Davis's ability to compete with Brownback in later stages of the race.

Davis did compete effectively with Brownback in one area where Kansas Democrats have often trailed their Republican rivals: fund-raising. In the Senate race, independent Greg Orman had been unable to match incumbent Republican Pat Roberts's fund-raising ability, with Roberts collecting more than $5.5 million to Orman's $3.1 million. For the entire 2014 campaign, Brownback raised $4,719,807, including a $500,000 personal loan from Lieutenant Governor Jeff Colyer. By most accounts, though, Brownback's campaign was struggling. Davis was consistently close to or ahead of Brownback in fund-raising, finishing the race with a total of $4,607,364 raised.

The close and contentious nature of the race led both campaigns to embrace a strategy based on comparisons with their opponent, with most messages taking a strongly negative tone. Brownback did little to promote his tax-cut plan on the campaign trail, choosing to focus on traditional Republican themes such as law and order. An important ad from Brownback's campaign featured Reginald and Johnathon Carr, Wichita brothers who had committed a series of violent crimes, including murder, and been sentenced to death. The Kansas Supreme Court, long a target of conservative ire, had vacated the death penalties for both Carr brothers. Brownback's ad, reminiscent of 1988's infamous "Willie Horton" presidential ad, associated Davis with the Kansas Supreme Court, hoping to rally conservatives against him. Brownback and Chief Justice Lawton Nuss became unspoken players in that ad. Brownback had often railed against the state supreme court for its school finance and death penalty decisions, and the ad implied that Davis's election would lead to the appointment of more justices like Nuss.

Outside money entered the race, with the Republican Governors Association running multiple ads. One tied Davis to President Obama, which was strategically counterintuitive, since Obama was no less popular than Brownback, according to multiple polls. Another ad implied that Davis's silence on whether he would advocate for a tax increase meant that he intended to raise taxes significantly.

Moderate Republicans also entered the fray with an outside group known as Kansas Values. Many of the Kansas Values members were former state legislators who had lost to Brownback's allies in 2010 and 2012. They focused on the negative effects of the Glide Path to Zero, including multiple bond-quality downgrades, K–12 education spending cuts, larger class sizes, and deteriorating buildings, to highlight the statewide concern over Brownback's signature plan. The National Education Association also ran ads attacking Brownback, focusing on how the tax cuts would affect spending on education.

According to the Wesleyan Media Project, the number of ads run during Kansas's 2014 election cycle was the seventh highest in the country.[57] The total was more than five thousand, and while Republicans held an advantage, it was not overwhelming: Republicans ran 54 percent of the television ads, and Democrats ran 46 percent. Republicans spent more money than Democrats, though: $1.17 million versus $850,000 worth of ad time for the 2014 Kansas governor's race.

Davis led in most polls throughout the campaign, but his advantage rarely exceeded the margin of error. After the August primary and the start of the campaign in earnest, neither candidate held a lead of more than eight points. Polls continued to show Davis ahead, but his lead shrank as the campaign progressed and more outside money flowed into the race. The Insight Kansas consortium's meta-analysis of polls in late October gave Davis a 4.2-point lead.

During a preelection symposium at the Dole Institute of Politics at the

University of Kansas, all participants on the panel predicted a Davis victory. On election night, many believed that a Democrat would take Cedar Crest and an independent would go to the Senate, but these expectations failed to materialize. As county after county reported their results, Brownback pulled ahead of Davis. Very quickly, a cascade of results put victory out of Orman's reach and then out of Davis's. Most importantly, Davis's failure to perform well in populous Johnson County sealed his fate. By a narrow margin of three points, Brownback won reelection in 2014, despite significant signs pointing to the contrary.

How Did Davis Lose (or Brownback Win)?

Among academics and political professionals, there is a belief that negative (or comparative) advertising is an important weapon in the campaign arsenal, but it must be used properly. Relatively few candidates can get away with sending exclusively negative messages about their opponents for an entire campaign. In fact, professionals suggest that campaigns balance their negative strategy with a softer, more personal approach to their own candidate. In short, since the public tends to distrust political candidates and their messages, a preponderance of negative ads about an opponent can backfire when the sponsoring candidate has not previously established him- or herself as a credible messenger.[58]

Davis's campaign made the fatal mistake of failing to establish his credibility before going on the attack against Brownback. Davis's campaign team had even created a five-minute introductory video discussing Davis's history, his struggles to conceive a child, and his vision for Kansas. The video, which was viewed only about two thousand times online during the campaign, could have been edited down into a brief ad to introduce Davis and establish his credibility. Davis's team opted instead to focus almost exclusively on Brownback; as a result, Davis's message likely came through to most voters as nothing more than noise.[59] Davis's attacks (and those of outside entities) added no new information or novelty to the voters' existing frames of reference.

Brownback, along with Republican-aligned outside entities, effectively portrayed Davis as a liberal ideologue by repeatedly connecting him to President Obama. Kansas Democrats are most successful when they campaign as moderates, making themselves more attractive to moderate Republicans who might switch party tickets. Kathleen Sebelius used that strategy to win the governorship. Davis, though, never appealed to the moderate Republicans he needed to propel him to victory. This problem was exacerbated by the immense infusion of money into the Senate race on behalf of Roberts; the nationalization of that campaign meant that the Kansas electorate reacted to both the Senate and the gubernatorial races from a partisan perspective. In a GOP state like Kansas, this benefited all Republican candidates, but none more so than Sam Brownback.

Moreover, Davis and analysts watching the race may have overestimated the importance of the Kansas economy to voters in 2014.[60] With a common enemy at the federal level in President Obama, ads that attacked the president helped both Roberts and Brownback.

Notes

1. J. A. Schlesinger, *Political Parties and the Winning of Office* (Ann Arbor: University of Michigan Press, 1994); D. M. Farrell and P. Webb, "Political Parties as Campaign Organizations," in *Parties without Partisans: Political Change in Advanced Industrial Democracies*, ed. Russell J. Dalton and Martin P. Wattenberg (Oxford: Oxford University Press, 2000), 102–128; J. F. Bibby, "State Party Organizations: Strengthened and Adapting to Candidate-Centered Politics and Nationalization," in *The Parties Respond: Changes in American Parties and Campaigns*, ed. L. Sandy Maisel and Mark Brewer (Denver, CO: Westview Press, 2002), 19–46.

2. P. Mair, "Party Organizations: From Civil Society to the State," in *How Parties Organize: Change and Adaptation in Party Organizations in Western Democracies*, ed. Richard S. Katz and Peter Mair (Thousand Oaks, CA: Sage Press, 1994), 1–22.

3. For the term "polar alliance," see H. E. Flentje and J. A. Aistrup, *Kansas Politics and Government: The Clash of Political Cultures* (Lincoln: University of Nebraska Press, 2010).

4. Michael Smith, "The Three-Party State of Kansas: What's in Store for Moore and Brownback?" *Campaigns and Elections* 13, 1 (2003): 18–20.

5. R. Kolodny, *Pursuing Majorities: Congressional Campaign Committees in American Politics* (Norman: University of Oklahoma Press, 1998); Daniel Shea, *Transforming Democracy: Legislative Campaign Committees and Political Parties* (Albany, NY: SUNY Press, 1995); Marjorie Randon Hershey, *Party Politics in America* (New York: Taylor & Francis, 2017).

6. Larry Sabato, *Goodbye to Good-time Charlie: The American Governorship Transformed* (Washington, DC: CQ Press, 1983); Sarah McCally Morehouse, *The Governor as Party Leader: Campaigning and Governing* (Ann Arbor: University of Michigan Press, 1998).

7. Tim Carpenter, "Kansas GOP Forming 'Loyalty Committee,'" *Topeka Capital-Journal*, March 8, 2007.

8. "FEC Audits Kansas GOP," *Topeka Capital-Journal*, January 28, 2010, http://cjonline.com/news-state-state-government/2010-01-28/fec-audits-kansas-gop.

9. Diana Dwyre and Jeffrey Stonecash, "Where's the Party? Changing State Party Organizations," *American Politics Quarterly* 20, 3 (1992): 326–344.

10. M. M. Conway, "Republican Political Party Nationalization, Campaign Activities, and Their Implications for the Party System," *Publius: The Journal of Federalism* 13, 1 (1983): 1–17.

11. David Byler, "Is the Ames Straw Poll Useless?" RealClearPolitics, February 9, 2015, https://www.realclearpolitics.com/articles/2015/02/09/is_the_ames_straw_poll_useless_125535.html.

12. "Brownback to Drop White House Bid," NBC News, October 7, 2007, http://www.nbcnews.com/id/21359819/ns/politics-decision_08/t/brownback-drop-white-house-bid/#.WgoABcanGUk.

13. Gerald Wright and Brian Schaffner, "The Influence of Party: Evidence from the State Legislatures," *American Political Science Review* 96, 2 (2002): 367–379.

14. Flentje and Aistrup, *Kansas Politics and Government*.

15. Theda Skocpol and Vanessa Williamson, *The Tea Party and the Remaking of Republican Conservatism* (Oxford: Oxford University Press, 2016).

16. Lawrence Rosenthal and Christine Trost, *Steep: The Precipitous Rise of the Tea Party* (Berkeley: University of California Press, 2012).

17. Sasha Issenberg, *The Victory Lab: The Secret Science of Winning Campaigns* (New York: Broadway Books, 2012).

18. Adam Schraeger and Rob Witwer, *The Blueprint: How Democrats Won Colorado and Why Republicans Everywhere Should Care* (New York: Fulcrum Publishing, 2009).

19. Clayton Barker, interview with the author, April 7, 2017.

20. Aman Batheja, "Lack of Texas Income Tax Draws Out-of-State Envy," *Texas Tribune*, May 24, 2013, https://www.texastribune.org/2013/05/24/lack-income-tax-texas-draws-envy/.

21. Ryan Wilson, "Brownback: State Needs to Grow to Come out of Tough Economy," *Clay Center Dispatch*, April 2, 2010.

22. "State and Local Tax Burdens, 1977–2012," Tax Policy Foundation, 2017, https://taxfoundation.org/state-and-local-tax-burdens-historic-data/.

23. "Rankings and Estimates of the States 2009 and Estimates of School Statistics

2010," National Education Association, August 31, 2011, http://www.nea.org/assets/docs/010rankings.pdf.

24. Michael McLendon, James Hearn, and Christine Mokher, "Partisans, Professionals, and Power: The Role of Political Factors in State Higher Education Funding," *Journal of Higher Education* 80, 6 (2009): 686–713.

25. Peter Roff, "Measuring the Size of Election 2010's Republican Sweep," *US News and World Report*, November 5, 2010, https://www.usnews.com/opinion/blogs/peter-roff/2010/11/05/measuring-the-size-of-election-2010s-republican-sweep.

26. Alan Abramowitz, "How Large a Wave? Using the Generic Ballot to Forecast the 2010 Midterm Elections," *PS: Political Science & Politics* 43, 4 (2010): 631–632.

27. Ric Anderson, "Bill Kurtis for Governor? Not Interested, TV News Icon Says," *Topeka Capital-Journal*, June 15, 2009, http://cjonline.com/opinion/2009-06-15/column-bill-kurtis-governor-not-interested-tv-news-icon-says.

28. John Hanna, "Brownback's Style an Issue in Governor's Race," *Topeka Capital-Journal*, September 6, 2010.

29. Tim Carpenter, "Brownback Arts Reform Ends $1.3m in Grants," *Topeka Capital-Journal*, August 25, 2011.

30. "Wave of Anti-Abortion Bills Advance in the States," *Bismarck Tribune*, March 24, 2011.

31. Mary Clarkin, "Brownback Pushes for Economic Change," *Hutchinson News*, December 6, 2011.

32. Tim Carpenter, "Legislature Digs into Tax Package," *Topeka Capital-Journal*, January 13, 2012.

33. Andy Marso, "Jordan Defends Tax Plan as Concerns Mount," *Topeka Capital-Journal*, January 19, 2012.

34. Andy Marso, "Brownback's 5-Year Budget Projects Big Surpluses," *Topeka Capital-Journal*, January 13, 2012.

35. Tim Carpenter, "Dems Blast Brownback Budget Assumptions," *Topeka Capital-Journal*, July 28, 2012.

36. Tim Carpenter, "Gov Pushes Again for Income Tax Cuts," *Topeka Capital-Journal*, February 5, 2012.

37. Tim Carpenter, "Senate Revotes, Passed Tax Reform Bill," *Topeka Capital-Journal*, March 22, 2012.

38. Tim Carpenter, "'Old Guard' of State GOP Revolts," *Topeka Capital-Journal*, April 26, 2012.

39. Sam Brownback, "Gov. Sam Brownback: Tax Cuts Needed to Grow Economy," *Wichita Eagle*, July 29, 2012.

40. Mary Clarkin, "Lawmakers Launch Work on Redistricting," *Hutchinson News*, June 2, 2011.

41. "Census Sure to Shuffle House, Senate," *Hays Daily News*, February 27, 2011.

42. "Senators Ask Kansas House Not to Mess with Senate Redistricting Map, Honor Tradition," *Republic*, February 29, 2012.

43. Andy Marso, "Redistricting Process Enters 'Uncharted Territory,'" *Topeka Capital-Journal*, May 13, 2012.

44. John Hanna and John Milburn, "Olathe Woman Files Federal Suit over Redistricting," *Lawrence Journal-World*, May 3, 2012.

45. Mary Clarkin, "Summary of Judges' Order on Kan. Redistricting," *Hutchinson News*, June 8, 2012.

46. "Brownback and Graves, Both Republicans, Take Sides in Kansas Senate Primary Battles," *Republic*, July 12, 2012.

47. David Mayhew, *Congress: The Electoral Connection* (New Haven, CT: Yale University Press, 1974); Alan Abramowitz, "Name Familiarity, Reputation, and the Incumbency Effect in a Congressional Election," *Western Political Quarterly* 28, 4 (1975): 668–684; Adam Gelman and Gary King, "Estimating Incumbency Advantage without Bias," *American Journal of Political Science* 34, 4 (1990): 1142–1164; Michael Krashinsky and William Milne, "The Effects of Incumbency in U.S. Congressional Elections, 1950–1988," *Legislative Studies Quarterly* 18, 3 (1993): 321–344.

48. Dennis Simon, Charles Ostrom, and Robin Marra, "The President, Referendum Voting, and Subnational Elections in the United States," *American Political Science Review* 85, 4 (1991): 1177–1192.

49. James King, "Incumbent Popularity and Vote Choice in Gubernatorial Elections," *Journal of Politics* 63, 2 (2001): 585–597.

50. Andy Marso, "Brownback: Numbers Plunge as Agenda Emerges," *Topeka Capital-Journal*, April 28, 2012, http://www.cjonline.com/news-legislature-state/2012-04-28/brownback-numbers-plunge-agenda-emerges.

51. Kelsey Ryan, "Jennifer Winn to Follow Failed Bid for Governor by Running for Wichita Mayor," *Wichita Eagle*, September 16, 2014, http://www.kansas.com/news/local/article2122748.html.

52. Bernard Grofman, Andre Blais, and Steven Bowler, eds., *Duverger's Law of Plurality Voting: The Logic of Party Competition in Canada, India, the United Kingdom and the United States*, vol. 13 (New York: Springer Science & Business Media, 2009).

53. Steven Rosenstone, Robert Behr, and Edward Lazarus, *Third Parties in America: Citizen Response to Major Party Failure* (Princeton, NJ: Princeton University Press, 1996).

54. Kenneth Vogel and Tarini Parti, "Billionaires for Orman," *Politico*, October 9, 2014, https://www.politico.com/story/2014/10/greg-orman-kansas-2014-billionaires-111764.

55. Tom Jensen, "Brownback Unpopular Heading into 2014 Re-election Campaign," Public Policy Polling, October 10, 2013, https://www.publicpolicypolling.com/polls/brownback-unpopular-heading-into-2014-re-election-campaign/.

56. Steven Ansolabehere and Shanto Iyengar, *Going Negative: How Political Advertisements Shrink and Polarize the Electorate* (New York: Free Press, 1997).

57. Wesleyan Media Project, September 30, 2014, http://mediaproject.wesleyan.edu/releases/gop-groups-keeping-senate-contests-close/.

58. Larry Bartels, "Messages Received: The Political Impact of the Media Exposure," *American Political Science Review* 87 (1993): 267–285; Daniel Stevens, "Elements of Negativity: Volume and Proportion in Exposure to Negative Advertising," *Political Behavior* 31 (2009): 429–454.

59. Ansolabehere and Iyengar, *Going Negative*.

60. Robert Stein, "Economic Voting for Governor and US Senator: The Electoral Consequences of Federalism," *Journal of Politics* 52, 1 (1990): 29–53.

CHAPTER EIGHT

Brownback's Red-State Governance

H. Edward Flentje

From the start, Sam Brownback was in a hurry to make his mark. Born into a farming family and raised in rural eastern Kansas, he became state president of the Future Farmers of America while in high school. He attended Kansas State University and was elected student body president as a senior. Subsequently, he served as class president at the University of Kansas Law School. In 1986, at age thirty and after briefly practicing law, Brownback was named secretary of agriculture by the Kansas Board of Agriculture.

Brownback's performance as head of a state agency revealed a progressive streak. He worked to rejuvenate a moribund organization into a positive force in the lives of Kansas farmers—helping farm leaders explore options for increasing farm income. Newly elected governor Mike Hayden named Brownback to the cabinet, where he advised the Hayden administration on drought response and rural development.[1] Hayden and Brownback formulated a plan to expand hunting access on private farmland, a potentially controversial program that other states later replicated and Congress eventually authorized for nationwide application. Brownback was named a White House fellow in 1990 and served for one year in the Office of the US Trade Representative during the first Bush administration. He then resumed his post as Kansas secretary of agriculture, eventually stepping down from that position in 1993.

In 1994, Brownback sought his first elective office, pursuing the Second District congressional seat after incumbent Jim Slattery announced a run for governor. That district covered the rural counties in the eastern quarter of the state, running from Oklahoma to Nebraska, with urban counties in the Kansas City metropolitan area carved out. During the campaign, Brownback characterized himself as a "mainstream conservative" aligned with emerging political forces in both Kansas and the nation that pushed to restrain government on economic issues, such as taxing and spending, and to extend the government's reach on social issues, such as abortion. He described federal government as too big and too intrusive, saying, "I want to cut the federal beast back."[2] He advocated shifting authority and funding for domestic programs to the state and local levels. Brownback also spoke in opposition to abortion, although both sides on that issue felt that he was shifting his position for political advantage.[3]

Brownback succeeded in his run for Congress, prevailing first in a three-person Republican primary and then defeating former governor John Carlin in the general election by a wide margin. He joined seventy-three newly elected US House members who elevated Newt Gingrich to Speaker and embarked on the Republican revolution of 1994.

Not one to hesitate when opportunity knocked, Brownback quickly stepped in to seek the US Senate seat vacated by Bob Dole, who resigned to run for president in 1996. Governor Bill Graves appointed his lieutenant governor, former state senator Sheila Frahm, to fill the seat less than two months before the August primary, but Brownback wasted no time in challenging her. He positioned himself to the right of mainstream Republican Frahm and tightened his alliance with right-wing forces on economic and social issues. He also pledged that, if elected, he would serve no more than two full terms in the Senate. He bested Frahm in the primary by a 55 percent–42 percent margin, with a third candidate drawing off a few votes. Brownback then faced a potentially difficult race against Democrat Jill Docking in the general election and won with 54 percent of the vote. In two years, he had moved from the private sector to the US Senate—a remarkable rise.

Brownback subsequently won two full terms to the Senate in 1998 and 2004, with no significant opposition. During his Senate service, Brownback made little progress on taming the federal beast, but he gained national notoriety on social issues, especially his highly visible display of faith in the public square. He became associated with fundamentalist and evangelical Christian leaders, and his religious affiliation shifted from mainline Protestant to evangelical to highly conservative Catholicism. He advocated a "culture of life" through legal actions such as removing constitutional protections for abortion, banning same-sex marriage, curtailing federal courts from ruling on official expressions of religious beliefs, encouraging the teaching of the evolution controversy in public schools, and allowing churches to endorse political candidates, among other propositions. His spiritual journey also included compassion for the oppressed, such as incarcerated felons who deserved a second chance, victims of human trafficking, casualties of genocide in Darfur, starving children of the Congo, and Native Americans who had suffered from past mistreatment, among others.[4]

After a short-lived presidential bid in 2007 and nearly two full terms in the Senate, Brownback announced his candidacy for Kansas governor in 2010. In the five gubernatorial elections since 1990, a combination of moderate Republicans and Democrats had prevented the Far Right faction of Kansas Republicans from electing one of their own as governor. In consecutive primary elections, incumbent governor Hayden prevailed over Nestor Weigand in 1990; Bill Graves then defeated Gene Bicknell in 1994 and David Miller in 1998. Candidates Tim Shallenburger and Jim Barnett aligned themselves with Far Right Republicans and survived primary contests in 2002 and 2006, only to be defeated in consecutive general elections by centrist Democrat Kathleen Sebelius.

The 2010 campaign would provide few clues as to what voters could expect from Sam Brownback as governor. His campaign "roadmap" broadly addressed mainstream issues—promoting economic growth, improving education, and relieving childhood poverty. His campaign ads claimed he would freeze spending and cut taxes, but the lack of strong competition allowed him to avoid specifics. He coasted to a landslide victory, 63 percent–32 percent, over a weak opponent in the national "red wave" of 2010. Once he was sworn in, Governor Brownback would initiate an aggressive agenda to reverse the broad political consensus previously established on fundamental issues such as taxation, federal aid, and state courts, among others. He sought to make Kansas a national laboratory for Far Right governance.

Red-State Governance

Although Kansas politics remained competitive between Republicans and Democrats from the 1950s through the 1980s, critical elements of state policy seemed immune from these interparty disputes. Key decisions made in different time frames during the twentieth century were reinforced and gained broad legitimacy, largely insulated from the rough-and-tumble of partisan challenges. This bipartisan consensus was mostly unwritten and generally unspoken. Candidates for office conducted competitive campaigns on numerous issues but rarely threatened the bipartisan agreement on achieving a balanced tax policy, making judicial appointments based on merit, and accepting federal aid. Brownback sought to undo this bipartisan consensus, telling the *Wall Street Journal*: "My focus is to create a red-state model that allows the Republican ticket to say, 'See, we've got a different way, and it works.'"[5]

Brownback's plan to remake Kansas into a national model for red-state governance would encompass a raft of social and economic measures promoted by Far Right Republicans on issues such as abortion and guns but largely blocked by centrist Republicans and Democrats over the past fifteen years. Brownback would happily embrace such actions, but his agenda would focus on turning Kansas toward the Far Right on foundational policies that had evolved over many decades through a centrist consensus of moderate Republicans and Democrats. Specifically, Brownback would seek to eliminate the state income tax, abandon merit-based selection of state court judges, and block the acceptance of federal funds. Although the governor's highly conservative agenda reflected his thinking, it also boosted a possible presidential run in 2012 or 2016 if his small-government strategies succeeded.

Eliminating the State Income Tax

In 1995, a blue-ribbon "tax equity" task force commissioned by Governor Graves issued the following recommendation on tax policy:

> The state and local tax system should be balanced and diversified. A diversified tax system offers a blend of economic tradeoffs. Because all revenue sources have their weaknesses, a balanced tax system will reduce the magnitude of problems caused by over reliance on a single tax source. It will also result in lower rates on each tax and reduce the pressure of competition from other states that have lower rates for a particular tax.[6]

The task force's statement formalized as policy what was commonly known in Kansas as the "three-legged stool" of state and local finance. This concept of a balanced tax policy had evolved over sixty years and held that Kansas was best served by maintaining property, income, and sales taxes as the three primary sources of revenue and moving these revenue sources toward relative balance. A bipartisan consensus believed that balance and diversity in taxes assured lower tax rates overall, reduced tax competition with other states, and promoted tax fairness based on income.

In 1932, during the depths of the Great Depression, gubernatorial candidate Alf Landon advocated the adoption of a constitutional amendment authorizing taxes on income that may be "graduated and progressive." Voters approved, and Governor Landon secured enactment of a state income tax in 1933, with the understanding that "the tax on property be proportionately reduced."[7] While running for president in 1936, Landon set the stage for enactment of a sales tax by calling for constitutional amendments to authorize Kansas's financial participation in the federal Social Security Act of 1935. Voters agreed, and shortly thereafter, state lawmakers enacted a sales tax to finance social welfare, but they allocated a major portion of the proceeds to reduce the state's reliance on property taxes.[8]

For the balance of the twentieth century, Kansas governors, legislative leaders, and state lawmakers—Republicans and Democrats—consciously shifted the state and local tax burden from the property tax to state income and sales taxes. The term "three-legged stool" entered the national discussion of state and local tax policy in the last third of the century. In the early 1970s, Professor Barry Flinchbaugh of Kansas State University introduced the term in a statewide discussion with state and local officials on this question: what should the tax mix be to fund state and local government?[9]

Tax policy was under discussion throughout the Carlin and Hayden governorships, but within the framework of achieving a balance among the three primary tax sources. Carlin justified changes in tax policy—for example, a severance tax and a sales tax increase—as one way to relieve reliance on the property tax. Hayden preferred to finance a comprehensive highway program through user fees that would avoid any additional tax burden on property owners by providing highway aid to local governments. During the Carlin and Hayden years, reliance on property taxes dropped from 42 to 32 percent of total state and local revenue.

By the early 1990s, a major revision of school finance was taking shape, and maintaining a balanced tax policy and the three-legged stool dominated the debate and the outcome. Income and sales taxes rose, and property taxes were substantially reduced statewide. By fiscal year 2000, state and local governments in Kansas relied on the three legs of property, income, and sales taxes in almost equal proportions.[10] A well-balanced three-legged stool of state and local finance had become a reality.

Brownback made no mention of eliminating the state income tax or undoing the three-legged stool during his 2010 campaign but hinted at "lowering income tax rates" in his first legislative message. The first signal of dramatic change was Brownback's hiring of tax-cut guru Arthur Laffer of the American Legislative Exchange Council (ALEC) in July 2011.[11] In September, at an annual gathering of the Kansas Policy Institute, a free-market think tank dedicated to low taxes, the governor embraced Laffer's "supply-side" dogma of cutting taxes to stimulate economic growth and explained to the friendly audience that cutting income tax rates would generate even more revenue for the government.[12] In his 2012 State of the State message, Brownback called for deep cuts in income tax rates and the elimination of income taxes on most businesses. Then, after his purge of moderate Republican state senate leaders in the 2012 primaries (discussed later), he began to speak boldly of a "Glide Path to Zero," his plan for the complete elimination of the state income tax.

Brownback's transition to a radical tax policy took a torturous route. To his credit, the governor started his tax initiative by proposing in his 2012 legislative message that lower tax rates be offset by a broader tax base through the elimination of credits, deductions, and exemptions. He wanted a "flatter, fairer, and simpler" state income tax, but that is not what he got. His hastily prepared tax bill surfaced late and contained huge gaffes, such as an $86 million tax hike on the working poor, and legislative consideration got off to a rocky start.[13] Erroneous and shifting projections by the revenue secretary added to the confusion. Eventually, a Republican impasse between the moderate senate and the conservative house stalled Brownback's tax bill in a conference committee in late May—at which point the house sought to force senate submission by passing a "nuclear option." Brownback's bill, intended to be a negotiating vehicle between the chambers, had passed in the senate in response to the governor's plea to move the tax issue along—it was never supposed to be the final product. In fact, the governor had promised senate leaders that the bill was just a vehicle for subsequent negotiation. However, as an impasse loomed, the governor, desperate to show progress and unable to reconcile the two chambers, double-crossed the senate leadership by signing an admittedly flawed bill into law.[14]

Politics had emboldened and encouraged Brownback to sign a defective tax bill. The 2010 elections had given him a thirty-point landslide and handed house Republicans a huge 92–33 majority in that chamber, the largest in more than sixty years. Further, key allies in the Far Right Republican coalition were demanding action. The Kansas Chamber of Commerce's 2012 legislative agenda abandoned long-standing support of a balanced tax policy and called for outright elimination of the state income tax. In doing so, the chamber aligned with entities associated with Charles and David Koch, such as ALEC, Americans for Prosperity, and the Kansas Policy Institute. The unified support of this anti-tax coalition likely convinced Brownback that the centrist, traditional Republican leadership in the state senate could be purged in the upcoming 2012 elections, and he was right.

Anti-tax business owners proceeded to pour cash into the campaign coffers of the Chamber of Commerce's Political Action Committee (PAC). The nearly $1 million raised in 2012 substantially exceeded the total PAC contributions for the five prior years. Koch Industries, along with Ivan Crossman of Columbus, David Murfin of Wichita, and Justin Hill of Lawrence and their respective business entities, contributed 58 percent of the PAC's total campaign chest in 2012.[15] They succeeded in ousting nine incumbent state senators, accounting for nearly all the key Republican leaders, in the August primary; Republicans retained their house majority. The 2012 elections profoundly altered the political complexion of the Kansas legislature. The Far Right was in full control of both the legislature and the governorship.

The anti–income tax Chamber of Commerce would continue its battle to preserve the tax gifts of 2012. In the five years between 2012 and 2016, its PAC would deploy $2.3 million to recruit and retain legislators friendly to the business tax exemption and provisions for the eventual elimination of the state income tax. Koch Industries alone would contribute $625,000 to the PAC's war chest, more than one-quarter of the total. Together, Koch, Crossman, Murfin, and Hill would make up 59 percent of the total campaign contributions.[16]

Once the thrill of a crowded bill-signing ceremony had passed, the harsh financial reality of the tax law became apparent. The governor's signature had eliminated state income taxes on at least 330,000 business and farm entities and would slash income tax revenue by $4.6 billion over five fiscal years, 2014–18, with no planned reductions in spending. The nonpartisan Legislative Research Department projected soaring deficits—amounting to $2.5 billion by the end of 2018.[17] The subsequent plunge in revenue would set off a downward spiral in state finance—a recurring cycle of unbalanced budgets, ad hoc tax increases, and record-breaking debt—with state lawmakers lunging from one financial crisis to the next for the balance of Brownback's time in office.

Brownback remained undaunted and even elevated his rhetoric. He crisscrossed the state during the 2012 election season declaring that his tax cuts would provide "a shot of adrenaline in the heart of the Kansas economy."[18] After his successful ouster of incumbent Republican senators in the 2012 primary, he declared in his 2013 legislative message: "Look out Texas, here comes Kansas!" That March, he paraded his radical tax policy in front of a national TV audience, boasting, "We'll have a real live experiment."[19]

After the 2012 elections, however, he would concede that state revenue would experience a "hard dip" in 2013. He proposed a sales tax increase, the first fix of his self-inflicted financial crisis. That fix allowed the governor to campaign for reelection in 2014 claiming that "the sun is shining in Kansas and don't let anybody tell you any different," only to acknowledge a few days after the election that Kansas was facing a financial abyss.[20] The governor would propose additional "fixes" throughout his remaining years in office.

The governor's financial remedies of 2013, 2015, 2016, and 2017 were all designed to preserve his signature tax experiment and had consistent themes: spend down balances, increase taxes on consumers, borrow money, and cut or defer spending on core services—schools, universities, highways, public pensions, and other essentials.

Brownback first responded to the gaping hole in state finances by spending down balances. To their credit, back in 2010, Democratic governor Mark Parkinson and a bipartisan legislative coalition had created a cushion by enacting a "temporary" three-year, one-cent sales tax increase in an effort to stabilize state finances reeling from the Great Recession. This gave Brownback $1.1 billion in additional cash, most of which he spent in his first three budgets (2012–14); he used what remained to help make up for the income tax shortfall in 2014. Even so, general fund balances plunged from $709 million in 2013 to $380 million in 2014 to $72 million in 2015 and to $37 million in 2016. In addition to running the state's general fund into the red, Brownback began to dip into other state funds, primarily the highway fund, to pay for the income tax cuts. In a series of sweeps in 2012 through 2017, $1.9 billion was diverted from highway improvements to plug the hole left by plummeting income tax revenue.[21]

In addition to spending down balances, Brownback resorted to raising taxes on consumers. He argued that taxing consumer spending was preferable to taxing income that could produce growth. In response, lawmakers increased the state sales tax from 5.7 to 6.15 percent in 2013 and then raised it again to 6.5 percent in 2015—making the Kansas sales tax on food among the highest in the nation. Taxes on cigarettes were also boosted in 2015 to $1.29 a pack—a 63 percent increase. Brownback continued to push for a broader income tax base and secured cuts in tax deductions in both 2013 and 2015.

The income tax cuts approved by Brownback in 2012, coupled with the sales tax increases of 2013 and 2015, dramatically shifted the state tax burden from wealthy Kansans to those with lower incomes. After passage of the 2012 tax law, the Kansas Department of Revenue estimated that the state's 285,000 low-income taxpayers—those with incomes of $25,000 or less—would be receiving a $46 tax cut, compared to a $9,792 tax cut for the 21,000 taxpayers with incomes of $250,000 or more. In other words, the wealthiest 2 percent of tax filers would take home $207 million in tax cuts, or 29 percent of the total.[22] National organizations, such as the Center on Budget and Policy Priorities and the Institute on Taxation and Economic Policy, concurred with the department's assessment, reporting that the 2012 tax cuts "were heavily tilted to the richest Kansans . . . [and] actually raised taxes for the lowest-income households."[23]

The full impact of Brownback's fiscal mismanagement was just beginning to be felt as the governor began his reelection bid in 2014. Even so, attentive voters were aware of depleted balances, downgraded credit, and higher sales taxes, and Brownback narrowly escaped defeat. Nearly 100,000 Republicans voted for the governor's unknown primary opponent in August, but in the general election, a huge influx of outside money into US senator Pat Roberts's campaign (estimated at $17 million) helped Brownback squeak by with slightly less than 50 percent of the vote.[24]

After the 2014 elections, the desperate antics of Brownback and his right-wing allies rose to new extremes as they attempted to save the income tax experiment. In 2015, they moved under the radar during the legislative session to suspend all statutory limits on highway debt; then, in November, they used that authority to borrow $400 million that was quickly swept from the highway fund to pay for their income tax cuts.[25] That new highway debt, coupled with $1 billion of new pension debt issued in August, ballooned the state's tax-supported debt to a historic high of $4.5 billion, an extraordinary jump of 38 percent in five short months.[26]

During the 2016 legislative session, with fund balances at zero, Brownback and right-wing lawmakers staged their final act of financial desperation. They enacted a 2017 budget in which spending exceeded revenue by $100 million. This unbalanced budget forced the governor to make immediate cuts and to defer spending for core services, but even that was not enough. The deficit would swell to $300 million.[27] Former governor Hayden expressed the growing disgust at a public forum in May: "They should be ashamed."[28]

Kansas voters had seen enough. Brownback's approval ratings sank to the lowest in the nation among governors. In 2016, voters rebuked the governor and elected a new class of centrist Republicans and Democrats who had campaigned to end the tax experiment. Forty contested legislative seats went against the governor and his allies. Thirteen incumbents aligned with the governor lost their races.

The 2016 election shake-up fundamentally changed the political complexion of the Kansas legislature. In the house, voters elected forty Democrats, with the remaining eighty-five seats roughly divided between moderate and Far Right Republicans. Democrats claimed only nine seats in the state senate, but Republican seats were rebalanced similar to the breakdown in the house. Centrist Republicans were elected to leadership slots and appointed to chair key committees in both chambers for the first time in six years.

Brownback began the 2017 legislative session as though nothing had changed. He proposed filling the $930 million budget hole with more debt and shifting current obligations to future taxpayers. His financial gimmicks, termed "payday loans" by newly appointed Senate Ways and Means Committee chair Carolyn McGinn, were promptly discarded by state lawmakers.[29]

A bipartisan coalition immediately went to work restoring state finances. By early February, the house tax committee had crafted legislation that would end Brownback's disastrous tax experiment and raise income tax rates, although they would remain lower than the rates in place in 1992–2012. Business exemptions from state income taxes and Brownback's Glide Path to Zero would be abandoned. The proposed legislation sought to reinstate balance and fairness in the overall tax structure and fill the deep financial hole left by the experiment.

An extraordinary house majority swiftly enacted the legislation, and a strong senate majority followed suit, but Brownback issued a quick veto. The house responded by overriding the governor's veto, but the senate's attempt at an override fell three votes short.[30] The governor prevailed in this early test, but members of the bipartisan coalition were confident that they were within reach of the votes needed to end Brownback's tax experiment.

In a further rebuke to Brownback, the Kansas Supreme Court ruled in early March that the governor's "block grant" scheme for funding schools enacted in 2015 failed to meet the constitutional standard of adequacy. It ordered the Kansas legislature to go back to the drawing board and draft a school finance law that met constitutional muster no later than June 30. The court's action reinforced the bipartisan coalition's case for restoring state finance. Additional state revenue would be required to meet court requirements for the adequate funding of schools.[31]

By early June, state lawmakers were writing an elegy for the Brownback tax experiment. Substantial majorities in both chambers enacted legislation patterned after that vetoed in February. On this second try, the bipartisan coalition prevailed. After a Brownback veto, supermajorities overrode the governor: 88–31 in the house, four votes more than required for an override; followed by a 27–13 vote in the senate, the bare minimum needed to override the veto. The bipartisan coalition of centrist lawmakers was joined by a handful of conservative Republicans formerly allied with Brownback.[32]

Brownback's six-year crusade to eliminate the state income tax—the foundation of his national model for red-state governance—came to an abrupt end. State lawmakers had taken the first steps toward rebuilding the three-legged stool of state and local finance in Kansas.[33]

Abandoning Merit-Based Selection of Judges

Historically, Kansas Supreme Court justices were elected by popular vote, and any vacancy was filled by the governor. Under this system, justices could become embroiled in partisan affairs from time to time.[34] Political shenanigans in 1956 and 1957, known as the "triple play" in Kansas politics, triggered reform and led Kansas toward the selection of justices based on merit. The triple play unfolded as follows: Governor Fred Hall sought reelection but was defeated in a divisive Republican primary in August 1956. On the last day of December, a friendly Republican justice resigned from the supreme court with the intention of preventing the incoming governor, Democrat George Docking, from making a court appointment. A few days later, Hall stepped down as governor, elevating Lieutenant Governor John McCuish. The new governor promptly appointed Hall to the Kansas Supreme Court.

In 1957, the Kansas legislature moved to insulate the state supreme court from partisan politics and proposed a constitutional amendment patterned after the Missouri Plan for the nonpartisan appointment of judges. Voters overwhelmingly adopted that proposition in 1958. The amendment, now part of the judicial article of the Kansas Constitution, provided for the selection of supreme court justices through a "nonpartisan nominating commission" composed of (1) one member to chair the commission, chosen by licensed members of the bar from among their membership statewide; (2) one member from each congressional district, chosen by members of the bar in the district; and (3) one member, who is not a lawyer, appointed by the governor from each congressional district. With four congressional districts in the state, the commission consists of nine members: five licensed members of the bar, one of whom chairs the commission, and four members of the public appointed by the governor.

Once a vacancy occurs on the court, the nominating commission screens applicants "possessing the qualifications of office" and submits the names of three nominees to the governor. The governor then appoints a new justice from that list of three nominees. If the governor fails to make an appointment within sixty days, the chief justice of the supreme court makes the appointment from the list.

Once appointed to the court, a justice must stand periodically for retention. Specifically, in a general statewide election, voters are asked on a judicial ballot, without party designation, whether the justice shall "be retained in office." If a majority of voters oppose the justice's retention, that position on the court is vacated at the expiration of the justice's term. Each newly appointed justice stands for retention after serving for one year. If that justice is retained, he or she serves a regular six-year term but must stand for retention again before the expiration of that term. Since adoption of the plan, no justice has lost a retention vote, although that record was seriously tested in 2016.

This procedure for the selection of supreme court justices is commonly referred to as merit selection, even though the word "merit" appears nowhere in the judicial article. However, the constitutional language clearly seeks to diminish, if not eliminate, partisanship in judicial selection. For example, both the selection procedure and the nominating commission are termed "nonpartisan," and commission members "may not hold any other public office by appointment or any official position in a political party." Any justice standing for retention is prohibited from having a "party designation" next to his or her name on the ballot. Further, sitting justices cannot engage in political activity. The constitution states: "No justice of the supreme court . . . shall directly or indirectly make any contribution to or hold any office in a political party or organization or take part in any political campaign."[35]

In 1975, Kansas lawmakers established the Kansas Court of Appeals to serve as an intermediate court between the Kansas Supreme Court and lower trial courts. In doing so, lawmakers also adopted a statutory procedure for the merit selection and retention of appeals court judges, patterned after the constitutional process for selecting supreme court justices. The supreme court nominating commission was assigned the duty of screening and nominating appeals court judges for appointment by the governor.

Since the implementation of merit selection of Kansas Supreme Court justices, every one of the eleven Kansas governors serving in that period (1964–2017) has appointed at least one justice to the supreme court. Each of the twenty-five justices appointed through merit selection has stood for retention on one or more occasions and has been retained by voters, as have all the appeals court judges appointed through the merit system.

Prior to the 2010 election of Sam Brownback, Kansas governors had honored the nonpartisan procedure for judicial selection and shown respect for judicial independence. That would change with Brownback. His antipathy toward merit selection would unleash a tirade of sustained attacks on the courts, court decisions, individual justices, and merit selection. These assaults, from various sources, would continue in one form or another throughout his time in office.

The precise origin of the campaign against the courts cannot be easily identified. Over the past fifty years, disagreements over court decisions on school finance, the death penalty, and tax issues had occurred from time to time, but they never led to deep-seated condemnations of the state courts or a furor to undo judicial selection. The Kansas chapter of Americans for Prosperity acknowledged in 2014 that it had been seeking to abandon merit selection for "the past several years."[36] Brownback did not campaign on the issue in 2010, but he expressed a preference for partisan selection of judges in a private conversation with state senator Tim Owens, chair of the Judiciary Committee, in 2012. Owens later reported that discussion as follows: "Governor Brownback pointed his finger at me and said, 'Tim, why can't you go along with us on this judicial selection issue and let us change the way we select judges so we can get judges who will vote the way we want them to?'" In response to a press query about Owens's comments, the governor's spokeswoman indicated that Brownback had "consistently advocated for a selection process, through Senate confirmation or direct elections, that made participants accountable to voters."[37]

The assault on state courts unleashed by Brownback unfolded in waves. In his first message to the legislature, he said, "Let the Legislature resolve school finance . . . not the courts." He returned to this theme repeatedly, and his denunciation of court interference in the funding of schools would continue throughout his seven years as governor. During his reelection bid in 2014, Brownback made the state supreme court a punching bag on the issue of the death penalty. His campaign ads charged that "liberal judges in Topeka" let convicted murders "off the hook."[38]

After Brownback's successful purge of nine incumbent Republican state senators in the 2012 primary, the governor and his legislative allies moved aggressively to undo merit selection. In his second State of the State message, the governor declared: "Kansans expect and are entitled to a government that is not beholden to any special interest group. . . . Unfortunately, our current system of selecting our appellate judges fails the democratic test. . . . Kansas is the only state that allows a special interest group [to] control the process of choosing who will be our appellate judges. That is not as it should be."[39] Concurrent resolutions to abandon the merit process surfaced immediately in the 2013 legislative session, and after perfunctory hearings, constitutional amendments to grant the governor the power to appoint supreme court justices and appeals court judges, subject to senate confirmation, moved hastily out of judiciary committees onto the house and senate floors. Before the end of January, the senate had adopted the proposition by the requisite two-thirds majority, but the proposal stalled on the house floor.

With action on a constitutional amendment checked by the house, the governor's legislative allies moved to change the selection of appeals court judges, which was statutory and required only simple majorities to revise. By midsession 2013, Brownback had signed legislation authorizing the governor to appoint judges to the court of appeals without screening by the nonpartisan commission, but subject to confirmation by the state senate.

Political allies of the governor also emerged to take a stand on judicial selection. Kansans for Life, a longtime critic of state judges and courts on the issue of abortion, targeted without success two supreme court justices up for retention in 2014 and lent its support to the proposal to change the method of judicial selection. Late in 2013, the Kansas Chamber of Commerce added backing for "judicial reform measures" to its 2014 legislative agenda.

After his narrow reelection victory in 2014, Brownback charged forward to end the merit selection of Kansas Supreme Court justices, stating in his 2015 legislative message: "It also is time we change the way we pick our Supreme Court." Still lacking the required votes for a constitutional amendment in the house, the governor's legislative partisans began to publicly harass the court and challenge its authority. They threatened to shut down the courts with budget cuts. They enacted legislation seeking to undo a constitutional provision for unified court administration, which was linked to court funding. They advanced constitutionally questionable legislation that would subject judges to impeachment for rulings that "usurp legislative or executive authority."[40] These moves garnered state and national publicity but had little real effect.

Having failed to achieve legislative action on constitutional change, Brownback and his allies turned their attention to a campaign against individual supreme court justices. Five of seven supreme court justices were on the retention ballot in 2016, and the governor and his allies targeted four of them for nonretention. Given his low approval ratings, Brownback tried to hide his involvement in the attempted purge, but his fingerprints were visible. Republican Party officials voted to make ousting the four supreme court justices a priority at their convention in May 2016.[41] The party platform stated: "Kansas should change its judicial selection process to reflect the federal model of legislative confirmation or by adopting direct election of judges statewide."

The governor's political action committee, Road Map PAC, transferred $110,000 to Kansans for Life to bolster its aggressive campaign on judicial selection. That organization blanketed the state with multicolored postcards shouting out: "WE MUST REMOVE ACTIVIST JUDGES on the Kansas Supreme Court. . . . These ACTIVIST JUDGES want to permanently LEGALIZE DISMEMBERMENT abortions of fully-formed, unborn babies while still alive in the womb—and have YOUR TAXES pay for it." Kansans for Justice spent $500,000 on highly emotional ads featuring family members of murder victims and slamming justices for delays on the death penalty.[42]

In response to this onslaught, Kansans for Fair Courts emerged to contest the ouster campaign, expose the governor, and defend the four justices.

The group distributed "fact sheets" documenting "the unprecedented number of attacks on our courts by Gov. Sam Brownback and his political allies" and rallied voters to "keep politicians out of the courts." Its executive director charged: "This is a full-out power grab by the governor."[43] The organization raised more than $400,000 for a TV commercial that warned voters: "We could have five Sam Brownback clones on the Kansas Supreme Court. If we fire our Supreme Court justices, Brownback can appoint up to five of the seven justices. Reject Sam Brownback's power grab."[44]

In a move that further isolated Brownback, four former Kansas governors, two Republicans and two Democrats, came together to publicly support the retention campaign. Former governors Carlin, Hayden, Graves, and Sebelius met with the media, appeared jointly at public forums, voiced strong bipartisan support for merit selection and judicial independence, and criticized the "unprecedented assault on the judiciary."[45] In a Wichita forum, Hayden spoke passionately: "When people come before the courts, they expect a fair and impartial hearing, and that's what they have gotten with these five justices." Further, the justices had "a stellar record worthy of retention," and their removal "would be catastrophic to justice in Kansas."[46]

The targeted justices survived the highly contested purge campaign, all four receiving close to 56 percent of votes in favor of their retention. The "power grab" theme, coupled with Brownback's rock-bottom approval ratings, bolstered their chances of survival. The retention elections drew a record turnout of 1.1 million voters, topping the presidential-year elections of 2008 and 2012 by well over 100,000 votes.

After seven years of controversy over merit selection and the courts in general, the 2016 retention outcome led to a period of calm, and the state supreme court quietly returned to the business of ruling on school finance and the death penalty. Brownback would leave office with a partial loaf, ending the merit selection of appeals court judges but failing in his single-minded crusade to accomplish the same in the supreme court. Moreover, in 2018, the supreme court ordered the state to add hundreds of millions of dollars to fund K–12 education, in accordance with the Kansas Constitution. In doing so, the justices acted from a position of strength, given their 2016 victories.

Blocking Federal Funds

Kansans did not immediately embrace grants-in-aid when they were first introduced by the federal government in the early decades of the twentieth century. The state's political culture preferred self-governance and instinctively resisted outside aid with strings attached. In time, however, the enticement of federal dollars softened the state's resistance. After a good bit of back-and-forth with federal officials, state lawmakers proposed and voters adopted constitutional amendments in 1928 authorizing the state to construct, maintain, and finance state highways and levy taxes on motor fuel and vehicles for road and highway purposes. These actions opened the door to federal aid for road building.[47] In the 1930s, Governor Alf Landon actively pursued every federal dollar available for emergency relief during the Great Depression, and in 1936 he campaigned for constitutional amendments allowing the state's financial participation in the Social Security Act of 1935. In response, state lawmakers enacted a state sales tax to match federal funds for social welfare and authorized state financing for unemployment compensation in 1937.[48] These actions allowed federal funds to flow into the state and established critical precedents for state officials to pursue and accept federal grants-in-aid for a broad range of purposes.

In line with these early actions, Kansas officials readily agreed to participate in Medicaid, which was authorized at the national level in 1965 and would eventually become the largest grant-in-aid in every state. Indeed, officials in Kansas determined from the start to match federal Medicaid funds and to offer services and extend eligibility beyond that required by the federal act. However, accelerated Medicaid spending quickly alarmed fiscally conservative state lawmakers. In 1977, the state's legislative post auditor issued a report on controlling Medicaid costs and noted that total state expenditures for Medicaid had "more than quadrupled from fiscal year 1971 to fiscal year 1977."[49] The auditor outlined cost-control measures, such as reducing enrollment and cutting back on services, but his recommendations to curtail Medicaid spending through cutbacks found few takers; nor has that tactic proved popular in subsequent years. Instead, state officials opted to restrain costs through low reimbursement rates for service providers.[50]

Even though state initiatives to control Medicaid spending continued throughout the program's fifty-year history, the policy of accepting federal matching funds to provide health care for poor, aged, and disabled Kansans gained broad political support. Over time, Medicaid grew to serve 400,000 Kansas residents each year, and by 2016, federal and state matching funds totaling $3.3 billion were widely distributed throughout the state to a diverse array of nearly twenty thousand health care providers. Medicaid, along with dozens of other federal grant-in-aid programs, became part of a bipartisan consensus on the acceptance of federal aid. Governor Sam Brownback, however, would attempt to depart from that tradition.

In his first State of the State message, Brownback proposed saving "Kansas taxpayers millions of dollars" through the elimination of state agencies, and he immediately targeted state funding for the arts—a minuscule piece of the budget. He ordered the elimination of the state arts agency and later vetoed appropriations intended to match federal grants. He declared that public funding of the arts was not a "core service," and the private sector would fill the void. That never happened, and federal matching funds were lost. The state director of Americans for Prosperity, however, cheered the governor's action.[51]

Brownback next moved to attack a larger target by blocking federal aid through the Affordable Care Act of 2010 (ACA). As a US senator, he had joined all congressional Republicans in opposing adoption of the act, and in his campaign for governor, he vowed to resist implementation of the law. After initial mixed signals, he ordered moderate Republican insurance commissioner Sandy Praeger to return a $31 million grant she had secured to help Kansans take advantage of benefits provided through the ACA (also known as Obamacare). Brownback explained that uncertainty surrounding the law "requires freeing Kansas from the strings attached," and he rejected the funds.[52]

Brownback also used his continuing opposition to Obamacare to block the expansion of Medicaid to 150,000 low-income working Kansans—a huge stream of federal aid available to the state through the ACA. Congressional Democrats had included provisions mandating that states extend Medicaid to uninsured populations and promising to underwrite no less than 90 percent of the cost. However, in a constitutional challenge to the law, the US Supreme Court, in a split decision, found that although the ACA was constitutional, states could opt out of extending Medicaid coverage.[53]

Brownback used numerous ploys to dodge the expansion of Medicaid, but pressure to do so mounted. By 2016, thirty-one states, including some with Republican governors, had approved the expansion of Medicaid. Health care providers in Kansas, particularly hospitals, promoted the acceptance of expanded aid. The Kansas Hospital Association documented that expansion would cover an additional 169,000 low-income Kansans; over three years, it would create four thousand jobs and inject $1.6 billion into the state economy.[54] But Brownback's key allies—Americans for Prosperity, the Kansas Chamber of Commerce, ALEC, and legislative leaders—vigorously fought any extension of the state's safety net for low-income Kansans.

Over time, legislative resistance began to thaw, and during the 2017 legislative session, it melted away. Sensing a reversal, Brownback warned legislators in his State of the State message "not to take the bait on Medicaid expansion." He asserted that the Trump administration would soon "repeal and replace" Obamacare, and an endorsement of expansion would be foolish, "akin to airlifting on to the Titanic." But state lawmakers were no longer inclined to listen to the governor, and by the end of March, both legislative chambers had voted to extend Medicaid by substantial margins. Brownback promptly vetoed the legislation. The house voted 81–44 to override the veto, falling three votes short of the necessary margin. By the skin of his teeth, the governor had prevailed in blocking the expansion of Medicaid.

Brownback's objection to accepting federal aid had the greatest adverse effect on the state's most vulnerable populations: children, seniors, the unemployed, and the disabled. The governor first ordered restrictions on eligibility for income maintenance through Temporary Assistance for Needy Families (TANF) in 2011 and signed legislation enacting further restrictions in 2015 and again in 2016. Similar eligibility restrictions were applied to the Supplemental Nutrition Assistance Program (SNAP), commonly known as food stamps. The administration also declined to participate in a federal program that encouraged eligible populations to apply for food stamps. Families receiving cash assistance through TANF dropped precipitously from 13,900 in 2010 to 4,900 in 2016, placing Kansas near the bottom of the fifty states. Participation rates for families eligible for food stamps fell steadily as well, with Kansas ranking forty-fifth in participation across the nation.[55] These actions departed substantially from those of previous administrations, whether Democratic or Republican. Brownback and his Far Right allies veered sharply from policies that had been endorsed for forty years by moderate-conservative majorities.

Brownback drew national attention with his claims that work requirements for cash assistance and food stamp recipients would lift those relying on welfare out of poverty. His actions were lauded by a conservative Florida-based think tank, Foundation for Government Accountability.[56] The governor's assertions were challenged, however, by the left-leaning Center for Budget and Policy Priorities, which found that "the vast majority of Kansas families leaving TANF did not find steady work opportunities that positioned them to make ends meet and avoid raising their children in poverty."[57] Further, according to the preliminary results of a study by University of Kansas professors: "As the Kansas TANF caseloads drop, the number of reports of abuse and neglect go up. And you see a similar relationship for foster care placements."[58] In sum, harsh reductions in welfare eligibility produced poor results for participants and increased costs in other parts of the state budget.

Other losses in federal aid could be attributed to outright incompetence in the administration of social services during Brownback's governorship. In December 2015, for example, state inattention to safety issues at Osawatomie State Hospital resulted in its decertification and the loss of $1 million a month in federal matching funds until the hospital was recertified two years later. Privatization of Medicaid in 2013, coupled with cuts in Medicaid reimbursement rates in 2016, reduced federal aid and contributed to a series of calamities, including delayed payments to health care providers, backlogged applications for nursing home care, and diminished services for children, seniors, and the disabled by other health care providers. In November 2017, press reports revealed that budget cuts, staff vacancies, secrecy, and glaring mismanagement in the Department of Children and Families had resulted in high-profile child deaths, missing foster children, and children sleeping in state offices.[59] Incompetent oversight of nursing home contractors forced the state takeover of fifteen nursing homes from a bankrupt contractor in 2018.[60]

As Brownback departed the governor's office in January 2018, he left his successor, Lieutenant Governor Jeff Colyer, a litany of administrative messes tied to his aversion to assisting vulnerable Kansans through federal grants-in-aid—in most cases exacerbated by maladministration of that aid.

Brownback Leaves the Governorship

After seven years in office, Sam Brownback vacated the Kansas governorship on January 31, 2018. After a six-month delay, his nomination by President

Donald Trump as US ambassador for religious freedom won approval in the Senate by a vote of 50–49. Vice President Mike Pence cast the deciding vote; no Democrat supported Brownback's confirmation.

In response to queries from the statehouse press corps on his legacy as governor, Brownback cited his fierce opposition to abortion as his greatest contribution: "We're a pro-life state and we're not going back. . . . The inherent dignity of human life is the central issue of our day."[61] He mentioned nineteen antiabortion measures enacted during his governorship.[62]

Brownback left office with one of the lowest approval ratings among the nation's governors and acknowledged that being governor was "the hardest job I've ever had."[63] After sixteen years in Congress, he had glided into the governorship with a landslide victory in the "red wave" election of 2010. He was determined to leave his mark on state government and vowed to make Kansas a national model for red-state governance. He sought to reverse the bipartisan consensus that had governed the state for the last half century and aggressively targeted tax policy, judicial selection, and federal aid. Upon leaving office, however, he made little mention of those key elements of his radical red-state agenda.

Brownback's tax experiment began in 2012 and ended in 2017 after five years of unbalanced budgets, unfair taxes, and record debt. A bipartisan coalition of legislators overrode his veto and discarded the governor's ideological illusion of eliminating the state income tax. A restoration of the state's historic reliance on a three-legged stool of public finance was under way.

Brownback also failed in his crusade to eliminate merit-based selection of Kansas Supreme Court justices. A bipartisan coalition in the Kansas House blocked the governor from securing the supermajority required to place a constitutional amendment before Kansas voters. Brownback achieved a smaller victory against merit selection when lawmakers enacted a statute giving the governor the authority to appoint judges to the Kansas Court of Appeals, subject to senate confirmation.

Brownback blocked federal aid for vulnerable Kansans—specifically, children, seniors, the unemployed, and the disabled—and he did substantial damage to the safety net supporting those populations. He vigorously opposed the extension of Medicaid under the Affordable Care Act of 2010 and succeeded in blocking it. Lawmakers adopted legislation to extend Medicaid in 2017 but failed to override the governor's veto. Brownback also gained national notoriety for restricting federal aid to provide cash and food assistance, putting Kansas near the bottom of the fifty states in taking advantage of such aid.

Notes

1. H. Edward Flentje, ed., *Selected Papers of Governor Mike Hayden: Advancing a Progressive Agenda* (Wichita: Hugo Wall School of Urban and Public Affairs, Wichita State University, 2002), 194, 196, 199, 204.

2. Judy Lundstrom Thomas, "Issues Are Obscured by Personal Attacks in 2nd District Battle," *Wichita Eagle*, October 9, 1994.

3. Mike Hendricks, "Politics Attracted Brownback Early," *Kansas City Star*, October 27, 1996.

4. Jeff Sharlet, "God's Senator," *Rolling Stone*, February 9, 2006.

5. Neil King Jr. and Mark Peters, "The Right Way? Party Eyes 'Red-State Model' to Drive Republican Revival," *Wall Street Journal*, February 5, 2013, A-1.

6. *Report of the Governor's Tax Equity Task Force*, December 1995, 13.

7. Cited in H. Edward Flentje and Joseph A. Aistrup, *Kansas Politics and Government: The Clash of Political Cultures* (Lincoln: University of Nebraska Press, 2010), 178.

8. Flentje and Aistrup, 180–181.

9. Email from Barry Flinchbaugh, July 1, 2016.

10. Kansas Legislative Research Department, *Kansas Tax Facts, Seventh Edition*, December 2000, 12.

11. Dion Lefler, "Brownback Plans Income Tax Cuts," *Wichita Eagle*, September 21, 2011; Brent D. Wistrom, "Economist Arthur Laffer Says Tax Cuts Will Help Kansas Grow," *Wichita Eagle*, August 14, 2012.

12. Lefler, "Brownback Plans Income Tax Cuts."

13. Brad Cooper, "Analysis: Poor Will Pay More under Plan," *Wichita Eagle*, January 18, 2012.

14. Tim Carpenter, "High-Stakes Tax Maneuvering in 2012 Haunts Deliberations on Deficit," *Topeka Capital-Journal*, January 30, 2015.

15. Kansas Chamber of Commerce Political Action Committee, Campaign Finance Reports, Kansas Governmental Ethics Commission, 2008–16.

16. Kansas Chamber of Commerce Political Action Committee, Campaign Finance Reports, Kansas Governmental Ethics Commission, 2008–2016.

17. Kansas Legislative Research Department, "State General Fund Profile, FY 2010–FY 2018," June 15, 2012; Kansas Legislative Research Department, "2012 Summary of Legislation," July 2012, 130.

18. Sam Brownback, "Tax Cuts Needed to Grow Economy," *Wichita Eagle*, July 29, 2012.

19. Brent Wistrom, "Brownback Touts Kansas to National Audiences," *Wichita Eagle*, March 8, 2013.

20. Campaign ad available at Kansas Institute of Politics, Washburn University, www.washburn.edu/reference/cks/politics/ads/html.

21. Kansas Legislative Research Department, "SHF Transfers to SGF and Other State Agencies, FY 2011–2019," n.d. See also Official Statement, Kansas Department of Transportation, Highway Revenue Bonds, Series 2015 B, 27–31.

22. Kansas Department of Revenue, "Tax Filers Paying Income Tax," HB 2117, n.d.

23. Michael Leachman and Chris Mai, "Lessons for Other States from Kansas' Massive Tax Cuts," Center on Budget and Policy Priorities, March 27, 2014, 7–8; Institute on Taxation and Economic Policy, "Latest Kansas Tax Bill Carries $680 Million Price Tag and Raises Taxes on Those Least Able to Pay," May 17, 2012.

24. Elahe Izadi, "Pat Roberts Pulls off a Resounding Win in Kansas," *Washington Post*, November 5, 2014.

25. Tim Carpenter, "KDOT Issues Record $400 Million in Bonds, Exceeds Previous Debt Cap," *Topeka Capital-Journal*, December 15, 2015.

26. Kansas Development Finance Authority, "State of Kansas 2017 Debt Study" (2018), 4.

27. Jonathan Shorman, "Gov. Sam Brownback Makes Cuts to Budgets of Universities, Medicaid, State Agencies," *Topeka Capital-Journal*, May 18, 2016; Bryan Lowry, "Lawmakers Call on Brownback to Make Cuts before Session," *Wichita Eagle*, November 28, 2016.

28. Jonathan Shorman, "Past Kansas Governors Rebuke Brownback and Lawmakers: 'They Should Be Ashamed,'" *Topeka Capital-Journal*, May 14, 2016.

29. Bryan Lowry, "Brownback Wants to Tap State Investment Fund, GOP Leader Says," *Wichita Eagle*, January 1, 2017; Tim Carpenter, "Brownback's Budget Raises Taxes, Alters Pension and Medicaid Funding," *Topeka Capital-Journal*, January 11, 2017; Bryan Lowry, "Brownback Seeks to Raise Alcohol and Cigarette Taxes, Sweep Highway Fund," *Wichita Eagle*, January 11, 2017.

30. Alan Blinder, "Kansas Lawmakers Uphold Governor's Veto of Tax Increases," *New York Times*, February 22, 2017.

31. Suzanne Perez Tobias and Dion Lefler, "Kansas Supreme Court Rules School Funding Inadequate," *Wichita Eagle*, March 3, 2017.

32. Jonathan Shorman and Daniel Salazar, "Lawmakers Override Brownback Veto of Tax Increases, Rolling Back 2012 Cuts," *Wichita Eagle*, June 7, 2017; Julie Bosman, Mitch Smith, and Monica Davey, "Brownback Tax Cuts Set off a Revolt by Kansas Republicans," *New York Times*, June 7, 2017.

33. For an interdisciplinary monograph on the Brownback tax plan, see Michael A. Smith, Robert J. Grover, and Rob Catlett, *Low Taxes and Small Government: Sam Brownback's Great Experiment in Kansas* (Lanham, MD: Lexington Books, 2019).

34. Brian J. Moline, "Bill Smith: The Jurist as Politician," in *Politics and Government in Kansas: Selected Essays*, ed. Marvin A. Harder (Topeka: Capitol Complex Center, University of Kansas, 1989), 263–268.

35. Kansas Constitution, section 8, article 3.

36. See americansforprosperity.org, March 3, 2016.

37. Tim Carpenter, "Ex-Senator Tim Owens: Ideology Drives Sam Brownback's Push for Judicial Reform," *Topeka Capital-Journal*, February 4, 2015.

38. Campaign ad at Kansas Institute of Politics, Washburn University.

39. Sam Brownback, "Kansas Is a Special Place," 2013 State of the State address, January 15, 2013.

40. Erik Eckholm, "Outraged by Kansas Justice's Rulings, Republicans Seek to Reshape Court," *New York Times*, April 1, 2016.

41. Sam Zeff, "Get Ready for a Raucous Kansas Supreme Court Retention Race," KCUR, May 26, 2016; Brian Lowry, "High Stakes in Kansas Supreme Court Retention Vote," *Wichita Eagle*, September 5, 2016.

42. John Hanna, "Spending Likely Hits $1M in Campaigns over Top Kansas Court," Associated Press, November 3, 2016; Jim McLean, "More Questions about Brownback's Role in Supreme Court Retention Battle," KHI News Service, November 3, 2016.

43. Eckholm, "Outraged by Kansas Justice's Rulings."

44. Campaign ad at Kansas Institute of Politics, Washburn University.

45. Brian Lowry, "Former Governors Launch Campaign to Retain Justices," *Wichita Eagle*, September 6, 2016.

46. Editorial, "Governors Are Correct: Retain Supreme Court Justices," *Wichita Eagle*, September 9, 2016.

47. Flentje and Aistrup, *Kansas Politics and Government*, 154–156.

48. Flentje and Aistrup, 156–158.

49. Kansas Division of Legislative Post Audit, "Controlling Medical Assistance Costs in Kansas, Part II: Options for Containing Costs," December 17, 1977.

50. Flentje and Aistrup, *Kansas Politics and Government*, 158–159.

51. "Kansas Governor Eliminates Arts Funding," *Los Angeles Times*, May 31, 2011.

52. Phil Cauthon, Dave Ranney, and Jim McLean, "Kansas Rejects $31.5 Million for Insurance Exchange," KHI News Service, August 9, 2011.

53. See *National Federation of Independent Business v. Sebelius*, 567 U.S. 519 (2012).

54. Kansas Hospital Association, "Expanding KanCare Makes Good Sense," brochure, July 2014.

55. Ife Floyd, LaDonna Pavetti, and Liz Schott, "TANF Reaching Few Poor Families," Center on Budget and Policy Priorities, updated December 13, 2017; Madeline Fox, "Welfare Remade under Brownback, but Still Debated," KCUR, January 16, 2018; Madeline Fox, "Report: Poor Families Struggling with Kansas Work Rules," KCUR,

January 25, 2018; US Department of Agriculture, "Reaching Those in Need: Estimates of State Supplemental Nutrition Assistance Program Participation Rates in 2015," January 19, 2018.

56. Foundation for Government Accountability, "Work Requirements Are Working for Kansas Families," July 31, 2017.

57. Tazra Mitchell, LaDonna Pavetti, and Yixuan Huang, "Life after TANF in Kansas: For Most, Unsteady Work and Earnings below Half the Poverty Line," Center on Budget and Policy Priorities, January 24, 2018, 16.

58. Madeline Fox, "KU Study Indicates Link between Kansas Welfare Restrictions, Foster Care Case Increase," KCUR, December 15, 2017.

59. Andy Marso, "Problems with Medicaid Eligibility System Leave Kansans without Care," KCUR, February 1, 2016; Andy Marso, "Medicaid Application Delays Are Forcing Kansas Nursing Homes to Turn People Away," *Kansas City Star*, December 15, 2017; Laura Bauer, "Secrecy inside Child Welfare System Can Kill: 'God Help the Children of Kansas,'" *Kansas City Star*, updated November 13, 2017; Jonathan Shorman, "KanCare Contractor Fails to Meet Medicaid Deadline," *Wichita Eagle*, June 9, 2018.

60. Kelsey Ryan and Andy Marso, "How a Small Company above a N.J. Pizza Parlor Put Kansas Nursing Home Residents at Risk," *Kansas City Star*, updated April 16, 2018.

61. Tim Carpenter, "The Brownback Legacy: He Touts Pro-Life Work; Skeptics Point to Damaging Tax Cuts," *Topeka Capital-Journal*, January 30, 2018.

62. In 2019, the Kansas Supreme Court struck down some of those restrictions in *Hodes & Nauser v. Schmidt*, ruling that the Bill of Rights of the Kansas Constitution "affords protection of the right of personal autonomy, which includes the ability to control one's own body, to assert bodily integrity, and to exercise self-determination. This right allows a woman to make her own decisions regarding her body, health, family formation, and family life—decisions that can include whether to continue a pregnancy." Republican lawmakers proposed a constitutional amendment to nullify the court's ruling, but Kansas voters overwhelmingly rejected the amendment in August 2022.

63. Bryan Lowry, Jonathan Shorman, Lindsay Wise, and Hunter Woodall, "Brownback Confirmed in Narrow Vote, Leaves Mixed Kansas Legacy," *Wichita Eagle*, January 25, 2018.

CHAPTER NINE

Kansas Voters Reverse Course

The 2016 and 2018 Elections

Patrick R. Miller

On paper, the 2014 election was a sweep for Kansas Republicans, especially conservatives. They prevailed in a hotly contested gubernatorial race, won every statewide constitutional office, retained a jeopardized US Senate seat, held every US House seat, and reduced Democrats to only twenty-eight seats in the state house—the fewest in decades.

Nonetheless, those victories disguised deeper troubles. Governor Sam Brownback barely won reelection, managing a 3.7-point victory in a generally Republican state in a year that was a disaster for Democrats nationwide.[1] Even in the most favorable preelection polls for Brownback, he earned negative job approval ratings from Kansans. And the 2014 exit poll showed that the same voters who gave him a second term thought the Brownback tax cuts mostly "hurt Kansas" (53 percent) rather than "helped Kansas" (41 percent).[2]

The Republican sweep did not fix the underlying issues that almost cost Brownback his governorship, especially given the headlines about revenue shortfalls and budget cuts to core state services such as public education and transportation. Nor did the sweep boost Brownback's popularity. The persistence of these problems set the stage for the 2016 and 2018 elections, which derailed the governing dominance of conservatives in Topeka.

Setting the Stage for 2016

Politically, Kansas conservatives experienced a downward spiral after 2014. Given their near total control over the legislature and governorship, the fallout from the budget crisis created by Brownback's tax-cut "experiment" fell squarely on them. Month after month, state revenue failed to meet the

Brownback administration's projections, even after those expectations were repeatedly lowered.[3] And news headlines consistently underscored for Kansans how these revenue failures affected the state.

For example, revenue in February 2016 fell $53 million short of expectations, creating a budget hole for the fiscal year.[4] In response, Brownback announced a $17 million cut to state universities, on top of previous cuts to higher education and tuition increases to compensate for the lost funding. Brownback claimed that the revenue shortfalls were not his fault, often blaming Democratic president Barack Obama or the economy in general. He said about the February 2016 shortfall, "This is an economic problem, not a tax policy problem"—a standard line for Brownback and his allies.[5] They sometimes modified the line, saying that Kansas had a "spending problem" rather than a revenue problem, implying that the state had simply not cut spending enough to eliminate the projected deficits.

Funding for education was ground zero for the tax controversy after Brownback's reelection. In February 2015, the governor reduced funding for public schools and universities by $44.5 million, amounting to a 1.5 percent cut for K–12 schools and a 2 percent cut for universities.[6] The legislature further reduced spending to compensate for a $344 million budget deficit. Brownback framed this cut as a response to a "dramatic increase in state education funding" in his first term, which he claimed was unsustainable.[7]

Nonetheless, the budget cuts were the headline. In 2015, Brownback signed a bill that replaced the state's school funding formula with block grants; this meant additional funding cuts for many school districts, including millions of dollars for some of the larger ones.[8] Brownback claimed this was a spending increase and a policy win for school districts, arguing that state funding for public education had actually increased under his tenure. In fact, per-pupil state aid for classroom spending declined under Brownback, while spending for nonclassroom items such as school construction and teacher pensions increased.[9]

These education cuts—and the ongoing school funding case in the Kansas Supreme Court—fueled headlines warning of potential and actual public school closures. In April 2015, for example, numerous districts announced plans to end the school year early because of insufficient funds to maintain operations.[10] Even though the districts would still exceed the minimum number of school days required under state law, the closures generated negative press, often including statements from superintendents, school board members, and parent groups excoriating Brownback. Dozens of school districts had already eliminated or cut programs in response to the budget cuts, making the early closures seem even more dire.[11] News of such closures continued into 2016.[12]

The ongoing crisis barely fazed Brownback. He continued to echo the line that Kansas's problem was spending, not his tax experiment. In public, a smiling Brownback often repeated his 2014 campaign slogan: "The sun is shining in Kansas." He blamed others but not himself. Nonetheless, many conservatives in the legislature were tired of the constant bad headlines. Indeed, conservatives had already cut spending so substantially that their public attempts to toe Brownback's line were often little more than vague calls for greater efficiency; they had no specific ideas on how to cut spending further.

Brownback finally bowed to reality in 2015 when he persuaded conservatives to pass a $400 million tax increase by raising the state sales tax from 6.15 to 6.5 percent.[13] Factoring in local sales tax rates and special tax districts, this increase brought the cumulative sales tax in some Kansas localities up to 11.5 percent.[14] Most troubling to some, this tax rate applied to food, giving Kansas the second highest sales tax on food in the nation. Conservatives labeled the increase "tax reform" rather than a "tax hike" and pinned the blame on the Obama administration or on Democrats and moderate Republicans in the state legislature for not consenting to additional unspecified cuts that even many conservatives could not stomach. News stories showed Representative John Whitmer, a conservative Republican from Sedgwick County, crying on the house floor as he explained his sales tax vote, one of many conservatives who broke their campaign pledges not to raise taxes.[15]

The sales tax increase and corresponding spending cuts could not resolve the budget crisis, and legislators entered 2016 facing revenue shortfalls with few attractive solutions. When Brownback delivered his State of the State address that January, however, it was as if the budget crisis did not exist. He did not mention it, touching on abortion, welfare, the Affordable Care Act, and the Guantanamo Bay prison camp, among other issues.[16] The reaction to his speech varied: conservatives tersely wished Brownback had addressed the budget, and his political opponents outright accused him of not caring and intentionally trying to devastate core state services.[17] Brownback made it clear that any rollback of his tax policies was not on the table, regardless of reality.

Whatever Brownback's motives or beliefs about the budget crisis, Kansans were developing a very negative view of their governor. A year after his reelection, Morning Consult, in its fifty-state gubernatorial approval poll, pegged Brownback as the nation's most unpopular governor, with 26 percent of Kansans approving and 65 percent disapproving of him.[18] He maintained that dubious honor for most of the remainder of his governorship. Brownback's approval ratings from 2015 onward generally hovered between 20 and 25 percent, while his disapproval rating typically stood between 65 percent and the low 70s.

The 2016 Election

Regardless of what happened with federal politics in typically Republican Kansas, the conservative Republican political brand was set to be more of a liability than an asset for state legislative candidates in 2016. Brownback was deeply unpopular, and conservatives had unapologetically circled their political wagons around his governorship and his signature tax policies. But most important, the consequences of the tax experiment were powerfully felt among Kansans. Schools were cutting services or closing early, college tuition was increasing, road projects were canceled or delayed, new fees were instituted at understaffed motor vehicle offices, and mental health services were cut, among other effects.[19]

The first test came in August in the Republican primary. Unlike higher-profile congressional elections, legislative primaries in Kansas usually receive little attention, but they attracted greater than normal fanfare in 2016, especially from the national media, which expressed interest in the Brownback tax experiment and its implications for national politics. That said, public polling in these races was nonexistent. Most individual contests received little to no attention even from the Kansas media, which preferred stories with a broader scope; there were only anecdotal mentions of a few high-profile contests. Spending in these races was relatively minor, given the small scale of Kansas legislative districts—roughly seventy thousand persons in senate districts and twenty-three thousand in house districts after the 2010 census.[20] The turnout for primaries was often no more than a few thousand voters per district. Tracking outside spending in these races is challenging, since Kansas does not require frequent or detailed campaign finance reports, unlike federal disclosure requirements. Thus, it is often impossible to determine how much outside groups, which tend to be active in state legislative contests, spent in particular races.

The challenges of constructing an election narrative aside, the perception heading into the primary was that moderate Republicans were on the offense against conservatives. Although conservatives aggressively challenged moderate incumbents in some races, most challengers ran as moderates, and many appeared to have enough financial support and grassroots mobilization to make them viable contenders. Qualitatively, the electoral mood seemed markedly different from the great purge of moderates in the 2012 primaries or even the 2014 primaries, when the ideological status quo reigned.

But moderate Republicans did not necessarily constitute a coherent bloc. While some were encouraged to run by established political leaders, others were self-starters moved by ambition and reacting to the Brownback tax controversy. There was no singular force recruiting them or coordinating a united agenda. Indeed, even the label "moderate" downplays the often substantial disagreement on issues within this faction. Although it implies centrism, in practice, moderate Republicans span the ideological spectrum, from those who are arguably strong liberals with voting records virtually indistinguishable from those of the most proudly progressive Democrats to those who are more center-right in the traditional conservative mold of former US senator Bob Dole, with others scattered in between. Conservatives are not politically homogeneous either; some are best described as business-oriented, free-market types with little interest in social issues, whereas others are primarily socially and religiously motivated, Tea Party aligned, libertarian leaning, or even Trump-style white nationalists.

What united moderates in 2016 was their shared opposition to Brownback's tax and education policies and a common concern about the fallout from the budget crisis. Some issues, such as the expansion of Medicaid under the Affordable Care Act or opposition to the gubernatorial appointment of judges, drew larger but not universal agreement among moderates. On other issues, such as abortion, LGBT equality, and guns, moderates were more divided, and many sided with conservatives on these matters. But when it came to Brownback, opposition led to unity, at least on the symbolism of what they opposed if not on the substance of how to fix the problems created by his policies.

The role of Brownback and his controversial policies was evident in one race that earned national attention in the *New York Times*: the Twenty-First Senate District primary in Johnson County. The contest featured freshman incumbent Greg Smith, a conservative and reliable supporter of the Brownback agenda. His opponent was Dinah Sykes, a first-time candidate and former local PTA president. Citing funding for education as her motivation for running, she told the *New York Times*: "We're getting a bad reputation: that our state doesn't care about public education. . . . We live in Kansas because of the great quality of life, the great schools, the great amenities. I want my boys to have the opportunity to have the same."[21]

The messaging in this race was echoed in primaries around the state. On her Facebook campaign page, Sykes stayed on message about her opposition to Brownback and his tax experiment–induced budget crisis, especially its effects on education.[22] In a June 2016 post about health care, Sykes wrote, "If the increased debt, increased tuition, increased property taxes, and canceled roadway projects weren't enough, we see here another high cost associated with my opponent and Governor Brownback's failed experiment." In another preprimary post, she commented, "The Kansas PTA provides a guide that shows that on key votes since 2012 on tax policy, my opponent has consistently sided with and helped Governor Brownback implement his policies. No matter what postcards in the mail may say, my opponent cannot run from his votes and his votes tell a clear story of his support for Brownback['s] failed experiment." Another consistent theme was her support among the local education community, especially several groups in Johnson County created to assist anti-Brownback candidates in the primary and general elections.

Despite framing her campaign around opposition to the "failed" Brownback tax experiment, Sykes, like many other moderate Republican challengers and Democrats in the upcoming general election, was less clear on how to end that experiment. Implicitly, anti-Brownback candidates favored repealing the 2012 tax cut, which would involve raising taxes back to their former levels. In theory, that would alleviate much of the revenue problem and restore funding to education. Understandably, however, these challengers did not characterize their positions as favoring a tax increase, and when conservatives pressed them, they typically employed generic language about "undoing" or "ending" the Brownback tax cut. Challengers commonly focus on what they oppose rather than the specifics of what they support, and that was the case in Kansas in 2016.

Brownback was notably absent from Greg Smith's primary campaign. Smith's Facebook campaign page almost completely ignored Brownback in the run-up to the primary.[23] Indeed, Smith generally omitted his own support of the governor's agenda and political positions, apart from several posts—either from him or from linked sources—that blamed the Kansas Supreme Court and public employees for the school funding problem or touted positive economic news in Kansas. Smith also tried to distance himself from some of the more high-profile controversies associated with Brownback, claiming that he was working to bring more funding to Johnson County schools, close the limited liability corporation (LLC) tax loophole, and reduce the sales tax on food. Tellingly, in both the primary and the general election, Smith and many other conservatives often refused to appear at candidate forums not sponsored by conservative organizations, allowing their opponents to attack them and Brownback unchallenged.[24]

Nonetheless, Brownback-related content was only a small part of Smith's message. He focused on crime and law enforcement. He also articulated his opposition to abortion rights and featured endorsements from antiabortion interest groups. As the primary campaign closed, his online content shifted to an attempt to paint Sykes as a liberal. He accused her of not being a real Republican, favoring increases in property and income taxes, and opposing "proof of citizenship" laws for voter registration. Smith cited Sykes's endorsements from a "public labor union," "pro-abortion advocates," and "gun control advocates" as purported proof of her liberal politics.

With no public polling in any primary races and with visible spending by both moderates and conservatives, it was unclear which message would prevail with Republican voters statewide: opposition to Brownback or support for conservative politics, Brownback aside. On primary day, Sykes decisively defeated Smith, 58 percent to 42 percent.[25] Indeed, moderate Republicans flipped nine state senate seats and approximately a dozen house seats, defeating several prominent conservatives. Every moderate-leaning legislative incumbent survived the primary. The disaffection reflected by Brownback's low statewide approval ratings penetrated the Republican base and dealt conservatives a strong blow in numerous races where the threat to core state services such as education was evident in campaigns, even if primary voters had concerns that anti-Brownback moderates were less than conservative.

The same dynamic that aided moderate Republicans in the primary helped

Democratic challengers in the general election. Democrats generally followed the same script as moderates, attacking conservatives for supporting Brownback and his policies and tying them to the fallout from the ongoing budget crisis. Indeed, the similarities between Democrats and moderate Republicans—their messaging, their issue positions, their donors, and the outside groups supporting them—were so striking that observers sometimes struggled to ascertain the genuine differences between the two factions, other than their partisan affiliations.[26]

Despite the commonalities between Democrats and moderate Republicans, the rift between the factions was deep. As I frequently observed during the campaign, prominent activists, especially those associated with the grassroots education community, professed their belief on social media and at community forums that Democrats and moderate Republicans would establish a formal coalition after the election to select legislative leaders and advance a common policy agenda. National media also fueled those speculations.[27] Although these unlikely coalitions have developed sporadically in other states, they are extremely rare and typically unplanned before the election, and they have never happened in Kansas. Some activists who seemed to wholeheartedly believe that Democrats and moderate Republicans were truly "the same team" reacted angrily when others pushed back on the prospects of such a coalition.

Many grassroots activists who were liberal in their policy preferences nonetheless identified as moderate Republicans. They expressed anger at Democrats for being on the ballot against moderate Republicans and often tried to shame the Democrats into dropping out of these races. They implored Democrats to focus their resources on defeating conservatives, many of whom were running in safely Republican districts that Democrats were unlikely to win.

After the election, these tensions between Democrats and moderate Republicans shifted to the legislative arena. Not surprisingly, the moderate Republicans caucused with conservative pro-Brownback legislators of their own party and often voted for these conservatives for legislative leadership positions. Although Democrats and moderate Republicans often voted together against key conservative bills, they often did not support each other in procedural and policy matters when one faction had an amendment or bill it wanted to advance. Personal tensions between Democratic and moderate Republican legislators often flared publicly on social media, in newsletters, and at community forums.

Factional politics aside, Democrats benefited from a crop of candidates whose campaigns were more aggressive and of higher quality than usual. The most successful candidates typically started their campaigns early in the year, well before the primary; consistently employed anti-Brownback messaging; mounted strong door-to-door grassroots campaigns; and raised substantial funds, at least by Kansas standards, where candidates in competitive races often raise as little as $20,000 in state house races and $50,000 in state senate races.

Conservatives responded to Democratic challengers much as they responded to moderates—ignoring or deflecting Brownback, emphasizing local connections and other issues unrelated to the governor, and portraying Democrats as extreme liberals. But just as those tactics largely failed conservatives in the primary, they failed in the general election as well, at least in the house. On Election Day, even as Kansas Republicans were sweeping federal races, Democrats flipped thirteen seats in the Kansas House, all but one from conservatives. They lost one open seat that had been trending strongly Republican, for a net gain of twelve seats. Of their thirteen victories, nine were in districts that had supported Democrat Paul Davis in the 2014 gubernatorial race. Curiously, some of those districts had supported Davis by more than twenty points while simultaneously ousting Democratic incumbents in favor of pro-Brownback conservatives—a testament to how poorly prepared Democrats were in 2014 to capitalize on anti-Brownback sentiment. In 2016, in a sign of notable ticket splitting, voters in eight of those flipped districts supported Donald Trump over Hillary Clinton—by margins of up to forty-eight points—while simultaneously replacing conservative Republican legislators with Democrats.

Minimizing their overall gains, Democrats flipped only one Kansas Senate district but held all their own seats, for a net gain of one and a total of nine seats out of forty in the chamber. Nonetheless, the cumulative damage to conservatives between the primary and the general election was substantial. The net changes in the house left that chamber divided roughly into thirds: forty Democrats and eighty-five Republicans about equally divided between moderate and conservative legislators, although the ideological leanings of numerous legislators varied based on the issue. Even though moderates caucused with conservatives, Democrats had ousted enough conservatives to strengthen the moderates' power within the Republican caucus. Conservatives now had to deal with moderates to advance their own goals in the house or face the prospect of moderates and Democrats uniting in majority opposition.

Conservatives still held a slim majority of the senate's forty seats—again, with some legislators swinging between factions on certain issues—but their power was substantially diminished. Conservatives in Topeka could no longer pass legislation unilaterally. They had to bargain, jeopardizing Brownback's policy agenda. And like it or not, Democrats and moderate Republicans needed each other to empower themselves: Democrats needed moderates to form majorities, and moderates needed Democrats to call conservatives' political bluffs and stop their legislation. Fulfilling their respective campaign promises to check Brownback necessitated an uneasy unity.

The Legislative Interim

Voters had reelected Brownback in 2014 with reservations. By 2016, doubts about his leadership finally translated to political change and ended conservative dominance of the legislature. This change was evident in the outcome of leadership elections. In the Kansas Senate, although conservative Susan Wagle of Sedgwick County was the consensus pick among Republicans for reelection as senate president, some members with more moderate records filled lower leadership positions.[28] In the Kansas House, conservative Ron Ryckman of Johnson County became speaker, but moderate Republicans won positions as majority leader, assistant majority leader, and caucus chair. Senate Democrats maintained their leadership, but house Democrats replaced their consensus-oriented minority leader with Jim Ward of Sedgwick County. Ward had gained a reputation as a feisty liberal who showed little interest in compromising with Brownback conservatives and a willingness to criticize moderate Republicans.

Given the campaign rhetoric of Democrats and moderate Republicans, expectations were high that they would not only stop Brownback from advancing his agenda further but also, as promised, repeal his signature tax cuts. But delivering on that promise was difficult. Conservatives still had influence, and although Democrats and moderate Republicans were united in their general opposition to Brownback's most visible failings, they did not necessarily agree on specific remedies.

After one of the longest legislative sessions in Kansas history, those expectations culminated in the legislature overriding Brownback's veto of a bill that largely repealed his tax plan. The bill halted the long-term plan to reduce tax rates further, restored three brackets of marginal tax rates, and increased tax rates in all brackets—for example, increasing the tax rate for the wealthiest Kansans from 4.6 percent to 5.2 percent.[29] It also eliminated the LLC loophole that had resulted in at least 330,000 entities—far more than the Brownback administration's forecast—using that exemption to avoid tax liabilities.

The road to override was contentious. Democrats and moderate Republicans were divided over the scope of the repeal. This often devolved into partisan bickering, but they ultimately found common ground after the two factions' women—calling themselves the Bipartisan Women's Caucus—brokered an agreement.[30] Conservatives were largely intractable in defending Brownback's policies, voicing doomsday warnings about the repeal and calling for additional unspecified budget cuts.[31] Ultimately, however, facing a projected $900 million budget shortfall over the next two fiscal years and Kansas Supreme Court rulings that education funding was inadequate, several conservatives—including house speaker Ron Ryckman and senate majority leader Jim Denning of Johnson County—joined Brownback opponents in overriding the veto when it became evident that conservatives had no counterproposal and that the overwhelming majority in both chambers supported repeal of the tax experiment.[32]

A more moderate legislature did not necessarily translate to more moderate policies on other matters. Medicaid expansion, which would have covered 150,000 lower-income Kansans and helped struggling rural hospitals, was a priority for many Democrats and moderate Republicans.[33] Expansion easily passed both chambers but fell just shy of veto-proof support. Brownback predictably vetoed Medicaid expansion, and the house failed to override.

While Medicaid united Democrats and moderate Republicans, other issues divided them and had moderates siding with conservatives. For example, many moderates supported a so-called font bill that required abortion providers to furnish patients with certain information about the physician in black ink on white paper using twelve-point Times New Roman font, a measure that proponents called "transparency" and opponents called unnecessary regulation.[34] Many moderates also supported a so-called religious freedom bill that allowed faith-based entities providing adoption and foster care services that received financial support from the state to deny services to gay and lesbian Kansans.[35] This bill passed by one vote in the state house, and moderate Republican support was decisive in its passage.

The 2018 Gubernatorial Race

Brownback had essentially built his governorship on his tax experiment. With that largely repealed, rumors arose that he would not finish his term. That speculation came to fruition in early 2018 when the US Senate confirmed Brownback—by a tie vote broken by the vice president—as ambassador-at-large for international religious freedom, a largely symbolic post that, at a minimum, spared Brownback from serving as governor for another year after his leadership had been repudiated.[36] Brownback resigned the governorship soon thereafter, elevating Lieutenant Governor Jeff Colyer once the resignation became effective.

After his nomination as ambassador, Brownback began transitioning administrative leadership to Colyer. When Brownback's nomination was delayed over his opposition to LGBT equality, the situation in Kansas became awkward: Brownback was still technically the governor, and it was uncertain for much of 2017 when or if he would be confirmed, yet Colyer was perceived as leading the administration. This situation focused attention on Colyer, who had kept a low profile since becoming lieutenant governor in 2011 and had not strongly defined himself as separate from Brownback before his anticipated gubernatorial bid.

The Republican Primary

The newly minted Governor Colyer would not be coronated as the Republican nominee in 2018. Prior to his succession, Colyer had not publicly established himself as a gubernatorial candidate, which attracted a crowded primary field.[37] The presumed front-runner at that point was secretary of state Kris Kobach, a controversial figure and an ally of President Trump. Kobach gained national attention with his anti-immigration politics, concern over largely imaginary election fraud, and focus on imposing new voter registration regulations.[38] Because of Kobach's "proof of citizenship" requirement, more than thirty thousand Kansans were unable to navigate a complicated and ultimately discredited voter registration process.[39]

After several prominent Republicans dropped out, the final primary field consisted of seven candidates: six conservatives and one moderate, former state senator Jim Barnett. Widely seen as a conservative when he was the

Republican gubernatorial nominee in 2006, Barnett had tracked more liberal in the interim, to the point that his public positions were barely distinguishable from those of Democrats.[40] Despite having the moderate Republican vote to himself, Barnett never gained much traction. He was largely self-funded and drew skeptical reactions when he selected his wife as his running mate.[41]

The Republican race essentially came down to a choice between Colyer and Kobach. As the primary campaign progressed, polling was relatively scarce. Polls affiliated with Kobach and his network generally showed him with a ten-point lead over Colyer, while polls affiliated with Colyer and his network indicated a tied race. Those numbers did not budge during the race, nor did most polls provide much information about the attitudes of potential primary voters.

The April 2018 Kansas Speaks survey offered data about how Kansans in general—not just potential primary voters—viewed the candidates.[42] Kobach was more well known than Colyer, with 85 percent versus 55 percent name recognition. The public's evaluation of the two candidates differed wildly. Only 30 percent of Kansans had a positive opinion of Kobach, whereas 51 percent viewed him negatively and 21 percent were neutral. For Colyer, 29 percent of respondents viewed him positively, 30 percent negatively, and 41 percent had no opinion. No other Republican candidate enjoyed more than 40 percent name recognition, and most respondents had no opinion on any of them.

Although the Kansas Speaks survey did not provide detailed breakdowns, it reported that respondents who self-identified as "strong Republicans"—potentially the most likely primary voters—liked Kobach somewhat more than they liked Colyer. This created a fundamental dilemma for Republicans. They could nominate the controversial Kobach, who was disliked by most Kansans but preferred by Republicans, consistently emphasized issues that were proverbial "red meat" for the party base, and shared Trump's talent for attracting media attention with his flamboyance. Or they could nominate the conventional Republican Colyer, who was more unknown and undefined, less controversial, and a safer politician who meshed well with the party establishment but was inextricably tied to Brownback.

The Republican primary campaign was surprisingly sedate, with no clear turning points. Kobach and Colyer differed greatly in style, but they were reasonably similar in ideology and issue preferences, which tamped down the negativity between the two. Indeed, given their political similarities, personality and style dominated the campaign.

One incident illustrates the centrality of persona. In June, Kobach appeared at the Old Shawnee Days parade in Johnson County, riding in a Jeep painted like the American flag.[43] Mounted on the Jeep was a replica of a machine gun—complete with ammunition hanging from it—which many spectators thought was real, and a Trump bobblehead doll. Marching behind Kobach was the gun-control group Moms Demand Action. It was the perfect storm for drama. Facing criticism, Kobach tweeted, "The outrage over the replica gun on the back of a patriotic jeep is the left trying to attack guns and your #2A rights. I will not back down in the face of a snowflake meltdown and outrage culture."[44] He labeled any criticism of his appearance as an attack on gun ownership itself.[45] The incident garnered national attention and dominated media coverage for a week, strongly associating Kobach with gun culture and arguably overshadowing the National Rifle Association's later endorsement of Colyer.[46]

The outcome of the primary seemed highly uncertain going into its final days, despite Trump's endorsement of Kobach on Twitter just days before the voting.[47] The results were extremely close on election night, and it appeared that provisional ballots, especially in populous Johnson County, would decide the race. Ironically, given Colyer's criticism of Kobach's performance in administering elections, the two campaigns quickly positioned themselves for a potential legal battle over the provisional ballots, the possibility of a recount, and delayed election certification.[48] In mid-August, in a surprising move, Colyer decided not to pursue his legal options, conceding the race and endorsing Kobach.[49]

In the final tally, Kobach defeated Colyer by 343 votes, 40.6 to 40.5 percent.[50] With such a close race, any number of factors could have altered the outcome. Most prominently, however, was the role of "spoilers." The moderate Barnett ultimately received 8.8 percent of the vote, and the other conservative candidates received about 10 percent cumulatively. Had a handful of those voters strategically cast their ballots for Colyer instead, even if he was not their first choice, he might have beaten Kobach. Instead, Kobach benefited from divided opposition and a strong base that responded to his flair.

Kobach's win, however, likely saddled Republicans with the less electable of the two major candidates—the one who was best known but most unpopular and had a knack for political theater. Despite the early perception that his national prominence would translate to political strength, Kobach turned out to be a poor fund-raiser, with less appeal among small grassroots donors than other candidates. His running mate, wealthy businessman Wink Hartman, loaned the campaign $2.3 million, constituting the bulk of Kobach's campaign fund.[51] And, as revealed after the general election, Kobach proved unwilling to take professional campaign advice and failed to assemble a professional staff.[52] Or, as one Republican operative told the *Kansas City Star*, Kobach's campaign was "the most dysfunctional thing I've ever seen in my life."[53]

The Democratic Primary

It is impossible to know whether Colyer would have been a better candidate than Kobach, but the latter's flaws gave Democrats an opening. As the Republican drama captured media attention throughout 2017, the Democratic primary proceeded quietly, with few headlines and no apparent front-runner. Major candidates included house minority leader Jim Ward of Sedgwick County, former Wichita mayor Carl Brewer, and former Kansas secretary of agriculture Josh Svaty, who had once represented rural Ellsworth County in the state house.

As 2018 approached, Kansas's gubernatorial race was the only one in the country with no female candidates (a factoid made even more bizarre by reports that six teenage boys had declared their candidacies for governor, since Kansas lacked an age requirement).[54] Strategically, this offered an opening for a woman to run, especially on the Democratic side. The #MeToo Movement and the political reaction to Trump, especially among women, was fueling a surge of female Democratic—but not Republican—candidates in congressional and state races.[55] And ultimately, the political environment was exceptionally conducive to these Democratic women winning primaries and general elections in record numbers.[56] Moreover, no Democratic candidate had emerged from the more urban eastern third of the state, where Kansas Democrats were more plentiful.

The details of the Democratic primary made the strategic space for a female candidate particularly inviting. Although Ward himself was not accused, when a former legislative staffer alleged sexual harassment and other inappropriate behavior toward women at the statehouse, the implication was that Ward had not addressed the situation adequately.[57] For Svaty, the challenge was abortion.[58] As a legislator, Svaty had voted with Republicans on numerous measures to limit abortion access, including preventing state college insurance plans from covering abortion, imposing licensing and facilities regulations meant to discourage abortion clinics from operating, defining a fetus as a legal person, and banning late-term abortion, among other measures.[59] Although Brewer had no obvious problems with female voters, he proved incapable of capitalizing on his opponents' vulnerabilities. Understandably, the murder of his grandson kept him off the campaign trail in late 2017, but observers noted that his campaign lacked energy and resources.[60]

Into this void stepped state senator Laura Kelly of Shawnee County in mid-December 2017. Kelly was a reluctant candidate, but prodding from former governor Kathleen Sebelius and other Democrats who were dissatisfied with the primary field lured her into the race.[61] Kelly had served in the legislature since 2005, defeating a conservative incumbent and consistently winning competitive races in her Republican-leaning district. She was usually one of the top fund-raisers in the legislature and had cultivated an image as a moderate Democrat who collaborated well with moderate Republicans.[62] The enthusiasm greeting her entry into the race was evident in the 2017 campaign finance disclosures, which covered the entire calendar year. Kelly raised $156,000 in just two weeks, with no self-funding.[63] This was more than the amounts raised by Brewer and by Ward, who dropped out before the primary,[64] but less than the $193,000 Svaty raised in seven months of campaigning. Kelly immediately became the front-runner, and this would be the case until the August primary election.

The Democratic primary progressed quietly. The only minor drama came from predictable but low-key dustups between Kelly and Svaty at forums where she criticized his abortion record and he criticized her gun record, especially her support for legislation that allowed concealed handguns to be carried on college campuses.[65] He also attacked her stance on Kobach's proof-of-citizenship voter registration law, which had attracted some Democratic support in the legislature before its actual implementation proved controversial.

The rare legitimate polling showed Kelly leading, Brewer in second place, and Svaty in third. Kelly accrued major endorsements from politicians and political groups, dominated fund-raising, and assembled a professional campaign team. Svaty was viewed as her nearest competitor—at least financially, given Brewer's unviable fund-raising levels. However, Svaty spent an unusually large share of his money on consultants—with little obvious benefit—and aired no television advertisements. Perhaps bowing to the inevitable, Svaty spent almost all his money before the primary, and the only polling his campaign released was an "informed vote" question that showed him effectively tied with Kelly, but only after respondents had been read statements about the candidates. The content of those statements was never disclosed in the polling report, further discrediting Svaty's already questionable survey data.

Predictably, Kelly won the primary with 51.4 percent of the vote, carrying many vote-rich urban counties by relative landslides.[66] Even though Svaty portrayed himself as the rural candidate, Kelly generally dominated rural Kansas, except for some clusters of sparsely populated counties that backed Svaty. Consistent with polling, Svaty placed third behind Brewer, probably due to Brewer's built-in name recognition in the Wichita metro area. This likely allowed Brewer to carry several populous counties near Wichita and place second behind Kelly in many rural counties in the Wichita media market, which covers central and western Kansas.

The General Election

After the primary, the race between Kobach and Kelly was not straightforward. The wild card was independent candidate Greg Orman. Orman had a long history with Democrats, financially supporting Barack Obama, Hillary Clinton, the Kansas Democratic Party, and Kelly herself during her brief run for Congress in 2010.[67] After his own short-lived run for the US Senate as a Democrat in 2008, Orman proclaimed himself a "centrist Independent" and linked himself to national organizations that promoted such candidates.[68] When he ran for US Senate in 2014 as an independent, Democrats saw him as a more viable candidate against unpopular Republican senator Pat Roberts, and they successfully fought Kobach in court—with the encouragement of US Senate Democrats—to withdraw their own nominee from the ballot so as not to split the non-Republican vote. Orman became the de facto Democrat.

Orman's candidacy in 2018 immediately caused speculation that he would be a spoiler, not earning enough support to win but drawing enough votes from nonconservatives to split the opposition and elect Kobach, just as Kobach had won the Republican primary in a divided field.[69] This speculation was based on two rationales. First, data from the 2014 exit poll indicated that Orman's support was essentially a smaller version of the same coalition that supported Democrat Paul Davis in the gubernatorial race. In both the exit poll and precinct-level data, there was no evidence of a widespread "uniquely Greg Orman" voter—someone who otherwise voted Republican but backed Orman for the Senate. Thus, Orman had no particular appeal among voters that Democrats were not already attracting, countering speculation that his candidacy might draw evenly from Kelly and Kobach.

Second, despite Orman's symbolic self-labeling as a "centrist" and a "moderate," on policy issues, he looked like a liberal. Orman justified his candidacy through his belief that the ranks of independent voters were growing, that those voters were disillusioned with the major parties, and that they wanted a moderate third option.[70] These beliefs do not fully square with actual patterns of party identification or voter behavior, even if that simplistic analysis sounds logical on paper.[71] During the campaign, Orman struggled to differentiate himself from Kelly on policy, and while he sometimes labeled her a liberal extremist and a Topeka "insider," he also attacked her from the left on guns, Medicaid expansion, and proof of citizenship.[72]

Indeed, at times it seemed that the centrist Orman was trying to out-liberal the Democrat: taking left-leaning policy positions, embracing the symbolism and platitudes of moderation, and basing his campaign more on frustration with politics than on policy per se. In this context, it is understandable why the media sometimes expressed frustration with Orman's frequent avoidance of policy specifics. For example, when the *Shawnee Mission Post* offered candidates space for a short essay on school funding, Orman's campaign ignored the offer.[73] Yet it later complained that the Kansas press "engages in multiple choice journalism demanding yes or no answers."[74] Later in the race, the Orman campaign promoted several largely noncontroversial ideas for political reform and promised a series of policy-oriented reveals on major issues that never materialized.[75]

Polls leading up to the general election showed just how serious a threat Orman posed to Kelly. In every poll from early August through Election Day, Kelly and Kobach were statistically tied, with neither enjoying a lead of more than four points.[76] The Orman vote varied from 9 percent to 12 percent in polling throughout the campaign; when asked, his voters generally preferred Kelly as their second choice, sometimes by as much as a three-to-one margin. Orman's campaign attacked the polling as biased and flawed but never released a poll showing him in a better position.[77]

Whatever Orman originally saw as his path to victory, as the campaign progressed, it was clear that Kelly had spoiled his narrative. Indeed, she was likely the Democrat he least wanted to face. Shortly before the primary vote, Grow Kansas Action Fund, a dark-money group linked to Orman's former campaign manager, attacked Kelly and Colyer, attempting to make them both look unappealing to their respective party bases.[78] Presumably, the goal was to indirectly support Svaty and Kobach, a general election matchup that would have allowed Orman to position himself to the left of the underfunded Svaty on abortion and frame himself as more appealing and more electable than Kobach.

Orman's team contended that his ability to self-finance made him a viable candidate and claimed that Democrats could not raise sufficient funds.[79] Orman spent about $1.3 million of his own money on the campaign and raised an additional $1 million in donations skewed toward large out-of-state donors. However, Kelly ultimately raised $3.5 million, with no self-funding and leaning heavily toward smaller donors in Kansas. Kelly roughly matched Kobach's $3.7 million war chest, $2.3 million of which took the form of loans—later forgiven—from his running mate. Moreover, the dark-money group Kansas Values Institute raised several million dollars in support of Kelly.

Orman made a strategic play for moderate Republicans by recruiting one of their own from the legislature as his running mate.[80] However, Kelly trumped that move by earning the endorsements of many key moderate Republicans. Most notably, two dozen current and former Republican lawmakers endorsed Kelly, as did former governors Bill Graves and Mike Hayden and former US senators Nancy Kassebaum and Sheila Frahm.[81] Neither Graves nor Kassebaum had ever previously endorsed a Democrat in a statewide race. Ultimately, Orman's own campaign treasurer and former moderate Republican state senator Tim Owens resigned from the Orman team to endorse Kelly, warning that Orman was risking a Kobach victory.[82]

With Orman neutralized, except for how his votes would ultimately affect the race, Kelly was free to focus on Kobach. Late in the campaign, however, a Republican super-PAC attempted to make the Orman spoiler element relevant again by airing an ad that depicted him as a more favorable choice than Kelly, while barely mentioning Kobach.[83] The interplay between Kelly and Kobach had certain moments that shaped the election narrative, but polls indicated that it was a stagnant fight, with voters seemingly equally divided between the two, and neither developed a clear lead. Despite marked media attention, there is no evidence that events such as Trump's visit to Topeka for a campaign rally, any of the debates between the candidates, or Kobach's statement that he thought Brownback had been a good governor had any appreciable effect on voters.[84]

Kelly and Kobach largely talked past each other in the campaign, emphasizing different issues and using lines of attack that rarely developed into deeper policy exchanges. Kelly's advertising focused on her image, touting her reputation as a moderate and her support from moderate Republicans.[85] On policy, her messaging emphasized the issues that had hurt conservatives under Brownback. She praised the repeal of the Brownback tax experiment and attacked Kobach for his desire to reinstate it, but she was committed to balancing the state budget without raising taxes and to cutting the sales tax on food. She cited her record on public education and support from education organizations while criticizing Kobach's comments that public schools were overfunded. Other less prominent themes in her advertising included reproductive rights, Medicaid expansion, government management, and the underfunding of both transportation and public safety under Brownback.

Kobach's advertising was markedly different on the issues, but like Kelly, he focused on creating a positive image: labeling himself a political "outsider" who would defy the Topeka "establishment," having friends and family attest to his personal character and strength, and showing pictures of himself on a farm in casual dress.[86] He also associated himself with conservative imagery: Kobach handling firearms, Kobach with President Trump and Donald Trump Jr., and a character endorsement from a veteran who called himself a "fighter in the Battle of Benghazi."

The central issue in Kobach's advertising was immigration. He touted his role as an immigration adviser to Trump and devoted an entire negative ad to Kelly, calling her an "open borders extremist" who "voted for sanctuary cities" and who "wanted to give illegal aliens welfare benefits" and in-state tuition at universities. Other issues included generic promises to increase blue-collar jobs, cut property tax appraisals and income tax rates, and lower electricity rates. One ad featured pictures of Kelly and former president Obama with an equal sign between them. Kobach largely avoided the issue of funding for education, though late in the campaign, one commercial included his commitment to spend 75 percent of education funding inside classrooms but no promise to increase the overall amount spent on education.

On Election Day, Kelly received 48 percent of the vote, Kobach received 43 percent, and Orman attracted only 6.5 percent—lower than his projected total in the polls.[87] A five-point win was consistent with the margin of error in most polls, but the size of Kelly's victory and the relatively early call of the race on election night surprised some observers. Kelly won only nine of Kansas's 105 counties, but they were generally the more populous and vote rich: Johnson, Wyandotte, Douglas, Shawnee, Riley, Lyon, Crawford, Sedgwick, and Harvey. Although Kobach swept smaller rural counties, often by landslide margins, his victories in many of the more populous counties such as Leavenworth, Reno, Cowley, and Finney were too narrow to overcome Kelly's 45,000-vote margin in Johnson County. Orman placed a distant third in every county.

When the last Democratic governor, Kathleen Sebelius, won her first term in 2002, her geographic coalition included much of rural Kansas, where Kelly lost, but it excluded Johnson County, where Kelly won convincingly.[88] This morphing map generally reflects changes in party coalitions nationally during that period, with Democrats orienting toward whites with college degrees, who tend to cluster in suburbia, and minorities, and Republicans orienting toward white evangelicals and whites without college degrees, who are often more rural.[89]

The Fox News/AP Voter Analysis survey reflected these demographic divides (table 9.1).[90] The Kelly coalition included women, voters younger than forty-five, whites, non-whites (about equally divided between Latinos and African Americans), college-educated voters, the lowest- and highest-income voters, non-evangelical whites, Catholics and seculars, suburban and urban voters, and voters living in households without guns. Kelly's margin among these groups varied, ranging from a one-point plurality among whites to a forty-nine-point win among the religiously unaffiliated. LGBT Kansans accounted for 7 percent of voters, too small a sample to reliably estimate their candidate support; however, given the typical voting patterns of LGBT Americans, they likely supported Kelly. Men constituted 48 percent of voters and supported Kobach over Kelly 47 percent to 45 percent.

Despite the strong gender narrative surrounding women and female candidates in 2018, other demographic divisions often trumped the gender divide. In Kansas, Kelly won men with college degrees by nine percentage points and women with college degrees by twenty-five points. However, her winning margin among women without college degrees was just three points, and among

Table 9.1. Voter Demographics in the 2018 Kansas Gubernatorial Race, Fox/AP Voter Analysis

	Voter Share (%)	Kelly (%)	Kobach (%)	Orman (%)	Other (%)
Gender					
Male	48	45	47	6	2
Female	52	51	40	7	3
Age (years)					
18–29	12	55	30	8	7
30–44	22	53	36	8	3
45–64	39	45	47	7	2
65+	27	46	48	4	1
Race					
White	87	46	45	7	2
Non-white	13	61	27	7	5
Gender among whites					
Male	42	44	48	6	2
Female	45	48	42	7	2
Education					
High school or less	23	45	45	7	4
Some college/ associate's degree	34	42	47	7	3
College graduate	27	51	42	6	2
Postgraduate study	16	61	32	6	1
Education by gender					
Male non–college graduate	25	39	50	8	3
Male college graduate	23	51	42	5	2
Female non–college graduate	32	46	43	7	4
Female college graduate	20	59	34	6	1
Income					
<$50,000	34	47	41	8	4
$50,000–$99,999	38	45	46	6	3
$100,000+	28	54	40	5	1
White evangelical					
Yes	29	28	61	8	3
No	71	56	35	6	2
Religious denomination among whites					
Protestant/other Christian	49	37	54	7	2
Catholic	16	48	45	6	2
None/unaffiliated	16	70	21	5	4

Gun in household					
Yes	57	41	51	7	1
No	43	58	33	7	2
Community type					
Urban	15	59	33	6	2
Suburban	40	54	39	5	3
Small town/rural	44	39	50	8	3

men without college degrees, she lost to Kobach by eleven points. The urban-rural divide also outweighed gender: Kelly won both men and women in urban and suburban communities, while Kobach won both men and women in rural and small-town communities.

Although Kobach won some voter groups, his winning margins were often small. He won by double digits only among men without college degrees, evangelical whites, Protestants, voters in households with guns, and voters in small-town and rural communities. Orman won no voter group.

As table 9.2 shows, partisanship and ideology were predictably gigantic divisions. Among voters identifying as Democrats or independents leaning Democratic, Kelly won 93 percent of the vote. But among voters identifying as Republican or independents leaning Republican, Kobach won only 75 percent, losing 17 percent of votes to Kelly and 6 percent to Orman. Pure independents, making up just 11 percent of voters, voted 56 percent for Kelly and gave 16 percent each to Kobach and Orman. On ideology, Kelly unsurprisingly won liberals and Kobach won conservatives, but nearly two-thirds of moderates voted for Kelly.

The "centrist" independent Orman failed to assemble a coalition of either centrists or independents, as both supported Kelly. Although only 14 percent of voters claimed to have a negative view of both major parties, 71 percent of them voted for Kelly, with Orman placing third. Perhaps one reason why Orman underperformed was that Kansans who made their decisions in the last few days of the campaign—8 percent of voters—preferred Kelly (50 percent) over Kobach (29 percent). These voters were likely a mix of long-term undecideds and perhaps Orman voters switching to Kelly due to fears of a Kobach victory.

The Fox/AP poll did not ask voters their opinions of Orman, but in tracking polls, respondents were often divided on him or leaned toward a

Table 9.2. Vote by Nonissue Factors in the 2018 Kansas Gubernatorial Race, Fox/AP Voter Analysis

	Total (%)	Kelly (%)	Kobach (%)	Orman (%)	Other (%)
Partisanship					
Democratic/lean Dem.	35	93	2	4	1
Republican/lean Rep.	54	17	75	6	2
Pure independent	11	56	16	16	12
Ideology					
Liberal	25	87	7	5	1
Moderate	33	63	24	9	4
Conservative	43	15	77	5	2
Opinion of Kelly					
Very favorable	30	97	3	0	0
Somewhat favorable	29	72	19	7	3
Somewhat unfavorable	18	5	79	12	3
Very unfavorable	22	5	87	7	2
Opinion of Kobach					
Very favorable	24	2	96	2	0
Somewhat favorable	21	5	91	3	1
Somewhat unfavorable	11	56	17	20	7
Very unfavorable	45	90	2	7	2
View of major parties					
Favorable of both	3	N/A	N/A	N/A	N/A
Favorable Rep; unfavorable Dem.	49	7	86	5	1
Favorable Dem.; unfavorable Rep.	35	96	1	2	1
Unfavorable of both	14	71	13	12	3
Trump job approval					
Approve strongly	32	5	89	4	1
Approve somewhat	20	24	60	12	5
Disapprove somewhat	9	64	21	11	4
Disapprove strongly	39	91	2	5	2

somewhat negative assessment. Sixty percent of voters saw Kelly positively, versus 40 percent negatively; Kobach's numbers were 56 percent negative to 44 percent positive. Very negative views of Kobach outnumbered somewhat negative views by a four-to-one margin, suggesting that he never altered Kansans' strongly negative preprimary views.

Table 9.3. Vote by Issue Attitudes in the 2018 Kansas Gubernatorial Race, Fox/AP Voter Analysis

	Total (%)	Kelly (%)	Kobach (%)	Orman (%)	Other (%)
Raising taxes to increase public school funding					
Strongly favor	20	81	13	4	2
Somewhat favor	39	58	33	6	3
Somewhat oppose	23	28	61	9	2
Strongly oppose	18	17	73	7	2
Brownback's tax policies					
Good	19	5	88	5	2
Bad	81	60	30	7	3
Condition of national economy					
Excellent/good	67	39	53	6	2
Not so good/poor	33	73	14	8	5
Affordable Care Act					
Repeal entirely	31	9	83	6	2
Repeal parts	30	38	49	9	3
Leave as is	9	76	14	6	4
Expand	30	89	5	4	1
Immigrants in the US					
Do more to help the country	60	73	19	5	3
Do more to hurt the country	40	20	67	10	3
Immigrants living in the US illegally					
Offer a chance to apply for legal status	70	62	29	6	3
Deport to the country they came from	30	15	75	7	2
US-Mexico border wall					
Strongly favor	33	10	84	4	2
Somewhat favor	17	31	51	13	5
Somewhat oppose	11	64	21	10	4
Strongly oppose	39	91	2	5	2
Abortion					
Legal in all cases	19	72	20	6	2
Legal in most cases	35	69	24	5	2
Illegal in most cases	32	24	64	8	4
Illegal in all cases	14	18	73	7	2
Gun laws					
Should be more strict	52	72	20	6	2
Should be less strict	8	N/A	N/A	N/A	N/A
Should be kept as they are	39	22	69	8	1

The survey included two issue questions particularly relevant to the campaign. As table 9.3 shows, when asked about "support for raising taxes to increase funding for public schools," voters favored doing so, 59 percent to 41 percent. Eighty-one percent of voters assessed "Brownback's tax policies" as a "bad thing," and just 19 percent thought they were a "good thing." On balance, voters' responses to these two questions reflected an electorate with a negative view of Brownback, which carried over to Kobach's defense of Brownback's policy legacy.

Other issues that were less central to the campaign also proved to be significant points of division. As strongly as Kansans had backed Trump in 2016, just 52 percent of voters approved of his performance as president. And despite the tendency of positive economic perceptions to benefit candidates of the same party as the president, Kobach managed only a fourteen-point win among the 67 percent of voters with "excellent" or "good" perceptions of the national economy.

Medicaid expansion under the Affordable Care Act played a role in the campaign, mitigating Republicans' general negativity toward Obamacare. Only 31 percent of voters were in favor of repealing the law entirely. Polling had typically shown that about 70 percent of Kansans approved of Medicaid expansion, despite its ties to Obamacare, suggesting that the "Obama" connotation did not hurt Kelly significantly.[91]

Although Kobach highlighted his anti-immigration views, Kansas voters did not necessarily share those sentiments, as evidenced by their responses to the three immigration questions in table 9.3. They were evenly split on support for a border wall with Mexico but felt that immigrants did "more to help the country" than hurt it and favored a pathway to citizenship for illegal immigrants.

Likewise, voters did not take a strongly conservative stand on abortion or guns, two minor issues in the campaign. Fifty-four percent supported legal abortion in all or most cases, and 46 wanted abortion to be mostly or entirely illegal. Despite Kansas's strong pro-life stereotype, only 14 percent of voters thought abortion should be totally illegal, and only 4 percent of voters said abortion was the most important issue facing the country. Those voters preferred Kobach over Kelly, 82 percent to 14 percent, suggesting that conservatives had more intense feelings about abortion, even though most voters were generally pro-choice. Only 6 percent of voters cited guns as their top issue, and they voted for

Kelly 78 percent to 14 percent. When asked specifically about guns, 52 percent of Kansas voters said gun laws should be stricter, 39 percent thought they should remain the same, and 8 percent thought they should be less strict.

The Aftermath

As a candidate, Kelly took positions that contrasted strongly with both Brownback and Kobach, but she was cautious not to promise too much. She made few bold statements about taking Kansas in a more liberal policy direction. Rather, she focused on key issues related to Brownback's legacy and good management of the state government. Post election, Kelly frequently used the term "triage" to describe her approach to governing, "listing K–12 education funding, Medicaid expansion, infrastructure and the state's foster care program" as top priorities, while recognizing that the state had many other policy and budget needs.[92]

In 2018, Kansas voters opted for a more liberal option than Kobach, voting 55 percent for Kelly and Orman combined. But they also elected a slightly more conservative state house. In the August primary, conservatives netted roughly five seats, defeating several freshmen from the 2016 moderate wave but losing a handful of seats themselves, including the conservative Whitmer (mentioned earlier).[93] In the November general election, Democrats lost five incumbents in Republican-leaning house districts but gained five seats—flipping three from moderates and two from conservatives—for a wash, leaving them steady at forty seats.[94] Among the new Democrats were Brandon Woodard and Susan Ruiz of Johnson County, the first openly gay and lesbian Kansas legislators, and Rui Xu of Johnson County, Kansas's first Chinese American legislator. But even as Democrats elected a younger and more diverse caucus, the number of women in the legislature declined.[95]

There was also a mini-wave of party switching after the election, as four moderate Republican women from Johnson County became Democrats: Senator Barbara Bollier, who had endorsed Kelly and appeared in a campaign ad for her; Senator Dinah Sykes, discussed earlier; Representative Stephanie Clayton; and Representative Joy Koesten, who lost her primary but switched parties before her term ended and endorsed Kelly.[96] All four came from districts that had been trending Democratic in recent years and where Kelly won more than 50 percent of the vote. Indeed, Johnson County bucked its Republican roots and voted Democratic in four of five races for statewide office plus the race for the US House, where Democrat Sharice Davids unseated incumbent Republican Kevin Yoder. These switches left the Democrats with eleven senate seats and forty-one house seats. And since all four women were on the more liberal side of the moderate Republican spectrum, their change in party resulted in conservatives gaining marginally more power in the Republican legislative caucuses.

Ironically, then, the election and its aftermath created a fundamental tension. Voters elected Kelly in a high-profile, high-turnout gubernatorial race, seeing her as a remedy to eight years of Brownback and his legacy. Simultaneously, through the peculiarities of lower-profile district-level elections, Kansans also elected a more conservative legislature that supported conservative policies, felt newly emboldened, and would not easily defer to Kelly.

Notes

1. Kansas Secretary of State, 2014 General Election Results, accessed April 29, 2019, https://www.sos.ks.gov/elections/14elec/2014%20General%20Election%20Official%20Results.pdf.

2. CBS News, Kansas Governor Exit Poll, accessed April 29, 2019, https://www.cbsnews.com/elections/2014/governor/kansas/exit/.

3. Peter Hancock, "Kansas Revenue Projections for Next Year Contributing to Even Bigger Budget Hole," *Lawrence Journal-World*, April 20, 2015, https://www2.ljworld.com/news/2015/apr/20/kansas-officials-preparing-issue-new-fiscal-foreca/.

4. Bryan Lowry, "Brownback Cuts Higher Ed Funding after February Tax Revenue Falls Short," *Wichita Eagle*, March 1, 2016, https://www.kansas.com/news/politics-government/article63340222.html.

5. Lowry.

6. Scott Neuman, "Kansas Will Cut Education Funding to Help Close Budget Gap," National Public Radio, February 6, 2015, https://www.npr.org/sections/the-two-way/2015/02/06/384278249/kansas-will-cut-education-funding-to-help-close-budget-gap.

7. Neuman.

8. Bryan Lowry, "Brownback Signs Bill Changing School Funding Formula," *Wichita Eagle*, March 25, 2015, https://www.kansas.com/news/politics-government/article16333310.html.

9. John Hanna, "Questions on Classroom Spending Cloud Kansas Schools Debate," *Shawnee Dispatch*, December 20, 2015, http://www.shawneedispatch.com/news/2015/dec/20/questions-classroom-spending-cloud-kansas-schools-/.

10. Christina Wilkie, "More Kansas Schools to Close Early for Lack of Funds," *Huffington Post*, April 22, 2015, https://www.huffpost.com/entry/kansas-schools-funding_n_7112702.

11. Andrew V. Pestano, "Schools in Kansas Closing Early Due to $800 Million State Budget Deficit," United Press International, May 4, 2015, https://www.upi.com/Top_News/US/2015/05/04/Schools-in-Kansas-closing-early-due-to-800-million-state-budget-deficit/9901430734358/.

12. Chris Arnold, "Kansas Schools Preparing for Shutdown as Funding Crisis Looms," KSN News, June 3, 2016, https://www.ksn.com/news/local/kansas-schools-preparing-for-shutdown-as-funding-crisis-looms/1024119140.

13. Andy Marso, "Sales Tax Hike Ends Marathon Kansas Session," KCUR News, June 12, 2015, https://www.kcur.org/post/sales-tax-hike-ends-marathon-kansas-session#stream/0.

14. Kansas Department of Revenue, Sales Rate Changes, accessed April 29, 2019, https://www.ksrevenue.org/salesratechanges.html.

15. Tim Carpenter, "Kansas Lawmakers Approve Historic Tax Increase, Ending Record Session," *Hutchinson News*, June 12, 2015, https://www.hutchnews.com/article/20150612/News/306129869.

16. Sam Brownback, State of the State address, 2016, http://media.graytvinc.com/documents/2016+State+of+the+State+address.pdf.

17. Russell Berman, "Kansas's Never-ending Budget Mess," *Atlantic*, April 22, 2016, https://www.theatlantic.com/politics/archive/2016/04/kansass-never-ending-budget-mess/479400/.

18. Reid Wilson, "How Do Voters Feel about Your Governor?" Morning Consult, November 20, 2015, https://morningconsult.com/2015/11/20/how-do-voters-feel-about-your-governor/.

19. Roxie Hammill, "Kansas Budget Trickle-down under Brownback Crimps Johnson County and Its Cities," *Kansas City Star*, September 20, 2016, https://www.kansascity.com/news/local/community/joco-913/article102745202.html.

20. Ballotpedia, Kansas State Legislature, accessed April 29, 2019, https://ballotpedia.org/Kansas_State_Legislature.

21. Julie Bosman, "Kansas Parents Worry Schools Are Slipping amid Budget Battles," *New York Times*, May 31, 2016, https://www.nytimes.com/2016/06/01/us/kansas-parents-worry-schools-are-slipping-amid-budget-battles.html; Mitch Smith, "Kansas Republicans Reject Gov. Sam Brownback's Conservatives in Primary," *New York Times*, August 3, 2016, https://www.nytimes.com/2016/08/04/us/kansas-republicans-reject-gov-brownbacks-conservatives-in-primary.html.

22. Senator Dinah Sykes, Facebook post, accessed April 29, 2019, https://www.facebook.com/Sykes4KS/.

23. Senator Greg Smith, Facebook post, accessed April 29, 2019, https://www.facebook.com/GregSmith4KS/.

24. Elle Moxley, "In Johnson County, Conservative Republican Incumbents Are Often No-shows at Forums," KCUR News, July 28, 2016, https://www.kcur.org/post/johnson-county-conservative-republican-incumbents-are-often-no-shows-forums?fbclid=IwAR0s-e_OJDmlgtAqm-EvBrC-NgYnbvHzTP4AKsOW_zYgW_P8TTl6Jtl85Lc#stream/0.

25. Kansas Secretary of State, 2016 Primary Election Results, accessed April 29, 2019, https://www.sos.ks.gov/elections/16elec/2016_Primary_Election_OFFICIAL_Results.pdf.

26. Elle Moxley, "Who's the Moderate? In Kansas, Republicans and Democrats Run to the Middle," KCUR News, October 5, 2016, https://www.kcur.org/post/whos-moderate-kansas-republicans-and-democrats-run-middle.

27. Associated Press, "GOP Governor's Allies Suffer in Backlash in Kansas Primary," *Chicago Tribune*, August 3, 2016, https://www.chicagotribune.com/news/nationworld/politics/ct-kansas-primary-backlash-20160803-story.html.

28. Stephen Koranda, Andy Marso, Jim McLean, and Amy Jeffries, "Who's Who: Kansas Legislature Selects New Leadership," KCUR News, December 6, 2016, https://www.kcur.org/post/whos-who-kansas-legislature-selects-new-leadership.

29. Max Ehrenfreund, "Kansas Republicans Raise Taxes, Ending Their GOP Governor's 'Real Live Experiment' in Conservative Policy," *Washington Post*, June 7, 2017, https://www.washingtonpost.com/news/wonk/wp/2017/06/07/kansas-republicans-raise-taxes-rebuking-their-gop-governors-real-live-experiment-in-conservative-policy/.

30. Sam Zeff and Matt Hodap, "How the New Women's Caucus Helped Shape a Tax Compromise," KCUR News, June 15, 2017, https://www.kcur.org/post/how-new-womens-caucus-helped-shape-tax-compromise.

31. Associated Press, "Lawmakers: Brownback Preferred a Tax Veto Override," *Lawrence Journal-World*, June 18, 2017, https://www2.ljworld.com/news/2017/jun/18/lawmakers-brownback-preferred-tax-veto-override/.

32. Tim Carpenter, "Senate, House Narrowly Override Gov. Sam Brownback's Veto of $1.2 Billion Tax Bill," *Topeka Capital-Journal*, June 6, 2017, https://www.cjonline.com/news/state-government/2017-06-06/senate-house-narrowly-override-gov-sam-brownback-s-veto-12-billion.

33. Abby Goodnough and Mitch Smith, "Kansas House Narrowly Upholds Governor's Veto of Medicaid Expansion," *New York Times*, April 3, 2017, https://www.nytimes.com/2017/04/03/health/kansas-brownback-veto-expand-medicaid.html.

34. Jonathan Shorman, "Brownback Signs Abortion Measure that Sets Font,

Info Requirements," *Wichita Eagle*, June 7, 2017, https://www.kansas.com/news/politics-government/article154847149.html.

35. Ian Simpson, "Kansas Lawmakers Pass Adoption Bill Critics Say Biased against Gay Couples," Reuters, May 4, 2018, https://www.reuters.com/article/us-kansas-adoption/kansas-lawmakers-pass-adoption-bill-critics-say-biased-against-gay-couples-idUSKBN1I524F.

36. Mitch Smith, "After Long Wait in Kansas, Gov. Sam Brownback Gets Ambassadorship," *New York Times*, January 24, 2018, https://www.nytimes.com/2018/01/24/us/sam-brownback-kansas-ambassador.html.

37. Allison Kite, "Gov. Jeff Colyer Enters 2018 Gubernatorial Race," *Topeka Capital-Journal*, August 8, 2017, https://www.cjonline.com/news/state-government/2016-elections/2017-08-08/lt-gov-jeff-colyer-enters-2018-gubernatorial-race.

38. Dan Margolies and San Zeff, "Kansas Secretary of State Kobach Running for Governor," KCUR News, June 7, 2017, https://www.kcur.org/post/kansas-secretary-state-kobach-running-governor.

39. Bill Chappell, "Judge Tosses Kansas' Proof-of-Citizenship Voter Law and Rebukes Sec. of State Kobach," National Public Radio, June 19, 2018, https://www.npr.org/2018/06/19/621304260/judge-tosses-kansas-proof-of-citizenship-voter-law-and-rebukes-sec-of-state-koba.

40. Ryan Brooks, "Barnett Lays out Plan for Kansas," *Emporia Gazette*, July 21, 2018, http://www.emporiagazette.com/latest_news_and_features/article_d8aab15b-e18f-5bbf-ae8f-74811be0921d.html.

41. Tim Carpenter, "Republican Jim Barnett Selects Wife as Running Mate in Kansas Governor's Race," *Topeka Capital-Journal*, May 31, 2018, https://www.cjonline.com/news/20180531/republican-jim-barnett-selects-wife-as-running-mate-in-kansas-governors-race.

42. Kansas Speaks, Kansas Governor's Race Poll, Spring 2018, https://www.fhsu.edu/docking/documents/kansas-governors-race-poll-spring-20181.

43. Nicole Chavez, "Kris Kobach Criticized for Riding in a Parade with a Replica Gun," CNN, June 3, 2018, https://www.cnn.com/2018/06/03/politics/kris-kobach-republican-kansas-gun-parade/index.html.

44. Sean McDowell, "Kobach Won't Apologize for Use of Jeep, Replica Gun in Shawnee Parade Despite Complaints," Fox4KC News, June 4, 2018, https://fox4kc.com/2018/06/04/kobach-wont-apologize-for-use-of-jeep-replica-gun-in-shawnee-parade-despite-complaints/.

45. Zoe Brown and Nick Sloan, "Kobach: 'Outrage' over Parade Appearance Is 'to Attack Guns' and Second Amendment Rights," KCTV5 News, June 2, 2018, https://www.kctv5.com/news/kobach-outrage-over-parade-appearance-is-to-attack-guns-and/article_b8d690e9-43bb-5d84-9341-f80b12a8113a.html.

46. Associated Press, "NRA Endorses Kansas Gov. Colyer in GOP Primary,"

KSHB News, July 16, 2018, https://www.kshb.com/news/state/kansas/nra-endorses-kansas-gov-colyer-in-gop-primary.

47. Zeke Miller and John Hanna, "Trump Breaks with Aides, Tweets Endorsement of Kobach," Associated Press, August 6, 2018, https://apnews.com/9dc2ed42fbc74738a6c12d1a06c9060a.

48. Madeleine Fox, Andrea Tudhope, and Stephen Bisaha, "Kansas Republican Governor Primary Turns to Provisional Ballots, One County at a Time," KCUR News, August 13, 2018, https://www.kcur.org/post/kansas-republican-governor-primary-turns-provisional-ballots-one-county-time#stream/0.

49. Associated Press, "Kansas Governor Colyer Concedes GOP Primary to Secretary of State Kobach," NBC News, August 14, 2018, https://www.nbcnews.com/politics/elections/kansas-governor-colyer-concedes-gop-primary-secretary-state-kobach-n900776.

50. Kansas Secretary of State, 2018 Primary Election Results, accessed April 29, 2019, https://www.kssos.org/elections/18elec/PrimaryElectionOfficialResults.pdf.

51. Nomin Ujiyediin, "Losing Campaigns for Kansas Governor Mostly Spent Candidates' Money," KCUR News, January 11, 2019, https://www.kcur.org/post/losing-campaigns-kansas-governor-mostly-spent-candidates-money.

52. Hunter Woodall and Bryan Lowry, "Inside Kris Kobach's Losing Kansas Campaign: 'Check Logic and Reason at the Door,'" *Kansas City Star*, November 9, 2018, https://www.kansascity.com/news/politics-government/election/article221350970.html.

53. Woodall and Lowry.

54. Amir Vera and Andrea Diaz, "Thanks to a Loophole in Kansas Law, 6 Teens Are Running for Governor," CNN, February 9, 2018, https://www.cnn.com/2018/02/09/politics/kansas-teens-running-for-governor-trnd/index.html.

55. Danielle Kurtzleben, "Is the Record Number of Women Candidates a 2018 Blip—or a Lasting Trend?" National Public Radio, September 25, 2018, https://www.npr.org/2018/09/25/651085628/is-the-record-number-of-women-candidates-a-2018-blip-or-a-lasting-trend.

56. Eli Watkins, "Women and LGBT Candidates Make History in 2018 Midterms," CNN, November 7, 2018, https://www.cnn.com/2018/11/07/politics/historic-firsts-midterms/index.html.

57. Allison Kite, "Sexual Harassment Allegations Prompt Proposals from Kansas Democratic Candidates," *Topeka Capital-Journal*, October 26, 2017, https://www.cjonline.com/news/state-government/2017-10-26/sexual-harassment-allegations-prompt-proposals-kansas-democratic.

58. John Hanna, "Anti-Abortion Past Haunts Kansas Democratic Governor Hopeful," Associated Press, July 6, 2018, https://www.apnews.com/906a0dd0bb894a3a9461f333399cffc4.

59. Vote Smart, Svaty Abortion Positions, accessed April 29, 2019, https://votesmart.org/candidate/key-votes/34793/joshua-svaty/2/abortion.

60. Rachel Skytta, "Governor Candidate Carl Brewer Now 'Focusing on the Future' after Grandson's Death," KWCH News, September 22, 2017, https://www.kwch.com/content/news/Governor-candidate-Carl-Brewer-now-focusing-on-the-future-following-grandsons-death-446949463.html.

61. Sherman Smith, "Kansan of the Year Laura Kelly: Colleagues, Friends Attest to Governor-elect's Competitiveness, Kindness," *Topeka Capital-Journal*, December 29, 2018, https://www.cjonline.com/news/20181229/kansan-of-year-laura-kelly-colleagues-friends-attest-to-governor-elects-competitiveness-kindness.

62. Jim McLean, "State Sen. Laura Kelly Jumps into Kansas Governor's Race," KCUR News, December 15, 2017, https://www.kcur.org/post/state-sen-laura-kelly-jumps-kansas-governor-s-race.

63. Kansas Ethics Commission, Campaign Fundraising, accessed April 29, 2019, http://ethics.ks.gov/CFAScanned/StWide/2018ElecCycle/SWLinks2018EC.htm.

64. Stephen Bisaha, "Jim Ward Drops out of Kansas Governor's Race; Will Run for Re-election to the House," KCUR News, May 9, 2018, https://www.kcur.org/post/jim-ward-drops-out-kansas-governors-race-will-run-re-election-house.

65. Sherman Smith, "Svaty, Kelly Exchange Shots over Past Votes on Guns, Abortion, Voter Rights," *Garden City Telegram*, July 5, 2018, https://www.gctelegram.com/news/20180705/svaty-kelly-exchange-shots-over-past-votes-on-guns-abortion-voter-rights/1.

66. Kansas Secretary of State, 2018 Primary Election Results.

67. Open Secrets, Orman Political Money, accessed April 29, 2019, https://www.opensecrets.org/donor-lookup/results?name=gregory+orman.

68. Peggy Lowe, "Orman Runs as Independent in Partisan Kansas Senate Race," KCUR News, October 9, 2014, https://www.kcur.org/post/orman-runs-independent-partisan-kansas-senate-race.

69. Dion Lefler and Bryan Lowry, "Greg Orman Prepping for Independent Campaign for Kansas Governor," *Kansas City Star*, October 9, 2017, https://www.kansascity.com/news/politics-government/article177959541.html.

70. Greg Orman, "Why I Remained an Independent Candidate," Real Clear Politics, January 4, 2019, https://www.realclearpolitics.com/articles/2019/01/04/why_i_remained_an_independent_candidate_139096.html.

71. Patrick Miller, "No, Voters Aren't Turning to Independent Candidates," *Kansas City Star*, October 31, 2017, https://www.kansascity.com/opinion/readers-opinion/guest-commentary/article181950851.html.

72. Mark Feuerborn, "Kansas Governor Candidates Face off in Final Debate," KSNT News, October 31, 2018, https://www.ksnt.com/news/local-news/watch-kansas-governor-candidates-face-off-in-final-debate/1564310622.

73. Jay Senter, "Kansas Gubernatorial Candidates on K–12 School Funding: Republican Jim Barnett," *Shawnee Mission Post*, February 14, 2018, https://shawneemissionpost

.com/2018/02/14/kansas-gubernatorial-candidates-k-12-school-funding-republican-jim-barnett-69764.

74. Orman for Kansas, tweet attacking the media, accessed April 29, 2019, https://twitter.com/OrmanforKansas/status/1010150664171872256.

75. Tim Carpenter, "Independent Governor Candidate Greg Orman Unveils Plans to Reform Kansas Government," *Garden City Telegram*, July 11, 2018, https://www.gctelegram.com/news/20180711/independent-governor-candidate-greg-orman-unveils-plans-to-reform-kansas-government/1.

76. FiveThirtyEight, Kansas Governor Polls, accessed April 29, 2019, https://projects.fivethirtyeight.com/polls/governor/kansas/.

77. Nick Viviani, "PPP: Kansas Governor's Race Is a 'Dead Heat,'" WIBW News, August 30, 2018, https://projects.fivethirtyeight.com/polls/governor/kansas/.

78. Jonathan Shorman, "Friend of Independent Greg Orman Tied to Group Attacking GOP, Democratic Candidates," *Wichita Eagle*, July 21, 2018, https://www.kansas.com/news/politics-government/article215808260.html.

79. Ujiyediin, "Losing Campaigns for Kansas Governor Mostly Spent Candidates' Money."

80. Mark Minton, "Doll Breaks Ranks, Joins Orman," *Garden City Telegram*, March 7, 2018, https://www.gctelegram.com/news/20180307/doll-breaks-ranks-joins-orman.

81. Sam Hartle, "Former Kansas GOP Gov. Bill Graves Endorses Democrat Laura Kelly," KSHB News, September 4, 2018, https://www.kshb.com/news/political/former-kansas-gop-gov-bill-graves-endorses-democrat-laura-kelly; Associated Press, "Kassebaum Supports Democrat Kelly in Kansas Governor's Race," KAKE News, September 18, 2018, http://www.kake.com/story/39115071/kassebaum-supports-democrat-kelly-in-kansas-governors-race.

82. Associated Press, "Orman's Campaign Treasurer Resigns to Support Democrat Kelly," Fox4KC News, October 30, 2018, https://fox4kc.com/2018/10/30/ormans-campaign-treasurer-resigns-to-support-democrat-kelly/.

83. Patrick Miller, tweet about Republicans using Orman as a spoiler, accessed April 29, 2019, https://twitter.com/pmiller1693/status/1059223847893897216.

84. Tim Hains, "Full Replay: Trump Hosts MAGA Rally in Topeka, Kansas," Real Clear Politics, October 6, 2018, https://www.realclearpolitics.com/video/2018/10/06/watch_live_trump_hosts_maga_rally_in_topeka_kansas.html; Roxana Hegeman, "Kansas Gubernatorial Candidates Trade Barbs in Debate," AP News, October 9, 2018, https://www.apnews.com/bf24d35ba0794ac8bd959d23b2f5a773; *Iola Register*, clip of gubernatorial debate, November 1, 2018, https://www.youtube.com/watch?v=UP8G35lZWFA.

85. Laura Kelly for Kansas, campaigns ads, accessed April 29, 2019, https://www.youtube.com/channel/UC5L-EctoRQU_rz2OqYDk6jg/videos.

86. Kris Kobach, campaigns ads, accessed April 29, 2019, https://www.youtube.com/user/KrisKobach/videos.

87. Kansas Secretary of State, 2018 General Election Results, accessed April 29, 2019, https://www.kssos.org/elections/18elec/2018_General_Election_Official_Votes_Cast.pdf.

88. Kansas Secretary of State, 2002 General Election Results, accessed April 29, 2019, https://www.sos.ks.gov/elections/02elec/2002GeneralOfficialResults.pdf.

89. Pew Research, "Wide Gender Gap, Growing Educational Divide in Voters' Party Identification," March 20, 2018, https://www.people-press.org/2018/03/20/wide-gender-gap-growing-educational-divide-in-voters-party-identification/.

90. Fox News Voter Analysis, Kansas Gubernatorial Race Exit Poll, accessed April 29, 2019, https://www.foxnews.com/midterms-2018/voter-analysis?filter=KS&type=G#.

91. Patrick Miller, "Rural Voters Hold the Key to Medicaid Expansion," *Hays Post*, April 5, 2019, https://www.hayspost.com/2019/04/05/insight-kansas-rural-voters-hold-the-key-to-medicaid-expansion/.

92. Dylan Lysen, "Gov.-elect Kelly Aware of State's Higher Education Issues, but They're Not Likely to Top Her Agenda," *Lawrence Journal-World*, January 2, 2019, https://www2.ljworld.com/news/ku/2019/jan/02/gov-elect-kelly-aware-of-states-higher-education-issues-but-theyre-not-likely-to-top-her-agenda/.

93. Andy Marso, "Koesten, Markley Ousted as Conservatives Make Gains in Johnson County GOP Primaries," *Kansas City Star*, August 8, 2018, https://www.kansascity.com/news/politics-government/article216293205.html.

94. Kansas Secretary of State, 2018 General Election Results.

95. Jonathan Shorman, "Kansas Legislature Losing Women as Other States Gain Female Representation," *Wichita Eagle*, December 24, 2018, https://www.kansas.com/news/politics-government/article223046860.html.

96. Jonathan Shorman, "More Kansas Lawmakers Switch Parties: Sykes, Clayton Leave GOP, Become Democrats," *Wichita Eagle*, December 19, 2018, https://www.kansas.com/news/politics-government/article223283450.html.

Conclusion
The Arc of Kansas Politics

H. Edward Flentje

Kansans grew up in an era of rugged individualism and laissez-faire, but that state of affairs was repeatedly punctuated by dramatic moments of political reform. The first settlers battled pro-slavery intrusions and prevailed to enter the union as a free state. Evangelical Protestants later sought to elevate moral conduct with a constitutional edict prohibiting the manufacture and sale of intoxicating liquors but then struggled for decades to enforce that decree. Toward the end of the nineteenth century, insurgent populists fought entrenched railroad and banking interests and captured most state offices but lacked unity in advancing their desire to equalize conditions. After the turn of the century, Main Street progressives wrested control of state politics and proceeded to enact a broad array of political and economic restructuring. These political adventures left an imprint on the state's body politic and consequently gave Kansas a reputation for being on the cutting edge of national political change.

By the 1920s, however, the political energy for reform had been exhausted, and state politics entered the doldrums. Passions waned, and retrenchment set in. The Great Depression wrought economic distress, unemployment, defaults, and foreclosures across Kansas. The Dust Bowl swept discouragement across the state. The population fell. Officeholders sought federal aid to address the emergency and to support roads, farms, and public welfare.

The imprint of the state's first century is evident in the arc of Kansas politics in modern times. Kansans' aspirations for progress have challenged deep-seated preferences for individual liberty and freedom from an activist state government. In the period from the 1960s through the early 1990s, elected leaders defied the status quo, rewrote the state constitution, augmented the powers of key political institutions, and deployed those powers to reshape public policy. In time, opposing partisans regrouped, steadily reclaimed power, and threatened to undo the change. The push and pull of these forces have characterized Kansas politics for the last twenty-five years.

Kansas Plays Catch-up

As Kansans celebrated the centennial of statehood in 1961, many realized that state government had fallen behind. The legislature was grossly malapportioned. The constitution was out of date. Statute books were littered with archaic laws that constrained progress. National reform groups were ranking the state's political institutions—the legislature, the executive, and the judiciary—as mediocre in terms of representation, accountability, and performance.

The US Supreme Court prompted immediate attention to these issues by ordering that the Kansas legislature be apportioned in line with the principle of one person, one vote. Reapportionment brought new faces and leadership to public office, and a broad-ranging self-assessment began. In the early 1970s, the Kansas legislature placed twenty constitutional amendments on the ballot, and voters ratified them all. This wholesale revision of the state constitution strengthened the chief executive, unified a fragmented judiciary, and cleared the path for legislative reforms. A progressive resurgence ensued.

Democratic governor Robert Docking and his successor, Republican Robert Bennett, moved promptly to deploy augmented gubernatorial powers and establish a cabinet structure in place of the fragmented and disorganized executive department. Agencies were consolidated into major cabinet departments, each headed by a secretary serving at the pleasure of the governor. Numerous semi-independent boards and commissions were abolished. Bennett continued executive reorganization by restructuring a notoriously politicized Highway Commission into a Department of Transportation headed by a professional secretary. Within five years, the two governors had brought agencies representing half the state budget under direct gubernatorial supervision.

Bennett was succeeded in the governorship by two policy activists—Democrat John Carlin and Republican Mike Hayden—both of whom had served as speaker of the Kansas House. As experienced legislative leaders, they believed that bipartisan majorities were essential in moving public policy in a new direction.

In his second term, Carlin confronted a stagnant state economy. He challenged lawmakers to rethink state government's role in stimulating economic growth and advanced a bold agenda for doing so. A bipartisan coalition was assembled to address the state's archaic liquor and banking laws. Carlin then proposed constitutional amendments authorizing a state-owned lottery, pari-mutuel wagering, and local property tax exemptions for economic development, plus a sales tax increase to fund new economic initiatives and future state obligations. The governor's broad economic blueprint effectively aligned urban interests and, most importantly, the normally contentious metropolitan centers of Kansas City and Wichita. Voters embraced the constitutional amendments, and a bipartisan alliance of state lawmakers enacted tax and budget measures that fundamentally transformed state government's role in economic development.

Hayden assumed the governor's office alert to the critical role of public infrastructure in economic growth and to reports that state investments in infrastructure had fallen off. During his campaign for governor, he advocated highway improvements to address the state's primary obligation to maintain essential public infrastructure and enhance regional development. As governor, Hayden immediately promoted an aggressive initiative of new highway construction, accelerated maintenance, and expanded aid for local roads. He also directed staff to develop a financing strategy for the state water plan that had been prepared by the Carlin administration but never funded. Hayden responded to a federal court order related to prison overcrowding and addressed the need for expanded correctional facilities, which had been deferred for years.

Action on infrastructure came to a head in the 1989 legislative session. In alliance with grassroots lobbyists, narrow bipartisan majorities enacted a landmark highway program. On the last day of the session, lawmakers agreed to construct a new prison, the first maximum-security facility to be built in Kansas in more than one hundred years. In the last hour of the session, Hayden and former governor Carlin rounded up the votes needed to enact long-term funding for the state water plan. The achievements in state infrastructure were historic: an eight-year $1.8 billion comprehensive highway package, a new $55 million high-security prison, and dedicated financing of the state water plan at $16 million annually.

After more than twenty years of policy activism by governors and lawmakers of both parties, Kansas voters signaled a desire to slow down and elected state treasurer Joan Finney as governor. An effective grassroots campaigner, she had triumphed over Carlin in the primary and Hayden in the general election but had little experience in public policymaking.

One issue that could not be ignored during Finney's term was school finance. District court judge Terry Bullock had ruled that state provisions for funding the public schools were inequitable and unconstitutional. He reminded state lawmakers that school finance was a state obligation and ordered them to fix the constitutional deficiencies by a specified time.

In the absence of gubernatorial leadership, policy activism on school finance shifted to the Kansas legislature. Democratic speaker of the house Marvin Barkis and Republican senate majority leader Fred Kerr moved into the leadership vacuum during the 1992 legislative session, carefully guiding proposals that bounced back and forth within and between the two chambers. Work on school finance legislation exemplified bipartisan sausage making at its best, as the legislature fundamentally rewrote the law and enacted the School District Finance and Quality Performance Act. K–12 funding was recognized as a state obligation, and school financing was substantially shifted from local property taxes to state income and sales taxes. State tax revenue increased by nearly $350 million, but local taxes to fund schools were cut in 291 of the state's 304 school districts. Governor Finney signed the legislation, and Judge Bullock applauded the legislature's work.

Partisans Regroup and Reclaim Power

While state politics was undergoing a transition during the Finney governorship, political undercurrents were emerging to contest the policy activism of the prior twenty-five years. Two distinct political forces had been smoldering nationally and were coming to the surface in Kansas. The first was ignited by the US Supreme Court's 1973 ruling in *Roe v. Wade*, which negated state laws restricting abortion, including Kansas's. In its 1989 ruling in *Webster v. Reproductive Health Services*, the court pushed the abortion issue squarely into Kansas politics by granting state lawmakers leeway in restricting abortion. Both rulings energized grassroots organizing by antiabortion activists, who began fielding candidates for state and local offices.

The second political force emerged in the 1970s as a small faction of libertarian ideologues encouraged by Charles and David Koch of Wichita. The brothers created several vehicles to advocate for individual liberty, limited government, and free markets, providing seed money for these endeavors. On a separate but parallel track, economist Arthur Laffer gained national notoriety beginning in the 1970s with his advocacy of tax cuts as a stimulus for economic growth, which became a focal point during the Reagan administration.

Ronald Reagan effectively brought these disparate political causes together by aligning social order with economic liberty. Early on, he endorsed a constitutional amendment to ban abortion and campaigned to make abortion a litmus test for judicial appointments. As president, he championed tax cuts as both a stimulus for economic growth and a limitation on government growth. Reagan crafted an appealing message that blended opposition to abortion with resistance to big government. Consequently, the Republican Party became the vehicle to apply the powers of government to ensure social order on the one hand and to enhance economic liberty by restricting governmen on the other.

Reagan's alignment of order and liberty resurfaced dramatically in the 1994 Kansas elections. During the primary phase, partisan activists quietly recruited allies at the precinct level, who in turn replaced local and state party officials. The polar alliance took control of the state Republican Party organization. Aligned Republicans also gained fourteen house seats in the general election, took control of the house Republican caucus, and ousted the sitting speaker.

In the wake of the 1994 elections, Kansas Republicans split into two camps. The faction galvanized by the alliance of economic liberty and social order controlled the party organization and the Republican caucus of the Kansas House. Moderate Republicans held on to key statewide offices, including the governorship, and maintained control of the Republican caucus of the Kansas Senate. This standoff continued through the mainstream governorships of Republican Bill Graves (1995–2003) and Democrat Kathleen Sebelius (2003–10). Both governors embraced the centrist consensus on tax policy, merit-based judicial appointments, and acceptance of federal aid. Graves extended the Hayden legacy with a second round of highway improvements, and Sebelius broke a deadlock on school finance based largely on the legislature's work in 1992.

The political standoff came to a head in the 2010 election. Sam Brownback led the polar alliance within the Republican Party and coasted to gubernatorial victory. That election also handed house Republicans a 92–33 majority, their largest in more than sixty years. Those conquests encouraged Brownback and his allies to turn their attention to purging centrist Republicans who continued their hold on the state senate. They were aided by anti-tax business owners who had taken control of the Kansas Chamber of Commerce and its political action committee (PAC). The chamber's PAC raised nearly $1 million to target the 2012 state legislative races, an amount that substantially exceeded the total raised in the prior five years. A handful of entities with deep pockets, such as Wichita's Koch Industries, contributed more than half the cash.

The purge succeeded. Nine senate incumbents—all centrist Republican leaders—were ousted in the 2012 primary. The house supermajority was retained and enhanced. The Far Right bloc now controlled both the Kansas legislature and the governorship. Kansas politics had changed direction.

Brownback was emboldened by his political success and vowed to remake Kansas into a national model for "red-state governance" and to shift the state from its path of the past fifty years. He called for elimination of the state income tax, partisan control of state courts, and rejection of federal funds. He and his allies immediately took steps on a new path.

Once Kansans experienced the day-to-day reality of Brownback's governance, however, they changed course. Most significant was the financial disaster resulting from his radical tax experiment. The governor's approval ratings began to fall, and in 2016, voters rebuked Brownback and his allies and elected a majority of centrist Republicans and Democrats who had campaigned to end the tax experiment. Voters also rejected an intense campaign to purge a majority of Kansas Supreme Court justices in retention elections.

In the 2017 legislative session, lawmakers reversed course and restored state income taxes by overriding a gubernatorial veto. However, they fell short of overriding the governor on his determination to block federal aid through expanded Medicaid. In 2018, Brownback vacated the governorship one year early under a cloud of public disapproval. And later that year, voters rejected the brash partisan politics of Kris Kobach and elected moderate Democrat Laura Kelly to the governorship. Far Right Republicans had ascended and then tumbled in the space of a decade, 2010 through 2019.

Reform and reaction characterize the arc of Kansas politics, both historically and in modern times. Cutting-edge political reforms in the state's early years were eventually restrained by Kansans' instincts for individual liberty and limited government. However, a progressive resurgence in the 1960s and 1970s ignited bipartisan policy activism that transformed public policy and continued through the mid-1990s. Political forces then emerged to contest and undo the reforms resulting from that resurgence. The last decade of Kansas politics reflects these earlier patterns—reform followed by reaction—in a compressed time frame, embodying the ongoing clash of competing political preferences in the arc of Kansas politics.

About the Contributors

H. Edward Flentje is professor emeritus at Wichita State University and former director of the Hugo Wall School of Public Affairs at the university. He has authored and edited numerous books and articles, including *Kansas Politics and Government: The Clash of Political Cultures* (with Joseph A. Aistrup) and *The Rise and Spectacular Fall: Radical Kansas Republicans, 2010–2020*. He served with Kansas governors Robert Bennett and Mike Hayden and later as interim city manager for the City of Wichita and interim president of Emporia State University.

The late **Burdett "Bird" Loomis** was an emeritus professor of political science at the University of Kansas. He wrote extensively on legislatures, interest groups, and political institutions. Loomis published thirty books in various editions, including *Time, Politics, and Policy: A Legislative Year* (1994). He lectured widely for the US State Department and held the Australian-American Distinguished Chair in American Politics at Flinders University. He founded the University of Kansas's Washington, DC, intern program in 1984 and directed the Topeka legislative intern program for more than thirty years.

Patrick R. Miller is an associate professor of political science at Kent State University. He taught at the University of Kansas from 2013 to 2023. His areas of specialization include political psychology, public opinion, electoral behavior, survey methods, and quantitative research methods. He received his PhD in political science from the University of North Carolina at Chapel Hill, with specializations in American politics and research methodology. He also received a certification in survey research methodology from the Howard W. Odum Institute for Research in Social Science and later served as a survey research associate at the Duke University Initiative on Survey Methodology.

ABOUT THE CONTRIBUTORS

Chapman Rackaway serves Radford University as professor and chair of the Department of Political Science. Previously, he taught at Fort Hays State University and the University of West Georgia. Rackaway is the author of *Civic Failure and Its Threat to American Democracy: Operator Error* (2016), coeditor of *Parties under Pressure* (2017) and *The Unorthodox Presidency of Donald Trump* (2021), and coauthor (with Joseph Romance) of *Primary Elections and American Politics: The Unintended Consequences of Progressive Era Reform* (2022), as well as other works on American state and local politics, political electioneering organizations, and political communication. His teaching interests include civic leadership and electioneering and campaigns at the state level, and he teaches classes in state and local government, political communication, Congress, and the presidency.

Michael A. Smith is a professor of political science at Emporia State University. His research involves voting laws, Kansas politics, and teaching methods. His teaching interests include American politics, political theory and philosophy, campaigns and elections, and state and local government. He is the author, coauthor, and editor of several books, most recently *Much Sound and Fury or the New Jim Crow?* (2022). Smith writes a newspaper column as part of the Insight Kansas group, and he regularly provides political analysis on television and radio programs in Kansas and western Missouri, including *Kansas Week* (KPTS), *I've Got Issues* (KTWU), and *Up to Date* (KCUR).

Index

abortion/abortion rights
   Alexa's Law regarding, 126
   Bill Graves's policies regarding, 104
   as campaign platform, 116
   controversy of, 82–83
   debates/disputes regarding, 3, 114
   election of 2018 and, 213–214, 224
   Kathleen Sebelius's policies regarding, 126
   Mike Hayden's policies regarding, 67
   murder of George Tiller and, 114, 125–126, 145
   Phill Kline and, 124–125
   Republican Party stance regarding, 95–96
   restrictions of, 5
   Sam Brownback's policies regarding, 152
Abrams, Steve, 108
Ackerman, Peter, 162
Adkins, Amanda, 146
Affordable Care and Patient Protection Act (ACA) (Obamacare), 130, 143, 146, 191
Agnew, Spiro, 38
agriculture, threats to, 7
Aistrup, Joseph, 94, 95, 132
Alexa's Law, 126
American Legislative Exchange Council (ALEC), 85, 148, 179, 180, 192
Americans for Prosperity, 85, 180, 186, 192
Anderson, John, 9, 17, 30
Anderson, Steven, 153
Armstrong, Warren, 75, 76
Avery, William, 18, 23

Baker v. Carr, 14, 15–16, 34
Ballard, Barbara, 97–98
Barker, Clayton, 146–147

Barkis, Marvin, 77, 78
Barnett, Jim, 119, 121, 176, 210–211
Base Realignment and Closure (BRAC), 120
base state aid per pupil (BSAPP), 4, 5
Bennett, Robert F.
   1974 gubernatorial election and, 40–43
   actions of, 2
   characteristics of, 46, 57
   election of, 13, 55
   as governor, 43–49, 235
   legacy of, 49, 59
   merit-based appointments and, 46–47, 71
   quote of, 44–45
   as senator, 11, 35, 38–40
Bibb, Jim, 53n57
Bicknell, Gene, 58, 176
Biden, Joe, 7
Biggs, Chris, 116
Bipartisan Women's Caucus, 209
Blue Cross and Blue Shield (BCBS), 115
Board of Social Welfare, 31
Bollier, Barbara, 225
Bond, Dick, 102
Boyda, Nancy, 128–129
Bremby, Roderick, 131
Brewer, Carl, 160, 213–215
Brier, Jack, 58
Brown, John, 1
Brownback, Sam
   abandoning merit-based selection of judges, 184–189
   as ambassador, 210
   approval rating of, 159, 202, 239
   background of, 174–176
   blame of, 201

244 INDEX

Brownback, Sam, *continued*
  blocking federal funding and, 190–193
  as cabinet member, 174
  campaign of, 147–151, 176
  characteristics of, 132
  as congressman, 174–175
  criticism of, 204
  economic decisions of, 200
  election of, 3–4, 87, 115, 127–128, 158–160, 163–169
  elimination of state income tax and, 177–184
  Glide Path to Zero and, 5, 153, 179, 183
  as governor, 152–155, 176–193, 238–239
  job change of, 6
  as leaving governorship, 193–195
  overview of, 5, 141–143
  platform of, 174–175, 176
  redistricting maps of, 156–157
  reelection of, 199
  religion of, 175–176
  sales tax increase by, 201
  in the Senate, 105–107
  support for, 143–144
Brown v. Board of Education of Topeka, 8, 122
Brungardt, Pete, 157
buffer zone legislation, 120
Bullock, Terry, 78, 122, 237
Burbank, John, 162
Burke, Bud, 66
Bush, George H. W., 55
Bush, George W., 107, 122

cabinet system, 11
campaign finance, procedure regulations for, 38–39
Campbell-Kline, Christine, 69
capital punishment, 79, 166–167
Carlin, John
  1990 election and, 68, 69–70
  appointment by, 141
  campaign of, 48
  death penalty and, 79
  economic plan of, 62
  election of, 2, 48, 49, 55
  gubernatorial contest of, 56–59
  loss of, 175
  merit-based appointments and, 71–72
  overview of, 235–236
  as policy entrepreneur, 60–62, 235–236
  property tax platform of, 57, 61–62
  severance tax platform of, 57, 61
  successes of, 74
  tax policy and, 178
  utility rate platform of, 57, 60–61
  water policies of, 66
Carlson, Frank, 52n35, 75
Carr, Johnathon, 166–167
Carr, Reginald, 166–167
Carter, Jimmy, 55
casinos, 123
CATO Institute, 84
Center for Budget and Policy Priorities, 193
Center for Legislative Improvement, 11
Center on Budget and Policy Priorities, 182
Chamber of Commerce, 151, 155, 180, 188, 192, 239
Charles Koch Foundation, 84
Cigler, Allan, 55
Citizens' Committee on Constitutional Revision, 30, 32–33
Citizens' Conference on Modernization of Kansas Courts, 32–33
Citizens Conference on State Legislatures, 29, 34, 38
Citizens for a Sound Economy, 85
Clayton, Stephanie, 225
Cleaver, Emmanuel, 117
climate change, 7
Clinton, Bill, 55, 87
Clinton, Hillary, 114, 207
coal-fired electric power plants, 131
Colyer, Jeff, 6, 166, 193, 210–213
Commission on Constitutional Revision, 30
Commission on Governmental Ethics, 36, 39
Commission on Intergovernmental Relations, 28–29
Concannon, Don, 41–42
concealed-carry permits, 4
constitutional amendments, 10–11
Contract with America, 106

corn industry, threats to, 7
Corporation for Change, 79
correctional facilities, plans regarding, 65
cotton industry, growth of, 7
Crawford County, 219
Crossman, Ivan, 180
culture wars, 3–4
cycles, defined, 92

Dailey, Dennis, 126
Davids, Sharice, 226
Davis, Paul, 5, 160, 163–169, 216
deadlines, defined, 93
death penalty, 79, 166–167
Democratic National Committee (DNC), 129
Democratic Party
    bipartisan consensus of, 69–72
    demographics of, 54
    fundraising by, 140
    House control of, 56, 87, 88
    Joan Finney and, 77
    primary of 2018 and, 213–215
    reapportionment effects on, 25
    rift with Republican Party by, 206
    Senate control of, 87
    statistics regarding, 54
    structure of, 138
Denning, Jim, 209
Department of Administration, 31
Department of Children and Families, 193
Department of Corrections, 44
Department of Economic Development, 44
Department of Health and Environment, 31, 36
Department of Health and Human Services (HHS), 130
Department of Human Resources, 44
Department of Revenue, 31
Department of Social and Rehabilitation Services, 31, 36
Department of Transportation, 44, 45, 235
Department on Aging, 44
Division of State Planning and Research, 31, 36, 47
Dobson, James, 108
Docking, George, 2, 9, 29, 30, 163, 184

Docking, Jill, 106, 107, 160, 163–168, 175
Docking, Robert, 2, 3, 9–11, 25, 30, 31–32, 40, 235
Dole, Bob, 13, 40, 55, 82, 115, 116, 141, 163, 175
Douglas County, 219
Doyen, Ross, 16
driver's licenses, 102–103
Dukakis, Michael, 55
Dvorak, John, 97

Economic Recovery Tax Act, 86
economy of Kansas
    audit for, 119–120
    budget in, 5, 9–10, 182–183, 200
    challenges of, 62, 200
    cuts in, 131
    down balances in, 181
    fiscal analysis of, 37
    during Great Depression, 178
    Great Recession and, 120, 123, 181
    Legislative Budget Committee for, 35
    liberty and, 83–86
    payday loans and, 183
    social order and, 86–89
    spending cap in, 97
    statistics of, 15
    three-legged stool concept and, 177–178
education
    budget proposal regarding, 9
    enrollment increase in, 8
    evolution teaching in, 108–9
    finance legislation for, 78
    funding for, 100, 119–120, 121–123, 131, 150, 154, 184, 200–201, 237
    for immigrants, 127
    legislation regarding, 78–79
    reform of, 9
egalitarianism, 95, 113
Eisenhower, Dwight D., 8, 29
elections
    1960, 8
    1974 gubernatorial, 40–43, 55
    1978, 55, 56–57
    1980s presidential, 55
    1982, 57
    1986, 55, 57–59
    1990, 68–69, 74

elections, *continued*
   1992 presidential, 55
   1994, 86–89
   2006, 118
   2010, 143–145, 151–152, 176
   2012, 155–158
   2014, 158–160, 163–169, 199
   2016, 6, 199–208
   2018, 210–225
environmental policies, of Mike Hayden, 65–66
Essex, Robyn, 156
evangelical Christianity, 1
evolution, 4, 108–109
executive branch
   1974 gubernatorial election in, 40–43
   changes to, 10–11
   conflicts of interest in, 46
   election reform regarding, 32
   reforms in, 30–32
   reorganization of, 44
   term limits of, 10. See also *specific governors*
Executive Reorganization Order No. 1, 31, 36
Executive Reorganization Order No. 3, 36

Fatzer, Harold, 32, 33
Federal, State, and Local Committee, 16
federal assistance, bipartisan consensus regarding, 71
Federal Election Commission (FEC), 139
Federal Election Committee (FEC), 5
federal funding, blocking, 190–193
federal grants, increase of, 9
Finney, Joan
   abortion rights and, 3, 83
   background of, 68–69, 75–76
   characteristics of, 77, 80, 98
   death penalty and, 79
   election of, 55
   as governor, 117, 237
   as manager, 79–80
   overview of, 3
   as policymaker, 76–79
   vetoes of, 77
First District, 7

Fisher, Glenn, 61
Flentje, Ed, 94, 95
Flinchbaugh, Barry, 177
Focus on the Family, 4
Ford, Gerald, 82
foster-care system, 102
Foundation for Government Accountability, 193
Frahm, Sheila, 105, 107, 141, 175, 217

gambling, 64, 123
Gingrich, Newt, 87, 106
Glasscock, Kent, 104, 118
Glickman, Dan, 55, 68–69, 87
Glide Path to Zero, 5, 153, 179, 183
Goldwater, Barry, 117
governmental ethics, procedure regulations for, 38, 39
governors. *See* executive branch; *specific governors*
Goyle, Raj, 120
grants-in-aid, 190–193
Graves, Bill
   appointment by, 141, 175
   campaign of, 116
   characteristics of, 97–98
   election of, 88, 115, 176
   endorsement by, 217
   as faction leader, 95
   as governor, 96–105, 238
   overview of, 3
   platform of, 92, 95
   reelection challenge of, 107–108
   same-sex marriage legislation and, 126
Great Recession, 120, 123, 181
Greensburg, tornado in, 120
Grow Kansas Action Fund, 217
gun rights, 4, 104–105, 117, 212, 218, 224–225

Hagaman, Frank, 52n35
Hagstrom, Jerry, 28
Haley, David, 98
Hall, Fred, 2, 29, 184
Hardage, Sam, 57
Harris, Dee, 75, 76
Harris v. Anderson, 18
Harris v. Shanahan, 14, 16, 17

Hartman, Wink, 213
Harvey County, 219
Hayden, Mike
   1990 election and, 68–69
   abortion rights and, 3, 67, 82–83
   achievements of, 66
   appointment by, 174
   campaign of, 116
   characteristics of, 64
   correctional facilities plans of, 65
   election of, 49, 55
   endorsement by, 217
   environmental policy of, 65–66
   gubernatorial contest of, 56–59
   highway program of, 63–65
   merit-based appointments and, 71–72
   overview of, 2–3, 236
   as policy entrepreneur, 63–67, 235
   property tax policies of, 66–67
   quote of, 66, 67, 183, 189
   successes of, 74
   tax policy and, 178
   water policies of, 66
health care, 4, 101, 119, 121, 130, 191–192.
        See also Affordable Care and Patient
        Protection Act (ACA) (Obamacare);
        Medicaid
health management organizations
   (HMOs), 114
HealthWave, 101, 119
Heffington, Joan, 151
Heller, Francis, 30
Hendricks, Mike, 131–132
higher education, 8, 10, 200. See also
   education
High Plains Aquifer, 7
Highway Commission, 44, 235
highway program, 63–65, 99–100
Hill, Clyde, 12, 23, 34
Hill, Justin, 180
Hodes & Nauser v. Schmidt, 73n36, 198n62
Holiday, Mary, 80
Holland, Tom, 151
House Bill 504, 22, 23
House of Representatives (Kansas)
   campaigns for, 151
   Democratic Party control in, 56, 87, 88

   malapportioning of, 12–13, 14
   one person, one vote in, 18–24
   party composition of, 144, 157, 207, 225
   party control in, 25, 56
   reform in, 34–40
   Republican Party control in, 56, 87, 88,
      104, 152
   statistics regarding, 14, 16, 24
   structure of, 14
Howard, Kenith, 20
Huelskamp, Tim, 147
Huntington, Terrie, 157
Hutchinson News (newspaper), 14–15

Illinois, election policy in, 22
immigration, 84, 93, 127, 138
income tax, 70, 177–184. *See also* taxation
infrastructure, 3, 236
Institute on Taxation and Economic
   Policy, 182
insurance commissioner, redefining office
   of, 114–115

Jameson, Henry, 43
Jenkins, Lynn, 129
Jennison, Robin, 102
Jindal, Bobby, 148
John Birch Society, 84
Johnson, Dan, 139, 157
Johnson County
   Democratic trend of, 7
   diversity in, 93–94
   election of 2018 in, 219, 225–226
   growth of, 6, 93–94, 156
   reapportionment in, 6–7, 20–21, 22, 23, 24
   Republican preferences in, 116–117
   rural conflicts in, 102–103
   as up to date, 102–103
   Wyandotte County rivalry with, 103
Johnston, Michael, 76
Jones, Larry, 58, 59
Journey, Phil, 127
judicial branch, 11, 29–30, 32–33, 71–72,
      184–189. *See also* Supreme Court
   (Kansas); US Supreme Court
Judicial Department Reform Act, 32
justice system, 101

Kansans for Fair Courts, 188–189
Kansans for Life, 187–188
Kansas
  development of, 84
  growth of, 93, 147–148, 156
  migration in, 94
  origin of, 81
  in westward expansion, 1. See also *specific locations*
Kansas Arts Commission, 152
Kansas Bar Association, 30, 32
Kansas Bioscience Authority, 121
Kansas Board of Education, 4
Kansas City, 128
Kansas Commission on Executive Reorganization, 30, 31
Kansas Court of Appeals, 33, 186
Kansas Department of Transportation (Bank of KDOT), 5
Kansas Development Finance Authority, 64
Kansas Health Authority, 121
Kansas Hospital Association, 192
Kansas Policy Institute (KPI), 85, 132, 179, 180
Kansas Turnpike, 8–9
Kansas Values, 167
Kassebaum, Nancy, 55, 105, 115–116, 117, 217
Kaw Valley Services, 102
Kelly, Laura, 6, 214–225
Kelly, Patrick, 83
Kemp, Jack, 86
Kennedy, John F., 8, 11–12
Kennedy, Ted, 106
Kensinger, David, 141–143
Kerr, Dave, 120
Kerr, Fred, 78
Kerry, John, 122
Kline, Phill, 5, 100, 116, 124–125, 145
Knight, Bob, 83, 123
Kobach, Kris
  as activist, 93
  background of, 210
  election of 2018 and, 6, 210–213, 215–225
  failures of, 4–5
  immigration and, 127
  overview of, 138
  platform of, 124–125
  redistricting trial and, 156–157
  as secretary of state, 96
  as state party chair, 138–139, 140–141
Koch, Charles, 84–85, 180, 238
Koch, David, 84, 85, 180, 238
Koch, Fred, 84
Koch Industries, 148, 180
Koesten, Joy, 225
Krider, Charles, 62
Kubler-Ross, Elisabeth, 13, 23
Kurtis, Bill, 151

Lady, Wendell, 34
Laffer, Arthur, 5, 84, 85–86, 153, 179, 238
Landon, Alf, 71, 117, 178, 190
LaTurner, Jake, 157
Lee, Janis, 139
Legis-50, 11
Legislative Apportionment Committee, 20, 21
legislative branch
  changes to, 11
  demographics of, 15
  factions in, 12
  Joan Finney's actions regarding, 77
  overview of, 92–93
  procedure regulations in, 37–38
  reform in, 34–40
  salaries in, 11
  statistics of, 15
  structure of, 13–14. See also House of Representatives (Kansas); Senate (Kansas)
Legislative Budget Committee, 35, 51n22
Legislative Coordinating Council, 11, 34, 35, 37
Legislative Council, 16, 34–35
Legislative Division of Post Audit, 2, 11, 37
Legislative Post Audit Committee, 37
Legislative Research Department, 11
local option budget (LOB), 100, 102, 122
Londerholm, Robert, 19, 23
Long v. Avery, 17, 18
Loomis, Burdett, 55, 60, 92–93
Loux, Pete, 11, 34, 35–36, 56
Lowry, Patrick, 162
Lyon County, 219

Maag, Jim, 34
malapportionment, 12–13, 14, 17. *See also* reapportionment (redistricting)
maps, for reapportionment, 21, 22, 156–157
Mays, Doug, 118, 120
McCuish, John, 29, 184
McGill, Duane "Pete," 11, 34, 35, 38–40
McGinn, Carolyn, 157, 183
McKinney, Dennis, 120
McMillan, Ashley, 146
Medicaid, 71, 101, 121, 130, 190–192, 193, 194, 209, 224
Mercatus Center, 85
merit-based appointments, of judges, 2, 71–72, 184–189
#MeToo Movement, 213
Miers, Harriet, 107
Miller, David, 4, 88, 93, 107–108, 176
Miller, Deb, 160
Miller, Robert H., 66, 78, 88
Miller, Vern, 13, 40–43
Missouri, roads in, 99
Missouri Nonpartisan Court Plan, 2
Moms Demand Action, 212
Mondale, Walter, 55
Moore, Dennis, 116, 117, 128
Moore, John, 138, 145
Moran, Jerry, 150
Morgan, Christian, 4–5, 139
Morris, Steve, 118, 132, 153, 157
Morrison, Paul, 125, 138, 145
Mullen, Leo, 96
Murfin, David, 180
Myers, Jan, 116, 117
Myron Orfield, 93

Native Americans, casinos and, 123
Naumann, Joseph F., 126
Neufeld, Melvin, 123, 131, 157
Nuss, Lawton, 122, 167
Nuss fuss, 122

Obama, Barack, 107, 129–130, 143, 200
Obamacare, 130, 143, 146, 191
Ogallala (High Plains) Aquifer, 94
oil industry, 7
Oleen, Lana, 117

O'Neal, Mike, 156
one person, one vote, 12, 18–24, 29
Orman, Greg, 5, 6, 160–163, 166, 215–225
Osawatomie State Hospital, 193
Owens, Tim, 157, 186–187, 217

Parkinson, Mark, 4, 92, 113–114, 126, 130–132, 138, 145, 181
Paul, Ron, 146
payday loans, 183
Peckham, Richard, 68
Pence, Mike, 194
Perot, Ross, 55, 161
Perry, Rick, 148
personal autonomy, rights to, 73n36, 198n62
personal privacy rights, 105
Phelps, Eber, 139
Phelps, Fred, 68, 108, 120
Pierce, Neal, 28
Pisciotte, Joe, 60
Planned Parenthood, 5
polar alliance, 4, 238
policy activism, 59–62, 63–67
policy entrepreneurs, 60
Political Action Committee (PAC), 180
political competition, 54–56
political undercurrents, 81–86
politics in Kansas, overview of, 3, 234–240
Poor, Scott, 137
Post Audit Committee, 37
Powell, Larry, 157
practical governance, 3
Praeger, Sandy, 4, 95, 101, 121, 191
progressivism, 28–33, 34–40
prohibition, 81–82
property tax, 57, 61–62, 66–67, 70, 97. *See also* taxation

Reagan, Ronald, 55, 59, 67, 82, 86, 238
reapportionment (redistricting)
    2012 elections and, 155–156
    denial and anger regarding, 15–18
    of districts, 12
    ground rules for, 19
    in House of Representatives (Kansas), 12–13

reapportionment (redistricting), *continued*
  lawsuit regarding, 156–157
  maps for, 156–157
  metaphors regarding, 18, 21, 23
  one-man, one-vote ruling regarding, 12, 18–24, 29
  overview of, 235
  population equality and, 14
  process of, 1, 13
  setting the stage for, 13–15
  stages of, 15–18
  statistics regarding, 24
  voting effects of, 128–129
Reardon, Joe, 160
Redwood, Tony, 62
Reed, Clyde, 42
religious freedom bill, 209
Religious Right, 83
Republican-Democratic alliance, 4, 6, 95, 132
Republican Party
  bipartisan consensus of, 69–72
  challenges of, 4–5, 137, 139, 140–141
  characteristics of, 28, 124
  conservatism in, 116
  decline of, 143–144
  demographics of, 54
  dominance of, 54
  faction in, 87–89, 137–138, 238
  financial challenges of, 139
  following redistricting, 13
  fundraising by, 139–140
  House control of, 56, 87, 88, 104, 152
  investigation of, 139
  moderate, 103–104
  partisan polarization and, 86–87
  platform of, 95, 104–105, 132
  polar alliance and, 4, 238
  primary of 2018 and, 210–213
  reapportionment effects on, 25
  rebels in, 93
  rebuilding of, 146–147
  rift with Democratic Party by, 206
  Senate control of, 55–56, 87, 88, 208
  statistics regarding, 54
  structure of, 137
  unification efforts of, 139
  vulnerability of, 138
Reynolds v. Sims, 17, 29, 34
Right to Life of Kansas, 82
Riley County, 219
Road Map PAC, 188
Roberts, Pat, 5, 105, 143, 159, 160–163, 166, 182
Robertson, Pat, 82, 83
Robinson, Forrest, 41–42
Roe v. Wade, 13, 82, 237
Rogers, Richard, 65
Romeo and Juliet law, 124
Roy, Bill, 55, 82, 116
Ruff, Candy, 127
Ryan, Jim, 128–129
Ryan, Richard, 35
Ryckman, Ron, 208, 209

Sabato, Larry, 29
sales tax, 70, 123, 131, 178, 181–182, 201. *See also* taxation
same-sex marriage, 126
Sawyer, Tom, 108, 115
Schmidt, Vicki, 157
Schodorf, Jean, 157
School District Equalization Act of 1973, 41
School District Finance and Quality Performance Act, 78, 237
Sebelius, Kathleen
  accomplishments of, 132
  background of, 114–115
  campaign platform of, 118
  egalitarianism and, 95, 113
  election of, 118, 137
  farm team of, 145
  as governor, 118–123, 238
  as insurance commissioner, 114–115
  nomination of, 118
  overview of, 4
  platform of, 92, 95
  as secretary of Department of Health and Human Services, 129–130
Second Congressional District, 127–129
Sedgwick County, 21, 22, 24, 219
Seltsam, Susan, 79–80

Senate (Kansas)
  Democratic Party control in, 87
  party composition of, 55–56, 144–145, 157, 207, 225
  reapportionment and, 14
  redistricting of, 16
  reform in, 34–40
  Republican Party control in, 56–57, 87, 88, 208
  statistics regarding, 16
Senate Bill 2, 17
Senate Concurrent Resolution 4, 16
Senate Concurring Resolution 1, 17–18
Senate districts, boundaries of, 1
severance tax, 57, 60
sex education, 126
Shallenburger, Tim, 88, 104, 118, 176
Shawnee County, 21, 38, 219
Shawnee Mission Post (newspaper), 216
Shriver, Garner, 55
Shultz, George, 85
Six, Stephen, 125
Slattery, Jim, 3, 55, 68–69, 87, 96, 127
Sloan, Tom, 98
Slocombe, Lawrence, 18
Smith, D. J., 161
Smith, Glee, 11
Smith, Greg, 157, 204, 205
Smith, William, 29
Snowbarger, Vince, 116, 117
social order, 81–83, 86–89
Social Security Act of 1935, 71, 178, 190
Sometime Governments, The, 34
Special Commission on a Public Agenda for Kansas, 63
Special Committee on Children's Initiatives, 78–79
State Children's Health Insurance Program (SCHIP), 101, 119
Steineger, Jack, 36
Stones, Harold, 39
Stovall, Carla, 88, 115, 117
Stubbs, Walter, 52n35
Summer of Mercy, 1, 3, 83, 95–96

Sunflower Electric, 131
Supplemental Nutrition Assistance Program (SNAP), 192
Supreme Court (Kansas)
  House Bill 504 and, 23–24
  justices selection for, 33
  merit-based selection of judges and, 184–189
  reapportionment cases of, 11, 12, 15–18
  reform in, 33. *See also* judicial branch
Svaty, Joshua, 145, 213–215
Sykes, Dinah, 204, 205, 225

task forces, 47–48
taxation
  bipartisan consensus regarding, 70
  changes to, 182, 208–209
  comparison of, 148–150, 152–153
  income, 70, 177–184
  Laffer curve for, 85–86
  property, 57, 60–61, 66–67, 70, 97
  reform of, 67
  sales, 70, 123, 131, 178, 181–182, 201
  Sam Brownback's policies regarding, 5, 152–154
  school finance and, 78
Taylor, Chad, 161, 162
Taylor, Jess, 13, 18–19, 20–22, 23, 24
Teagarden, George, 76
Tea Party, 146–147, 151
Temporary Assistance for Needy Families (TANF), 192–193
Third District, 7
Thornburgh, Ron, 88, 97, 151
three-legged stool concept, 177–178
Tiahrt, Todd, 3, 87, 107–108, 150
Tiller, George, 114, 145
Timmer, Gloria, 79–80
Topeka, 94, 127–129
Topeka Capital-Journal (newspaper), 57, 75
tornadoes, 120
Towns, Leroy, 41, 46
trend, defined, 92
Trump, Donald, 194, 207, 218
Trump, Donald, Jr., 218

University of Kansas, 10, 126
US Supreme Court, 13, 14, 29, 67, 82–83, 237
utility rates, as campaign issue, 57, 60–61

vetoes, 77
voter registration, 210
Vratil, John, 157

Wagle, Susan, 126, 208
Wanniski, Jude, 85–86
Ward, Jim, 208, 213–215
Warren, Rick, 107
Watergate scandal, 38
water policies, 65–66
water supply, 7, 94
Webster v. Reproductive Health Services, 67, 82–83, 237
Weigand, Nestor, 68, 69, 176

Westboro Baptist Church, 108, 120
White, William Allen, 28
Whiteman, Donna, 77
Whitmer, John, 201
Wichita, 94
Wichita Eagle (newspaper), 132
Wichita State University, 10
Wiesner, Patrick, 161
Willkie, Wendell, 116–117
Winn, Jennifer, 159–160
Wolf, Milton, 161
women, in Kansas politics, 117–118. *See also specific women*
wrap-up session, of Bill Graves, 101–102
Wyandotte County, 6–7, 21, 22, 103, 219

Yoder, Kevin, 226

Zahnter, Alvin, 161

www.ingramcontent.com/pod-product-compliance
Lightning Source LLC
Chambersburg PA
CBHW030535230426
43665CB00010B/898